MW00851335

Serbian and Greek Art Music

Serbian and Greek Art Music
A Patch to Western Music History

Yannis Belonis, Biljana Milanović, Melita Milin,
Nick Poulakis, Katy Romanou, Katarina Tomašević

Edited by Katy Romanou

Intellect Bristol, UK, Chicago, USA

First published in the UK in 2009 by
Intellect Books, The Mill, Parnall Road, Fishponds, Bristol, BS16 3JG, UK

First published in the USA in 2009 by Intellect Books, The University of
Chicago Press, 1427 E. 60th Street, Chicago, IL 60637, USA

Copyright © 2009 Intellect Ltd

All rights reserved. No part of this publication may be reproduced,
stored in a retrieval system, or transmitted, in any form or by any
means, electronic, mechanical, photocopying, recording, or otherwise,
without written permission.

A catalogue record for this book is available from
the British Library.

Cover designer: Holly Rose
Copy-editor: Heather Owen
Typesetting: Mac Style, Beverley, E. Yorkshire

ISBN 978-1-84150-278-6

Printed and bound by Gutenberg Press, Malta.

Contents

Contributors

YANNIS BELONIS is member of the Faculty of Music Technology at the Technological Educational Institute of Epirus and chief editor of the music periodical *Polyphonia*. He has done considerable research, publishing and music editing on Greek music of the first half of the 20th century.

BILJANA MILANOVIĆ is research assistant at the Institute of Musicology of the Serbian Academy of Sciences and Arts. Her main field of research includes Serbian heritage of the first half of the 20th century. Currently, she is interested in cultural studies, especially, in collective identities. She was editor of the music magazine *Pro Musica* and is member of the editorial board of the journal *Muzikologija*. She has published many articles in scientific periodicals, the more recent being "Analogies between the Works of George Enescu and Modern Serbian Composers" (2006); "Stevan Stojanović Mokranjac et les aspects de l' ethnicité et du nationalisme" (2006). She has published the book *Milenko Paunović – Two modalities of the work*.

MELITA MILIN is senior researcher at the Institute of Musicology in Belgrade. She was editor of the journal *Muzikologija* in 2001–2005. She has published the book *The Intertwining of the Traditional and the New in Serbian Music after the Second World War (1945-1965)*, as well as many articles and chapters in collective editions. Recent publications: "Les Compositeurs serbes et le nationalisme musical. L'évolution des approaches créatrices aux XIXe et XXe siècles", *Etudes Balkaniques*, Paris 2006; "Poetic texts in the Works of Ljubica Marić", *History and Mystery of Music*, Belgrade 2006.

NICK POULAKIS is a musicologist and composer. He is at present Ph.D. candidate in ethnomusicology at the University of Athens. He has worked as a special scientist on ethnomusicology, popular film music, ethnographic film and musical multimedia in the Faculty of Music Technology at the Technological Educational Institute of Epirus. He has participated in several musicological research and music editing projects. He is member of the editorial board of the journal *Polyphonia* and the International Music and Media Research Group.

KATY ROMANOU is a musicologist teaching in the Music Faculty of the University of Athens. She has done considerable research on Greek music and is the author of several books and many articles. She is on the editorial and the advisory boards of the periodicals *Musicologia* and *Polyphonia*, respectively, and associate editor for the Greek language in RIPM. Her most recent book is *Greek Art Music in Modern Times* (2006).

KATARINA TOMAŠEVIĆ is researcher at the Institute of Musicology of the Serbian Academy of Sciences and Arts in Belgrade and assistant professor in the Department of Musicology and Ethnomusicology of the Academy of Arts in Novi Sad. She is the present editor of the journal *Muzikologija*. Author of the book *At the Crossroads of the East and the West. On the Dialogue between the Traditional and the Modern in Serbian music (1918–1941)*, she published numerous essays on Serbian music, among which more recent are: "Musical Modernism at the 'Periphery'? Serbian Music in the First Half of the Tweniteth Century" and "Petar Konjović – Pro et contra Wagner. A Contribution to the Study of the History of National Musical Drama".

Foreword

This book is about the assimilation and development of western art music in Serbia and Greece during the 19th and 20th centuries. It gives information on music education, music life and music creativity in the two nations, since they gained their freedom from the Ottomans. It relates the efforts of local musicians to synchronise their musical environment with the West and achieve the inclusion of Serbian and Greek music in western music history: an aim that seemed consistent with overall progress and, at various historical stages, attainable.

One may certainly talk of a terminal failure, because both "art music" and the "history of Western music" have deeply changed their meaning in current musicology and this aim has not been accomplished.

However, it is some of the causes that have brought this irreversible change of context in "music history" and "art music" (such as globalisation aesthetics or overflowing academic fields and swarms of doctoral dissertations) that account for current interest in the Balkans. This interest compels us, local musicologists, to narrate in English the story of western music's assimilation in our countries; after all, we are convinced that what is not said in English is as if not said at all.

So, this book may be seen as mending an unfulfilled aim; or else, as a patch to western music history.

Being part of the Balkans, Serbia and Greece belong to the European area that was the latest to be westernised. Under the Ottomans for long centuries, they won their independence early in the 19th century and founded their tiny states with the intervention of major European powers interested in the area; they also postponed the expectation for a great Greece and great Serbia and foiled the dream of the union of all Balkan Christians. The new tiny states, inhabited by a small percentage of nationals living in surrounding and far remote areas, went through their race of westernisation with the conflicting sentiments of an awareness of inferiority compared to western powers and a fear of losing the "eastern" qualities of their identity.

Traditional music, developed in those areas during their isolation from the West, consists of folk music and the music of the Orthodox church (a purely vocal art music, with its own theoretical system and notation, which the Serbs have replaced by stave notation, but the Greeks continue to apply to this date). Both had attracted the interest of western scholarship since early in the 18th century, being European traditions singularly untouched by western institutionalised art music. Folk music of those areas was appealing because of its uncommon richness and diversity and because it strongly suggested originating from ancient Greek music. Béla Bartók, writing in 1942, attributes this wealth to "racial impurity" (that in our *ethical* age might be called "racial enrichment"), produced by the political (and military) upheavals that divided and dislocated peoples of numerous ethnicities forcefully or subtly in dense frequency, varying in pace, neighbours and influences.

But this racially impure – or rich – treasure was used by urban composers to demonstrate national unity. Because it is in urban music that national antagonism and politics in general are reflected. To bring in again Béla Bartók's experience from his contact with neighbouring peasants of different nationalities in 1943: "there is not – and never has been – the slightest trace of hatred or animosity against each other among those people".

Privileged with rich, still functional local music traditions, Serbia and Greece developed a corpus of art music that bore from its earliest examples interesting marks of national identity. The aim as well as the problems of uniting the traditional with the progressive (or the eastern with the western), motivated all initiatives in music education, music life and creativity, and this is a theme reverberating in nearly all chapters of this book.

Serbs and Greeks have been the lesser adversary among Balkan nations; one could even say the friendliest. Their common historic process continued in the first half of the 20th century, where they fought on the same side in both World Wars and in both Balkan Wars. It was the Cold War and recent globalisation policies that brought the two nations into opposition.

However, these latter policies have not hindered friendships and teamwork. The authors of this book have been in close collaboration since 2002, when we participated as a team in the International Musicological Society's Conference in Leuven.

The Serbian musicologists of the team are affiliated to the Institute of Musicology of the Serbian Academy of Sciences and Arts in Belgrade, and the Greek musicologists, to the Music Department of the University of Athens.

In the first part of this book the history of Serbian music is unfolded. Biljana Milanović writes on stage and symphonic music in Serbia. She describes the complex political situations since the 19th century that caused continuous population movements in the area, clarifying the situations and the influences that moulded the Serbian national music idioms and the composers' personal styles. Katarina Tomašević gives a comprehensive account of the history of the most important Serbian institutions of music education, performance and dissemination in the first half of the 20th century. Melita Milin has a chapter on the significant female composer Ljubica Marić, the centenary of whose birth is celebrated this year. Melita Milin has also contributed with a chapter on the trends that attracted Serbian composers in the second half of the 20th century, and on the political situations and dramatic events (including the 1999 war) that moulded and filtered their expression.

The second part of the book relates three successive stages of recent Greek music history. Katy Romanou describes musical life in the Ionian Islands: the sole area of Greece that was not under the Ottomans and which developed, in the 19th century, a music culture nearly identical to that of neighbouring Italy. Yannis Belonis transports us to Athens and Thessalonica, the cultural centres in the 20th century. Speaking on the composers dominating the scene, he skilfully interweaves the crucial political events of the period and their impact on society and culture. Following is a chapter on Nikos Skalkottas, who died sixty years ago and whose music is recently gaining recognition. (We have not included in this book chapters on Maria Callas, Dimitri Mitropoulos and Iannis Xenakis, who are already vastly explored in western bibliography.) In the final chapter of this book, Nick Poulakis writes about Greek music after World War II. He develops his subject through the paradigmatic cases of three composers who adopted different music trends from a stylistic and a philosophical point of view: Jannēs Chrēstou, Michalēs Adamēs and Periclēs Koukos.

Achieving homogeneity in the footnotes, bibliography and various aspects of language within this book was a task undertaken by the Greek musicologist Alexandros Charkiolakēs of the Music Library of Greece "Lilian Voudouri". Knowing the great difficulties he faced, I consider his contribution of supreme importance and thank him for his great care.

Katy Romanou
Athens, 13 May 2009

A Note on the Transliteration of Names

Serbs widely apply the Latin alphabet, with diacriticals, and this is how all Serbian names are written in this book.

Transliterating the Greek alphabet is a problem to which no solution may be practised consistently, without irrational results.

We chose the ALA Standard System because so many Greek names and words are spelled in English according to it; whereas the phonemic system does not show the connection between Greek and other European languages (it is doubtful if one could connect Omiros to Homer, Aggelos to Angel, Psikhi to Psyche and so on).

Greek names in bibliography are given both in Greek and in their transliterated form. The names of certain Greek authors might appear in two slightly different ways (Demertzis and Demertzēs). This is so in cases where the person is author of a Greek and a foreign edition (where another system of transliteration is followed).

Greek spelling is missing in names that were originally in some other language, as is the case with names of most early composers in Corfú, where Italian was the language spoken by educated Greeks. We write their names in Italian, instead of proceeding to a double conversion, which does not lead back to the original (for example: Manzaro – Μάντζαρος – Mantzaros).

In the index – uniform for all chapters in this book – Greek names are written in the Latin alphabet only.

The chapters of this book are signed as the authors themselves spell their names in English.

Katy Romanou

Part I: Art Music in Serbia

Chapter 1

Serbian Musical Theatre from the Mid-19th Century until World War II

Biljana Milanović

Petar Konjović's autograph from his *Miloš's Wedding* (1903).

The development of a modern Serbian musical theatre was comparable to that of other countries involved in nation-building within the revolutionary-Romantic context of the 19th century. However, the specific situation in Serbia was influenced by the complex political and socio-economic circumstances of the Austro-Hungarian and Turkish empires, by variable geographic and symbolic borders, and by the enduring struggle to unite the Serbs within a single state. Though several stages of liberation from the Turkish rule enabled the formation of first an autonomous Principality and then the Serbian Kingdom, a great many regions inhabited by Serbs on the territories of present-day Vojvodina, Croatia, Dalmatia, Bosnia, Kosovo and Metohija were still part of the Habsburg and Ottoman empires right up to the Balkan wars (1912–1913) and World War I. The legitimacy of Serbian statehood was then transferred to a multi-ethnic Yugoslav state (1918) characterised simultaneously by polycentric national cultures and a centralising (supra) national tendency towards the homogenization of an imagined Yugoslav identity. Therefore, the complex layers of collective cultural identities, as well as the multiple traditional strands of cultural life, represent an important context for the investigation not only of musical theatre but of the entire culture of the Serbs in the 19th and 20th centuries. Since the national musical scene had also been developing inside the Serbian state and among the Serbian population in Vojvodina from the beginning of this period, its foundation had been formed in relation to the experience of several different cultures, which meant overcoming numerous obstacles. However, certain regions were marked even prior to this by an expressive continuity of changes, so that the dynamic process of change within social and economic contexts, lifestyles, spiritual values and competing models of national culture had its foundation in an earlier period. This offered a unique potential for creativity.[1]

Researches into Serbian musical theatre developed within independent studies of institutions and repertoire on the one hand and compositional-stylistic or dramaturgical features of different musical-dramatic genres on the other. Though a consideration of individual works has been predominant, the resulting extensive corpus of knowledge only serves to emphasise that a detailed and integral insight into the history of the national musical scene in Serbia has yet to be developed in Serbian musicology.

As in earlier stages, from medieval jongleurs' theatre to Jesuitical dramas and verteps in the 18th century, Serbian musical theatre of the new era is inseparable from the dramatic theatre with which it shares its history. The initial impulses begin with the activity of the versatile Joakim Vujić (1772–1847), who organised stage performances among the Serbs of Hungary and the Principality of Serbia.[2] There were Serbian theatrical companies in the first half of the century in Novi Sad, Pančevo, Kikinda, Sombor and other places in

Vojvodina. At that time, the Theatre of the Princedom of Serbia (1834) was established, and its foundation, together with the slightly earlier orchestra (the Band of the Principality of Serbia (1831)), was an important part of the institutionalisation of culture and society in Kragujevac, the then capital of the newly formed Principality. The first developmental phase of a Serbian musical culture began with the cooperation of the two leading figures in these institutions, Joakim Vujić and Josif Šlezinger (1794–1870). It continued also when the capital was moved to Belgrade (1841) through the short-term activities associated with the theatres at Đumruk and at Jelen, and ended with the appearance of the first musical-stage works created by professional composers at the time when national theatres in Novi Sad (1861) and Belgrade (1868) were established. This initial period was characterised by the amateurism of composers, orchestral players and singer-actors alike, as well as by numerous organisational-technical problems and a patriarchal audience that was just beginning to construct its national and cultural identity.

Conditioned by multiple needs, Šlezinger performed various types of music: marches, dances, potpourri, fantasies from foreign, predominantly contemporary, operas (Mozart, Bellini, Donizetti, Halévy), as well as his own pieces dedicated to the theatre, often inspired by folk melodies.[3] His activity and cooperation with Vujić were influenced by the wishes, inclinations and autocratic demands of Prince Miloš Obrenović, who was not keen on performances without songs. Beside the royal family, the audience also included top-ranked dignitaries, clerks and officials and, on special occasions only, other citizens too. The prince used to drink coffee and smoke the chibouk, talk to the actors during the performance and demand certain songs regardless of the content of the play. Generally

the audience in the first part of the century expressed openly and aloud their dissatisfaction or approval regarding the activities on the scene, identifying dramatic persons with people around them and seeking the very life of the people inside the theatre. For the audience, the theatre represented a direct transposition of real life, of life itself divested of all illusions. (Tomašević 1990: 69)

Responding to spectators' taste, Šlezinger composed music for many plays by domestic authors and therefore became the creator of the favourite and dominant stage genre in Serbia in the 19th century: a play with music similar to the Singspiel and operetta.[4] One of the projects of that time, *Czar Dušan's Wedding* (1840), with numerous songs and dances by Šlezinger, was described in the press as a work "constructed [...] on the form of Italian operas", so historically it represented the first attempt at operatic composition in Serbia (Djurić-Klajn 1956: 114). However, six more decades would pass before the suitable creative, performative, technical and receptive conditions necessary for the emergence of the Serbian opera existed. The main preparatory stages took place by way of the play with music, or Singspiel.

With the establishment of national theatres in Novi Sad and Belgrade, better opportunities for the development of music for the stage appeared amongst the Serbs. The absence of

Davorin Jenko.

professionalism, due to a long period without educational music facilities and trained staff, was partially solved by hiring foreign, usually Czech, musicians and by giving training to singer-actors. In addition to the existing military orchestra, an opera orchestra was established in Belgrade.[5] These ensembles often worked together, and occasionally cooperated with the First Belgrade Singing Society, which was the main seed-bed of Serbian musical culture in the second half of the 19th century. In spite of more difficult conditions for musical activities, there was also an improvement in the level of performance in Novi Sad.[6] This theatre had particular importance because "the Serbian Athens" continually paid visits to numerous places inhabited by Serbs on Habsburg territory, thus undertaking a unique cultural mission. Moreover, the theatre, with its performances in Belgrade in 1867/68, gave a direct incentive for the establishment of the theatre in the capital of the Principality.[7]

The repertoire of Novi Sad at first influenced Belgrade, but more favourable conditions in the Serbian capital and the continuous activity of the bandmaster and composer Davorin Jenko brought the Belgrade Theatre to the forefront with a greater number of premieres and a richer programme. Both institutions followed the tradition of older theatres by performing plays interspersed with music. This most favoured and frequented theatrical genre was addressed by almost all composers of that time, even those whose art was not primarily directed towards the theatre. Davorin Jenko was particularly dedicated to the genre, writing innumerable plays with music.[8]

A major expansion of the "music sections" of Serbian theatres enabled the performance of operettas, beginning with Jenko's *Sorceress* in Belgrade (1882) and continuing with works by Offenbach, Suppé, Sullivan and Millöcker. At the same time, one-act plays started being performed, and opera appeared on the Belgrade stage in 1884 (*Jovanka's wedding guests* by Victor Masseé); while in 1903 the first Serbian opera was performed (*At Dawn* by Stanislav Binički). The premieres of several works given at the Belgrade and partly the Novi Sad theatres pointed towards a future repertoire based on different traditions including Italian, French, Slavonic, German and Serbian operas.[9] Considering the way the national theatres were organised, however, opera was constantly struggling to survive. Representatives from "drama section" considered "that vaudevilles and operettas had taken over enough audience from more serious literature and that there was no room for opera in the national theatre" (Mosusova 1995: 9).

This situation, together with the lack of a high-quality operatic ensemble, led composers to prefer genres which foregrounded musical performance. Moreover, the few Serbian operas that had been created by 1914 could not find their way on to the national theatrical stages.[10] Within that context, the short-lived, private opera on the Boulevard (1909–1911) of the singer Žarko Savić was of great importance. Due to this institution, the Belgrade audience could see the works of Srećko Albini's *Barun Trenk* (1909), *Mother* (1910) by Jovan Urban and *Prince Ivo of Semberija* by Isidor Bajić (1911), in addition to many foreign works.[11] Due to the enthusiasm of Stanislav Binički at the National Theatre, there were many operatic projects in 1913/14, such as *Il trovatore*, *Djamileh* and *Tosca*, *Der Freischütz*, *Verther* and *Mignon*. This sudden take-off was interrupted by World War I, and the work was not continued until the season of 1919/20.

The "music section" in the first decade after the war was soon promoted due to the emigration of Russian artists, who contributed to the Belgrade scene not only with their professionalism in operatic production but also by helping establish the ballet.[12] In the third phase of the development of Serbian music theatre, which took place in the context of the new Yugoslav state between the two wars, theatrical culture in Belgrade became the equal of national theatres in Ljubljana and Zagreb, whose "music sections" had a more long-standing and more evolved tradition. However, the cultural policy of the newly-established state was unfavourable to the activities of the Novi Sad theatre, so in spite of the positive effects of Russian singers, operatic activity was terminated in this theatre at the end of the third decade. At the same time, Belgrade acquired a significant number of opera conductors, a good choir and orchestra and vocal soloists of considerable potential.[13]

At the beginning of the inter-war period, the Belgrade Opera established something of a standard repertoire dominated by Italian works. But the repertoire was continually enriched by new operas. During the first seasons, works like *Der fliegende Holländer*, *Lohengrin* and *Boris Godunov* were performed. Then the repertoire was expanded with Slavonic works (*Jenůfa*, *Tsar Saltan*, *Rusalka*, *Prince Igor*, *Queen of Spades*), German classics (*Die Zauberflöte*,

Stevan Hristić (1815–1958).

Fidelio), Grand opera (*Turandot, Thais, Les Huguenots*), and less well-known operas (*Salomé, Der Rosenkavalier, Katerina Izmaylova, Khovanshchina*), all of which prepared the ground for the reception of works with a more modern musical-dramatic character. At first, national stage works (*Miloš's Wedding* by Konjović in 1923, *Dusk* by Hristić in 1925, *Oppressor* by Krstić in 1927, *Prince of Zeta* by Konjović in 1929, *Koštana* by Konjović in 1931) were performed at a measured pace. During the 1930s, however, Serbian works were neglected, so a substantial number remained unperformed and forgotten.[14] The national orientation at the time was represented rather by Croatian operas. They did not enrich existing domestic repertoire stylistically and aesthetically, but their prominence on the Yugoslav stage strikingly documented the policy of constructing a Yugoslav national identity: a policy that found very fertile ground in the multi-ethnic cultural context of Belgrade.

A Yugoslav orientation was strongly associated with ballet production, which, thanks to Russian choreographers, led to the establishment of a national ballet, whose musical, choreographic and scenic aspects could be truly marked with epithets of "Yugoslav" and/or "Balkan" cultural particularity. These folk-inspired forms created by Serbian and Croatian composers had a much better reception than domestic opera.[15] The entire world of ballet between the two wars in Belgrade, though without any previous tradition, impressed many with its quality and its contemporary repertoire, even when viewed within a wider European context. Rich choreographic and dancing experiences, starting from the classical stage of Saint Petersburg and continuing up to the influence of Djagiljev's troupe and other contemporary choreographers, played their part in the creation of a domestic ballet production. It started with the ballets *Nutcracker*, *Scheherazade* and *La Sylphide* (1923), and carried on with other works of the standard repertoire (e.g. *Coppélia*, *Swan Lake*, *Giselle*), but it also included novelties (e.g. *Firebird*, *Petrushka*, *Daphnis et Chloé*, *Boléro* and *Golden Cockerel*), and some were presented very soon after their world premieres. This unexpectedly sudden and prolific development led to an early climactic achievement for Serbian ballet, which, during the 1930s, began to give its first guest performances abroad (in Greece, Romania and Bulgaria). Operatic production reached a good professional level in the period between wars but its "golden era" was to come after the post-war years, when the Belgrade ensemble received international acknowledgement at festivals in Wiesbaden, Lozano, Paris, Florence, Osaka and Edinburgh.

During the early period of the development of Serbian music, from Šlezinger's works up to first national operas, there was a steady increase in the technical and artistic quality of music in plays, and a more explicit awareness of the need to make a close connection between the text and music. Contributions by Šlezinger and Djurković, authors who were not sufficiently qualified technically to achieve the level of early-Romantic Italian opera, were distinctive as naive and semi-amateur attempts. A clear advance in quality was observed in the only stage music of the first Serbian professional composer Kornelije Stanković and in the rich oeuvre of Davorin Jenko, who improved constantly in dealing with compositional techniques and developing an early-Romantic style with occasionally more advanced harmonic devices as well as in relating text and music (Tomašević 1982: 67–77).

In the works of the most significant composers of the 19th century in Serbia, Josif Marinković and Stevan Mokranjac, the basic principles of music dramaturgy had been already established: characterisation, initially through leitmotiv; linking musical numbers to former larger dramaturgical wholes; developing the orchestra's role in dramaturgy; the functional use of set numbers; and the dramaturgical treatment of musical folklore. Even though these composers were mainly involved with other genres, producing their best work in the field of Romantic solo song and choral music, two isolated examples of their stage music unmistakably indicate the final stages of the maturing process of the play with music. Actually, everything established by Marinković and Mokranjac in the music for the plays *Suđaje* and *Ivko's Saint Patron's Day* became characteristic features of the Romantic national operas by Joksimović, Vedral, Binički, Bajić and Krstić.

Serbian plays with music and the first operas can be included within various historical, social-anthropological and cultural researches. Serbs who lived north of the Danube had a direct opportunity at the beginning of the 19th century to adopt and adapt elements of a practice that flourished in German and Hungarian theatres. In the Principality, this tradition was of course a real novelty alongside existing town-music by Gypsy and Turkish ensembles. At that time, elements from the musical heritage imported from the West, the traditions

The Royal Guard orchestra, after a concert in Mostar (1909).

of Serbian folklore, and the Turkish inheritance present in urban settings all met on this territory. Different testimonies from those days referred to strong inclination towards Šlezinger's work in contrast to the "primitive and exotic" music associated with an Ottoman 'other'. Often presented within a typical orientalist discourse, they represented natural reactions to symbols of a centuries-old empire with all its customs and temperaments, as well as the adoption of western ideas on nationhood and progress which denoted images of their own Europeanism in the formation of a Serbian national identity. However, more detailed study reveals that the newly-arrived western cultural practices were not entirely immune to an existing oriental heritage. Considering contemporary post-colonial discourses on the Ottoman experience as a legitimate part of European identity, redefinition of attitudes in that respect is overdue in musicology.

Plays with music represented an extremely popular political theatre, so that the use of elements from the earlier musical stage in Serbia could not easily be isolated from the wider European context of revolutionary turmoil in the middle of the 19th century. Songs themselves had the strongest influence. They often trespassed beyond the boundaries of the play, gaining popularity and even becoming striking revolutionary symbols.[16] The presentation on stage of historical heroes and the evocation of the Serbian medieval empire had a very real immediacy because empire was a present reality – with the southern regions under the Ottomans and the northern territories under the Habsburgs for a very long period. Therefore it was not accidental that topics of the first Serbian operas were often based on the conflict between the Christian and Muslim worlds, stereotyped in musical dramaturgy through a contrast between Serbian folk melodies and oriental, sevdalinka-type music.

Predominant themes in plays with music were either national-historical in character or themes from popular life which were achieving popularity in the latest musical-stage works. Operas, musical dramas and ballet by the time of World War II could be organised typologically into historical or pseudo-historical, folkloric, legendary-fantastic or social topics. Unlike the romantic themes of the first operas, the librettos of the more recent works were constructed on the basis of modern theatrical tendencies, covering a wide range from drama with a moral thesis (*Divina tragoedia*), drama of the individual (e.g. *Prince of Zeta*, *Koštana*), and lyrical drama with elements of symbolism (*Dusk*), right up to utterly contemporary, surrealistic approaches (the ballet, *Le balai du valet*).

Textual diversity has its counterpart in the music. Where musical drama is concerned, early Serbian modernists advocated three different species: the first is based on the German, Wagnerian heritage; the second on a synthesis of elements of verismo, impressionism and French lyrical musical drama; and the third one on the tradition of Slavonic opera and a late-Romantic stylistic framework enriched by elements of Expressionism.

Paunović's *Divina tragoedia* (1912) appeared only one decade after the first Serbian opera, marking a sudden professional and creative leap in relation to previous practice. Its composer, who set his own dramatic text, had in mind Wagnerian postulates, so he omitted choruses, ensembles and set numbers, and based his work on dialogues and monologues, carefully organised leitmotiv and a densely symphonic orchestral texture. Even though his harmonic language is closest to *Der fliegende Holländer*, Paunović occasionally develops and dissects his leitmotiv material, simultaneously incorporating it in the vertical and horizontal dimensions of the music, in ways that point directly to elements of younger Austro-German composers such as Mahler and Strauss.

Paunović's second musical drama *Čengić-aga* (1923) establishes a more mature musico-dramatic language starting from a complex, dramatically functional structure where the triadic basis of the larger form is consistently transferred to the grouping of scenes and to segments within them. This is done through multiple relations among the musical symbols organised in leitmotiv families, to a dramaturgical role of musical folklore which was not present in the first musical drama, no doubt because of the universality of its text. Folklore in *Čengić-aga* is usually surrounded by other material which does not have features of folk music and through variation and transformation often loses its initial character. Thus, heterogeneous sound dimensions are not treated as elements of different traditional layers but as a part of the integral sound corpus. The incorporation of folklore into the atmosphere of a Wagnerian musical drama in this highly skilful way shows how Paunović has achieved a marked individuality of expression and indicates his remove from early musico-dramatic stereotypes, as well as suggesting analogies with the achievements of Konjović, yet to come (Milanović 1995: 173–181; Milanović 2006: 251–266).

By eschewing folklore and choruses, by employing only a small cast, by using closed numbers rarely and only with precise dramaturgical effect, and by combining a chamber dramatic atmosphere with minimal outer action (contrary to the strong dramatic potential explored by the orchestra), *Divina tragoedia* could be compared with Hristić's *Dusk* (1925). This other work is, however, an organic synthesis of late-Romantic, veristic and impressionistic elements, which make it an isolated example in the Serbian musical stage. Hristić relies on the semantic function of leitmotivs, and treats them, like Debussy, as symbols of certain states, moods and atmospheres. Even though his harmony is late-Romantic, he uses it for its colouristic value, and his proximity to Debussy's work is made even clearer by the orchestral style. In shaping the vocal parts, Hristić only occasionally achieves impressionistic simplicity. More often, he goes for an arioso-declamatory principle characteristic of Massenet's lyrical dramas, as well as for a melodic style close to Verismo, Puccini's in particular (Popović 1995: 182–191).

The works of Paunović, Hristić and Konjović are interwoven with more general features of the genre in which all the components of musical expression have a dramaturgic role. For Konjović, however, folklore is the primary source of the music. His music dramas contain many folk-influenced numbers and explore many different ways of incorporating these within wider musical-dramatic paragraphs. Beside different ways of connecting the material with surrounding compositional tissue (announcement, reminiscence, overlapping or concatenation) he reveals a wide range of procedures in the organisation of double-scenes, which is a quality less evident in Paunović's *Čengić-aga*. Considering its content, *Koštana* especially demanded the presence of such songs, and it triggered Konjović's gift for subordinate ornamentation, melodic profusion and colour to the dramaturgical potential of song as *per se*. Using different interventions in the middle of the songs – less frequently between verses, and more often by layering comments which represent the influence of the song on the inner world of certain characters – the composer achieves a multi-layered quality of musical expression. Simultaneously, he sustains an opposition of collective and individual feelings and achieves a counterpoint of different psychological and emotional states belonging to the protagonists. Developing such ideas far beyond their presentation in the original textual source, Konjović creates complex double scenes, some of which can be visually perceived. In shaping the vocal parts, the composer relates the music constantly to the text, and besides the use of folk melodies, achieves a kind of 'folk' quality by following closely the latent melodic flexions of the spoken words. This specific arioso-recitative principle can be correlated with Janaček's procedures (Veselinović-Hofman 1989: 51–56). In *Prince of Zeta*, it is an important methodological principle, and in *Koštana* it stands for the spontaneous synthesis of sounds and words (Tomašević-Jovanović 1983: 59–68). Leitmotivs in *Prince of Zeta* are actually leit-themes characterising the 'personalities' of two climates, Venetian and Montenegrin. In *Koštana*, they form three leitmotiv complexes, the first one (Fate motives) being on the symbolic level, and other two participating in the characterisation of the inner and outer worlds of the main characters, as well as providing the foundation for the symphonic musical tissue of the whole work (Mosusova 1971: 153–167).

By comparing these different stylistic tendencies with patterns of reception and later resonance, inasmuch as these have been researched, we may conclude that the greatest chance for the modernisation of Serbian national repertoire for the musical stage belonged to works based on the Slavonic heritage. This terrain was prepared concurrently on the levels of performance and repertoire. Such achievements in the local context included composing with Serbian folklore, which had its roots in the oldest layers of a common Slavonic tradition. Since Serbian musical folklore enabled a point of contact between older works (which made use of this music) and contemporary reception (which was favourable to it), it was logical to develop it further in the context of Slavonic musical drama. However, the encounter between inevitable generic starting points (in the German tradition, for example) and Serbian folklore meant that composers had to overcome various problems. Beside Paunović, more traditionally oriented composers such as Petar Stojanović and Svetomir Nastasijević tried out various temporary solutions to these problems. The conservative profile of their music – a restricted 'romantic' style in the case of Stojanović or insufficient technical acumen in the case of Nastasijević – led inevitably to limited creative results. Serbian facilities, both in technical and performance terms, at the time when Paunović's first musical drama appeared were not sufficiently developed to perform a work with a predominantly quadruple woodwind symphonic orchestra. Moreover, the controversial, even shocking, libretto of his opera, telling of Christ's resurrection perverted into fraud, made it highly unlikely that there could have been a positive reaction in the context of Serbian culture of that time. Paunović's second musical drama was not orchestrated and both works were suppressed and forgotten soon after the composer's sudden death. Thus, for a combination of different reasons, works based on German traditions had slim prospects of surviving in a Serbian environment. On the other hand, the Slavonic music drama represented by Konjović's works did survive, due mainly to the continuity it achieved with his post-war music. Even though it was slow to gain acceptance, in time it came to be regarded as a true classic of Serbian music.

If the blasphemy theme of the first Serbian music drama signalled exclusivity in Serbian art as a whole from the early century (it can "be interpreted today as the paradoxical presence of one avant-garde dimension inside the most conservative music genre" (Milanović 2006: 262)), then a yet more striking and unique modernism came with the first Serbian ballet. Milojević's *Le balai du valet* (1923) is an example of the earliest strivings for experiment in Serbian music. This multimedia project, with music, dancing, singing, stylised declamation and spoken text, belongs with that circle of contemporary European artistic achievements created in the wave of anti-romanticism, and, on ideological-aesthetic, compositional and technical grounds, suggests an analogy with Satie's *Parade*. Actually, the highly surrealistic text of Marko Ristić, organised as a succession of pictures with seemingly absurd characters and situations, was an ideal basis for the application of music collage and compositional principles close to cinematic technique. Milojević, maintaining both an associative and a formal relationship with the text, simulates or quotes a collage of music from present and past (e.g. foxtrot, waltz, quotations from works by both Wagner and Strauss), non-musical effects (a pistol shot) as well as music from popular Serbian urban songs. His approach to collage also includes direct creative intervention, involving the parody treatment of music parameters inadequate for the given model. On the other hand, as in Satie's aesthetics, this work deliberately 'places' ready-made, unchanging models in musically inappropriate environments, producing diverse results that range from mild irony to the grotesque and persiflage. It is important to note the composer's distance from the stylistic elements of romanticism, impressionism and expressionism (the groundwork for his other achievements) and his approach rather to an aesthetic based on the quotation of 'concrete' or 'found' sounds. Milojević treats his quotations as musical objects that enable him to reshape the constant features of his own creative work and to take them in a new direction. Even though we talk about his one and only visit to this land of experiment, this ballet ensures that the composer takes his place within a world of contemporary, neoclassical enterprises designed to present avant-garde novelty in a wider European context (Milanović 1998: 262–277).

It is interesting that Milojević, who, in the role of a critic, carefully kept track of opera and ballet production, did not compose for the stage; nor did he offer his *Le balai du valet* to the management of the National Theatre. He probably thought "that this work would have no chance to remain in the repertoire due to its 'eccentricity'" (Milin 1999: 73). His estimates were certainly realistic, as later Serbian ballets were conceived along the lines of Romantic aesthetics, with the cautious acceptance of innovation only in certain works. A rural ambience and a dramatic contrast of real and surreal worlds, as well as more collective conflicts (Serbian – Turks or Serbian – Albanians) are dominant themes in most of these works, but there are major differences of quality in their music realisation. While Pordes and Nastasijević (*Fire in the Mountain; In the Morava Valley*) composed picturesque set numbers for different characters, with a simple ordering of dances and without any more ambitious compositional agenda, Hristić (*Legend of Ohrid*) created a work of powerful symphonic dynamism. One ballet by a composer of the second generation of modernists, Milenko Živković's *Green Year*, although it uses a dissonant harmonic language, testifies with its theme and its southern folklore dance rhythms its essential proximity to these works. Today, however, it is difficult to reconstruct the first one-act version of what later became four-act *Legend of Ohrid* (1947), which with its noble melodic character, its folklore quotations that also function as leitmotiv, its irregular rhythms, and its refined harmony and orchestration, stands on the crossroad of romanticism and impressionism, and represents one of the most important works of Serbian art music in general (Milin 1999: 75; Mosusova 2002: 108–117).

If these works are seen in the context of the stylistic diversity of the time, it becomes obvious that, despite certain examples, they stand apart from the most radical tendencies. They are especially far from the atonal, athematic and quartertone compositions that can be found in other musical genres by younger composers whose early, avant-garde phases are not only anti-Romantic but anti-folklore as well. Still, the youngest composers (whose musical and dramatic gifts would come to fruition after World War II) directly indicate, even at this time, their personal inclination toward music theatre. It is, however, symptomatic that Stanojlo Rajičić with his ballet *Under the Ground* marks the beginnings of his latter, "quieter" compositional style. Interpreting the programme (a tragedy in a mine), which is one of the first socially rooted themes in Serbian music of that time, he spices an easily accessible tonal idiom with dissonant harmony, and makes highly convincing dramatic use of a folk music idiom as a novel element in his work (Peričić 1971: 35). It is also characteristic that Mihovil Logar, the least radical composer among the representatives of the youngest generation, dedicates himself to the stage. His artistic nature led him already in the pre-war period to composition of a musical farce *Phantom in the Saint Florian Valley* (1938), a work that finds its musical progeny in the contemporary comic operas of later Serbian music. On the other hand, Logar's *Four Scenes from Shakespeare* (1927–1931) are marked as a "symphony for orchestra and stage", with pantomime and oratorio-like non-acting roles for the vocal soloists, marking the beginning of a rich scenic production of later years when the crossroads of various genres would provide a context for new creative challenges and artistic quests.

As the field of art mostly conditioned by the manner of its reception, modes of transmission and numerous technical and material prerequisites, Serbian musical theatre changed its profile slowly and in the face of some resistance. The transition from an already rooted and accepted style into a newer, younger language of artistic expression really represented a change in the whole model of culture and a complete change in the mode of reception. The tastes of audiences who were raised on the stereotypes of folkloric plays with music changed slowly. The ballets reached audiences more easily thanks to their choreography, but modern and professional music dramas were difficult to accept. The works that stand out by their quality from many others composed in the Balkans in the period between the two wars, such as *Dusk*, *Prince of Zeta* or *Koštana*, initially had only a short life on stage.

The modernisation of Serbian music and theatre did not bring any direct profit, so theatre managements did not support it. There were no opera contests or other forms of organised state support that could stimulate artists or influence the tastes of the audience. However, compared to the music and theatre tradition in many other national environments that were undergoing various phases of development, the survival and maturing of the entire cultural world associated with this difficult, all-absorbing and immensely time-consuming genre is remarkable. In a period of little more than a century, Serbian musical theatre has attained levels of performance and creativity, and produced works in a diversity of idioms, that certainly merit our serious attention.

Notes

1. For example, Belgrade itself, separated from Serbs from Vojvodina only by the Danube at the crossroads of Ottoman and Austrian imperial strategies, changed its outer appearance with each new conquest. The Turks conquered it in 1521, 1690 and 1739, and the Austrians in 1688, 1717 and 1791. During the First Serbian Uprising, the town was taken over by Serbs but it remained under Serbian-Ottoman reign until the Turkish retreat in 1867. (On the different layers of the imperial heritage in the Balkans, see Bakić-Hayden 2006.)
2. Vujić was translating, modifying and making plays performed on European stages, especially works of German authors (August fon Kotzebue, Joseph Richter, Carl Erckartshausen, Emanuel Schikaneder etc.). His adaptation of Kotzebue's *Parrot*, presented to the Serbian population in Pest in 1813, was the first secular civil play performed in Serbian language.
3. Šlezinger's *Band* was essentially a wind orchestra. At first, it had sixteen members, but it grew bigger with time, and by 1839 it had fifty instrumentalists. In the absence of other ensembles, the *Band* played in all state celebrations and military parades, for plays at the court theatre as well as for balls and popular parties. From the mid-century and onward it was described as the "military band", then the Belgrade Military Orchestra since 1899, and in 1904 it became Royal Guard Orchestra.
4. Šlezinger composed music for the plays *Tailor's journeyman* (1835) by Joakim Vujić (translation of the play *Die Schwestern von Prag* – Joachim Perinet); *Kraljević Marko's Dream, Battle on Kosovo, Highwayman Veljko, Miloš Obilić* by Jovan Sterija Popović; *Erecting of Ravanica, Tsar Dušan's Wedding* (1840), *Kraljević Marko and the Arab* (1842), *Death of Serbian Prince Mihajlo Obrenović* (1869) by Atanasije Nikolić. His pioneer endeavours were soon followed by similar works by the versatile Nikola Đurković (e.g. *Drunkard, Miloš Obilić, Battle on Kosovo, Kraljević Marko's Dream* by J. Sterija Popović).
5. The theatre orchestra was formed shortly after the theatre was established. The theatre management occasionally dismissed it, and hired instead the military ensemble. Very often its numbers varied because the military musicians were often used to fill vacancies. In the beginning, the orchestra and choir were conducted by the Austrian Karl Resch and during three whole decades (1871–1902) by the Slovenian Davorin Jenko. Oskar Malata, Dragutin Pokorni, Petar Krstić, Stevan Hristić were also conductors. Stanislav Binički worked from 1912, whereas Pokorni stayed for the longest period of time (1897–1909). In the military orchestra Šlezinger was followed by the Czech Dragutin Čižek (from 1868 till 1899). Thanks to him, string instruments were introduced, enabling performances of significant works of symphonic literature. The Czech Josif Brodil

conducted from 1894, and from 1899 Josif Rožđalovski and Dragutin Pokorni were conductors. Between 1889 and 1920, Stanislav Binički was active and he especially contributed to flourishing of symphonic and musical-dramatic repertoire.

6. Even before the standing theatre was established, the citizens of Novi Sad had a chance to see performances by the Flying Amateur Theatre and Principality Theatre. The National Theatre, however, did not have its own piano or orchestra for years. The first bandmaster was the Czech Adolf Lifka, followed by Aksentije Maksimović, Alojzije Milčinski, the Czech Hugo Doubek and (from 1899) another Czech Antonije Tuna Osvald.

7. Foreign artist paid visits to Belgrade as recently as the 1940s, and among them there were people performing music from operas. The eagerness to have a professional national theatre was influenced by visits from German national companies (1857, 1858, 1867), as well as the above-mentioned theatre from Novi Sad. Further expansion is referenced in files from 1894, when there were seven theatres in Serbia and five outside of its borders. Various theatre companies were active, usually as part of singing societies or with their help. They cooperated with local amateurs, military ensembles and the different amateur orchestras that started appearing from the 1880s of that century (Pejović 2001: 135; Djurić-Klajn 1977: 21).

8. The most significant Serbian composers of the 19th century made one contribution each to this genre: Kornelije Stanković (1831–1865) composed music for Đorđe Maletić's drama *Precursor of Serbian liberty or Serbian Highwaymen* (1856); Josif Marinković (1851–1931) for Ljubinko Petrović's play *Suđaje* (1894); Stevan St. Mokranjac (1856–1914) for Stevan Sremac's play *Ivko's Saint Patron's Day* (1901). The most important of Jenko's contributions are stage music for the plays *Đido*, *Village hard-drinking rake*, *Girl's curse*, *Chase*, *Pribislav and Božana*. Isidor Bajić (1878–1915), a composer from Novi Sad, was also prolific in this field, writing music for fifteen plays (*Čučuk-Stana*, *Brandy*, *Wild woman*, *Village hard-drinking rake* etc.). Even though this form of work subsided with the arrival of the new century, many composers returned to it later on.

9. The opera *Inside the well* by Smetena's contemporary William Blodek was performed in 1894, followed by *Cavalleria Rusticana* (1906), *Pagliacci* (1908), *Sold bride* (1909), *Bastien und Bastienne* (1911), and *Enchanted shooter* (in Novi Sad in 1900). Due to production and technical limitations, ballets or Wagnerian musical dramas were out of question (Mosusova 1995: 6–7).

10. *Miloš Obilić's Wedding* by Božidar Joksimović (1902), *Pitija* by Vaclav Vedral (1902), and *Miloš's Wedding* by Petar Konjović (1903).

11. During the thirteen months of work on Savić's Opera, over 250 plays were performed – twenty-five operas and operettas, fifteen comedies and vaudevilles. Žarko Savić, the world-famous bass, was the first Serbian singer with an international reputation (Turlakov 2002: 119–180).

12. Among the numerous Russian emigrants who arrived in Serbia after the October revolution there were many first-class artists: the singers Ksenija Rogovska, Liza Popova, Lav Zinovjev, Djordje Jureljev, Pavle Holodkov; the directors Jurije Rakitin, Teofan Pavlovski, Evgenije Marijašec; the scenographers Vladimir Žedrinski, Leonid Brailovski; the dancers and choreographers Nina Kirsanova, Aleksandar Fortunato, Jelena Poljakova, Anatolij Žukovski, and Margarita and Max Froman.

13. Stanislav Binički was director and conductor of the opera until 1924, Stevan Hristić from 1924 till 1936. Later on, Ivan Brezovšek and Jovan Bandur took the role, and in 1938 and onwards Lovro Matačić. Mirko Polič, Ilija Slatin, Alfred Pordes, Krešimir Baranović and Predrag Milošević also conducted in the opera. Among singers, outstanding figures were Evgenija Pinterović, Rudolf Ertl, Dragi Petrović, Stanoje Janković, Vladeta Popović, Žarko and Nikola Cvejić, Melanija Bugarinović, Bahrija Nuri-Hadžić, and Anita Mezetova.

14. Serbian operas made their mark again in 1940 when *Đurađ Branković* by Svetomir Nastasijević was performed, as well as a new performance of *Miloš's wedding*. Unperformed music dramas included *Divina tragaedia* (1912) and *Čengić-aga* (1923) by Milenko Paunović, *Treasure of Međulužje* (1927) by Svetomir Nastasijević, the operas *Blaženka's oath* (1935) by Petar Stojanović, *Female slave* by Ljubomir Bošnjaković, and *Phantom in the Saint Florian Valley* by Mihovil Logar.

15. The repertoire included Croatian ballets such as *Licitar's heart* (1927), *Imbrek with nose* by K. Baranović and *Devil in the Village* (1938) by F. Lhotka, Serbian works such as *Legend of Ohrid* (1933) by S.Hristić, *Fire in the mountain* (1941) by A. Pordes and *In the Morava Valley* (1942) by S.Nastasijević. The more modernist work *Le balai du valet* by M.Milojević stands apart from all these ballets, and it was presented in 1923 in the hall of the Casino Hotel, but it was not part of the repertoire of the National Theatre. Unperformed ballets included *Mirjana and nine candlesticks* by P. Stojanović and two ballets which were fully presented only as concerts – *Green year* (1937) by Milenko Živković and *Under the ground* (1940) by Stanojlo Rajičić.

16. Certainly the most popular song was *Rise, rise, Serbian man*. This joint composition of Šlezinger and Djurkovic, performed in the play *Kraljević Marko's Dream* in 1847 in Belgrade, became the "Serbian Marseillesse" and the war cry of the Serbian resistance during the revolution of 1848. Sterija included the song in his play *Patriots* and Kornelije Stanković, after harmonising it for choir, used it as a theme for his piano variations. So it became one of the most loved pieces in the concert repertoire of Serbian pianists of the 19th century. The same song arrived in Croatia, where the Illyrianist Andrija Bastašić rewrote and published it as a song *Rise, rise, Croatian man*, and in this version Vjekostav Kostić later incorporated it in his anthology of choir compositions (Djurić-Klajn 1981: 32).

References

Bakić-Hayden, M., *Varijacije na temu "Balkan"* [Variations on the Theme "Balkans"], Belgrade, Institut za filozofiju i društvenu teoriju, 2006.

Djurić-Klajn, St., *Muzika i muzičari* [Music and Musicians], Belgrade, Prosveta, 1956.

——, "Orkestri u Srbiji do osnovanja Filharmonije" [Orchestra in Serbia by Foundation of Philharmonic Orchestra] in *Beogradska Filharmonija 1923/73* [Belgrade Philharmonic Orchestra 1923/73], Belgrade, Beogradska Filharmonija, 1977, pp. 15–27.

——, *Akordi prošlosti* [Chords of the Past], Belgrade, Prosveta, 1981.

Milanović, B., "Uloga Vagnerovih ideja u muzičkim dramama Milenka Paunovića" [The Role of Wagner's Ideas in the Musical Dramas of Milenko Paunović] in *Srpska muzička scena* [Serbian Music Stage], Belgrade, Muzikološki insitut SANU, 1995, pp. 173–181.

——, "*Sobareva metla*: bliskost sa evropskom avangardom" [Le balai du valet: Proximity to the European Avant-garde] in *Kompozitorsko stvaralaštvo Miloja Milojevića* [The Works of the Composer Miloje Milojević], Belgrade, Muzikološki institut SANU, 1998, pp. 262–277.

——, "Proučavanje srpske muzike izmedju dva svetska rata: od teorijsko-metodološkog pliralizma do integralne muzičke istorije" [Studying Serbian Music Between the Two World Wars: From Theoretical-methodological Pluralism to Integral Music History], *Muzikologija*, 1, 2001, pp. 49–92.

——, "Kontekstualizacija ranog modernizma u srpskoj muzici na primeru dva ostvarenja iz 1912. godine" [Contextualization of Early Modernism in Serbian Music: Case Studies of Two Works from 1912], *Muzikologija*, 6, 2006, pp. 251–266.

Milin, M., "Tipologija srpskog muzičko-scenskog stvaralaštva 20.veka" [Typology of the 20th Century Serbian Compositions for the Music Stage] in *125 godina Narodnog pozorišta u Beogradu* [125 Anniversary of National Theatre in Belgrade], Belgrade, Srpska akademija nauka i umetnosti, 1997, pp. 337–347.

——, "Prvi baleti jugoslovenskih kompozitora na beogradskim scenama (1923–1942)" [Yugoslav Ballets on the Belgrade Stages (1923–1942)], *Zbornik Matice srpske za scenske umetnosti i muziku, Zbornik Matice srpske za scenske umetnosti i muziku*, 24–25, 1999, pp. 69–77.

Mosusova, N., "Najnovije delo Petra Konjovića – opera 'Otadžbina" [The New Work of Petar Konjović – The Opera *Otadžbina*], *Zvuk*, 58, 1963, pp. 367–373.

——, "O *Koštani* Petra Konjovića" [About *Koštana* of Petar Konjović], *Arti musices*, 2, Zagreb, 1971, pp. 153–167.

——, "Srpska muzička scena" [Serbian Music Stage], in *Srpska muzička scena* [Serbian Music Stage], Belgrade, Muzikološki insitut SANU, 1995, pp. 5–36.

——, "Are Folkloric Ballets an Anachronism Today?", in *Dance as Intangible Heritage*, Corfu and Athens, International Dance Council CID-UNESCO, 2002, pp. 108–117.

Pejović, R., *Srpsko muzičko izvodjaštvo romantičarskog doba* [Serbian Musical Performance of the Romantic Period], Belgrade, Univerzitet umetnosti, 1991.

——, *Opera i Balet Narodnog pozorišta u Beogradu (1882–1941)* [Opera and Ballet of the National Theatre in Belgrade (1882–1941)], Belgrade, Fakultet muzičke umetnosti, 1996.

——, *Srpska muzika 19. veka* [Serbian Music of the 19th Century], Belgrade, Fakultet muzičke umetnosti, 2001.

Peričić, Vl., *Stvaralački put Stanojla Rajičića* [The Creative Development of Stanojlo Rajičić], Belgrade, Umetnička akademija, 1971.

Popović, T., "Stilske koordinate muzičko-scenskog stvaralaštva Stevana Hristića, sa akcentom na elementima impresionističkog stila" [Stylistic Coordinates in the Musical Stage Works of Stevan Hristić with an Accent on Impressionistic Elements], in *Srpska muzička scena* [Serbian Music Stage], Belgrade, Muzikološki insitut SANU, 1995, pp. 182–191.

Tomašević, K.,"Nastanak srpske nacionalne opera" [The Creation of Serbian National Opera], *Zvuk*, 4, 1982, pp. 67–77.

——, "Muzika u pozorišnom radu Joakima Vujića" [Music in Joakim Vujić's Theatrical Work], *Zbornik Matice srpske za scenske umetnosti i muziku*, 6-7, 1990, pp. 171–182.

Tomašević-Jovanović, K., "Muzička dramaturgija Petra Konjovića" [Musical Dramaturgy of Petar Konjović], *Zvuk*, 3, 1983, pp. 59–68.

Turlakov, Sl., *Iz muzičke prošlosti Beograda* [From the Musical Past of Belgrade], Belgrade, Author's edition, 2002.

Veselinović-Hofman, M., "Konjović i Janaček – odnos izmedju stila i metoda" [Konjović and Janaček – The Relationship between Style and Method], *Život i delo Petra Konjovića* [The Life and Work of Petar Konjović], Belgrade, Srpska akademija nauka i umetnosti, 1989, pp. 51–56.

Chapter 2

Musical Life in Serbia in the First Half of the 20th Century:
Institutions and Repertoire

Katarina Tomašević

The famous soprano Bahrija Nuri-Hadžić as Manon in Jules Massenet's *Manon Lescaut*. Archive of the Institute of Musicology SASA.

The first half of the 20th century undoubtedly represents one of the most dynamic and exciting epochs in the recent political, social and cultural history of the Serbian people. A century-long dream about liberation from Turkish power finally came true following Serbia's victory in the Balkans wars (1910–1912). On the other hand, the great contribution and sacrifices of the Serbian army, which in World War I fought on the allies' side, were awarded in 1918 by the leading roles granted to the Serbian King and to Belgrade, which became the capital of the newly-established state of all South Slavs – the Kingdom of Serbs, Croats and Slovenians (later the Kingdom of Yugoslavia).

The new position of Belgrade in the Balkans, as well as the new status of the Yugoslav state in Europe and worldwide, significantly contributed to the rapid development and reformation of Serbian cultural institutions. Acquiring in a relatively short period of time the characteristics associated with a West European urban physiognomy, yet at the same time retaining its ample Oriental charm, Belgrade remained at the heart of artistic life in Serbia, and retained its status as the most important musical centre of the Kingdom and an important stop in the itineraries of numerous important artists from abroad. The foundation of the major institutions of musical life, the establishment of music journals, the development of new media – all these unmistakable signs of social modernisation – were symptoms of the integration of the Serbian people and their culture into the family of modern nations of Europe.

This article is not devoted exclusively to the history of the most important institutions of musical life in Belgrade in the first half of the 20th century; information about repertoire, as well as data about the visits made by Serbian artists and ensembles abroad, will hopefully indicate something of the currency and significance of Serbian music in its broader, European context.[1] Special attention will be given to the opera and ballet, symphonic and chamber instrumental ensembles, choirs, the development of music schools, the popularising of classical music, music on the radio, and the developing phenomenon of mass musical culture.

Opera and ballet

Opera, the first major musical institution of national importance, was officially founded in 1920. Opera performances, just like ballet, which was introduced three years later, were staged in the National Theatre (founded in 1868). Until the opening of the Kolarac foundation in

1932, the hall at the National Theatre served as not only the most representative concert stage, but also as a specific focus of the capital's artistic life. The pioneering steps in the operatic life of Serbia were made by Serbian artists – gifted actors-singers, orchestral musicians and bandmasters of the national theatre – but there is no doubt that the responsibility for the increase in the quality and frequency of operatic productions, as well as for the establishing of a ballet repertoire in the decades between the two World Wars, goes to the Russian theatre artists who had arrived in Belgrade with the great wave of immigration that followed the October revolution.[2]

At the end of World War I Serbian opera audiences were mainly familiar with the works of Italian masters. The arrival of the Russian artists created an opportunity for broadening the horizons towards the operatic world of Eastern Europe. In the course of only ten years or so (1924–1935), among the premieres of the works of Mozart, Verdi and Puccini, Belgrade saw productions of most the significant operas of the Russian classical repertoire: *Queen of Spades* (1924) by Tchaikovsky, *Emperor's Bride/Mlada* (1925) and *Tsar Saltan* (1928) by Rimsky-Korsakov, *Boris Godunov* (1926) and *Khovanschina* (1935) by Mussorgsky and *Prince Igor* (1928) by Borodin.

Besides Yuriy Rakitin (a director with modern views), numerous operatic singers, chorus singers and orchestral musicians, experienced set and costume designers, the Belgrade stage was honoured by the performances of Yelena Polyakova and Margaret Froman, the ballet dancers who were well known as the second best in the famous ballet troupe of Sergei Diaghilev. Thanks to Polyakova, as early as 1923 Belgrade saw *Scheherazade* in the same version that had taken Paris by storm in 1910. The close contacts maintained by the "Belgrade" Russians with immigrants throughout the world, as well as the international acquaintances of the active concert agent Evgeny Zhukov, brought the most prominent guests – solo ballerinas Anna Pavlova (1927) and Tamara Karsavina (1928), as well as the legendary opera singer Fyodor Shalyapin (1935).[3]

The professional musical circles did not have such a positive view of this domination of the theatre by Russian artists. Since the Russians sang exclusively in their mother tongue, the leading critic of the era, Miloje Milojević, started the fight for the use of the Serbian language in the opera (Mosusova 1995: 11–13). However, it was yet another gesture of impatience in the struggle to make the musical theatre *national* in the full sense of the word, and at the earliest possible moment. In truth, it could become national not just when performances could be given by Serbian artists, but when a genuine national repertoire had been formed.

In the turbulent history of the Belgrade Opera, whose development was burdened by many problems in the first decades, it is worth mentioning that the first singing "stars" – tenor Vojislav Turinski, soprano Draga Spasić and mezzo-soprano Teodora Arsenović – were gifted amateur singers with no formal education whatsoever. Neither the chorus nor the orchestra was skilled for tasks that were altogether more ambitious. It was only when the opera stage saw the next generation of educated artists, some of whom later achieved world fame – Anita Mezetova, Melanija Bugarinović, Vladeta Popović, Aleksandar Marinković, Stanoje Janković, Milorad Jovanović, Žarko and Nikola Cvejić – that a new phase in the development of the opera began.

The appearance of distinguished foreign singers did a great deal to improve the quality of the performances, and here we should mention only two privileged moments: Pietro Mascagni as the guest conductor in *Cavalleria rusticana* and *Aida* (1925), and the performance of Bahrija Nuri-Hadžić in Richard Strauss's *Salome* (1931).

The appearance of the first generations of outstanding Serbian ballet dancers (Nataša Bošković, Anica Prelić, Danica Živanovic, Milorad Jovanović, Miloš Ristić) was partly the result of the work of the first ballet schools in Belgrade: the "classical" school of Yelena Polyakova (who cherished the classical ballet on 'points') and the "modern" school of Maga Magazinović, who followed the concept of dance introduced by Isadora Duncan (Magazinović 2000). The rapid development of ballet is demonstrated by the fact that the National Ballet troupe was the first of the theatre ensembles to make a foreign tour in 1933 to Athens.[4]

Orchestral and chamber music

Although the expansion of orchestral, and especially symphonic, music after World War I represented a huge leap in comparison to the earlier stages of this art form in Serbia, it was really a logical outcome of pre-war steps that were taken in a very short period.

Belgrade welcomed the beginning of the 20th century with nominally two and really only one active orchestra, since the Military Orchestra and the National Theatre orchestra joined forces for significant musical events. Low-quality instruments, a small number of educated musicians and the generally poor social status of musicians, represented a major obstacle to the development of a symphony repertoire. The first staging of a Beethoven symphony (the *Pastoral*) in Belgrade in 1899 was marked as "a milestone in history". Thanks to Stanislav Binički, who in the same year commenced his prolific work with the Belgrade Military Orchestra (from 1904 – *Music of the Royal Guards*), the repertoire was soon enriched by Schubert's *Symphony* in B minor, Wagner's Overture to *Rienzi*, Dvořak's *Slavonic dances* (1901) and Mendelssohn's *Italian Symphony* (1903). As early as 1904, in cooperation with the Singing Society "*Stankovic*", an oratorio was given for the first time: *Seven Last Words from the Cross* by Joseph Haydn. A real performance peak followed in 1910, when Beethoven's demanding *Ninth Symphony* was performed with great success.

There are valuable data illustrating the role of the Orchestra of the Royal Guards in World War I.

Having lost all the precious instruments and music archive in the painstaking and tragic crossing of Albania [...] Binički managed to collect new instruments, reconstruct the scores and make a concert in the Corfu National Theatre. The next seat of this orchestra after 1916 was Thessalonica, where it did credit both to the Serbian army and to Serbian art [...] No important celebrations or prestigious musical events in Thessalonica could be imagined without the participation of this orchestra. (Đjurić-Klajn 1981: 151–152).

First performance of Beethoven's *Ninth Symphony* in Belgrade, in 1910. Conductor: Stanislav Binički. Archive of the Institute of Musicology SASA.

As is well known, the participants of the Albania Golgotha sailed from Greece to recover under the protection of France, where Binički organised a triumphant tour, beginning with three concerts in Paris. After the war, the orchestra, then the most representative Yugoslav ensemble, took part in a six-month tour in the towns of a newly founded Kingdom. Shortly afterwards, there were as many as 27 new military orchestras throughout the country!

The most significant event in the history of Serbian orchestral music was the foundation of Belgrade Philharmonic (1923). The Philharmonic initially gathered the most experienced Belgrade musicians, as well as some gifted amateurs. Since the orchestra had no permanent financial support, the musicians were given small sums of money to prepare special concert programmes alongside their regular duties, and sometimes they were not paid at all. Ambitiously planned as a leading national symphony orchestra, the Philharmonic started its work without a music library and with no adequate premises.[5] Although Hristić did not lack enthusiasm in promoting a relatively high number of concerts, in giving other conductors a chance to work,[6] and in the constant expansion of repertoire, crises were inevitable.[7]

These difficulties and a wide variation in quality also accompanied the work of others orchestras. Although, frankly speaking, in Belgrade there were enough musicians for only one symphony orchestra, the period between the wars witnessed the activity of orchestras at the opera, the Royal Guards and the Music Society *"Stanković"*. In 1937, yet another symphony orchestra was founded, this time in Radio Belgrade, led by Mihailo Vukdragović. Apart from the slowly forming taste of the audience, the number of available musicians was no doubt a second major factor in designing the repertoire.

As we can see from all this, the orchestral scene in Serbia during the 1920s and 1930s was not a promising one. A completely different impression is gained, however, when we look at the impressive lists of concerts, visiting Yugoslav and foreign conductors and soloists, as well as of repertoire premieres. By the beginning of World War II, practically all important symphonic works of classicism and romanticism had been performed, while appearances by young Serbian soloists and numerous eminent guests from abroad[8] encouraged a rich and varied production of concerto genres. Close ties with Slavic cultural circles abroad resulted in a proportionally rich presentation of the works of Russian and Czech composers, while the desire for a more rapid progress in the development of musical culture stimulated the activity of young Serbian and Yugoslav conductors and composers.

After Hristić, whose enthusiasm for conducting seems to have outweighed the results he achieved, the Philharmonic was significantly improved by the appointment of an experienced chief-conductor, Lovro Matačić (1937–1941). But the chance to conduct was constantly offered to several leading younger musicians who were also composers, and this practical insight into the problems of the orchestral sound doubtless presented an irreplaceable experience in the creative development of composers such as Ljubica Marić, Vojislav Vučković, Jovan Bandur and M.Vukdragović.

As the conductor of the Singing Society *"Obilić"*, Bandur was responsible for making the Philharmonic successfully participate, in 1933, in the important premieres of several outstanding works of the contemporary repertoire: the opera-oratorio *Oedipus Rex* by

Stravinsky, *Věčné evangelium* by Janáček and *Religiofonija* (Religiophony) by Josip Slavenski. The shift to a modern sound world was also made by Vukdragović, when in 1938 the Philharmonic performed Roussel's G-minor *Symphony* (1929/30) and the composition *Pacific 231* (1925) by Arthur Honneger. Then a memorable event followed; thanks to the great affection of the famous Enrico Mainardi for the Belgrade music circle,[9] on 2 February 1939 the Radio Symphony Orchestra participated in the world premiere of Gian Francesco Malipiero's *Cello Concerto*.

The cumulative effects of this work in the field of orchestral music are best seen in the fact that concerts were attended by a large audience which, having "mastered" the 19th century repertoire, during the 1930s became interested in the works of a more "experimental" character. Despite the attempt to overcome the "historical delay" and join as soon as possible the current stylistic trends of "the West", the newly-developed orchestral music in Serbia was not, however, open to the "experiments" of the Viennese expressionists. The extreme limit of "modernity" was marked by the music of Prokofiev, Stravinsky and Shostakovich.[10]

A similar situation shaped the profile of the national repertoire. The most popular music was that of the generation of middle-aged composers whose works, mainly inspired by folklore, maintained some continuity with the Romantic tradition, while at the same time discretely adopting contemporary idioms, and thus contributing significantly to the history of modern "national schools" in the 20th century. When promoting national symphonic music abroad, those works that had won affirmation "at home" were always selected first: during the first tours in Romania and Bulgaria in 1937, the Philharmonic performed the works of the "national repertoire classics": Milojević, Binički, Krstić, Hristić, Baranović, Slavenski and Stojanović.[11] Even when the Vienna Symphony Orchestra performed in Belgrade in 1938, the conductor Vukdragović, honoured to lead the outstanding guests, opted for the most famous, representative compositions by Konjović, Slavenski and Hristić.

More radical expressionistic sound worlds were doomed to failure in Belgrade, as representatives of the youngest generation of composers in the late 1930s soon discovered when they brought their "ambitious" youthful scores from Prague, where they had studied. However, their success was hindered not only by the conservative taste of the audience. The performing musicians themselves were the first to reject these "avant-garde" works, primarily because they were technically too demanding.[12]

The rise in the quality of Belgrade orchestras, particularly the Philharmonic, was due in no small part to the work they did with visiting foreign conductors. There is no doubt that Belgrade musicians, led by the best masters such as Paumgartner, Baton, Fitelberg and Mitropoulos,[13] gained extensive knowledge from this, enhancing the general sound quality of the orchestra.

Just as elsewhere, the shifting "horizons of expectation" of symphonic performance production was equally a product of visiting orchestras from elsewhere in the country and from abroad. The picture of Belgrade concert life – its quality, dynamics and variety of genres – gains a new dimension when we take into consideration that during a single decade Belgrade was visited by the Berlin Symphony Orchestra (1928), Zagreb (1930), Czech (1931), Romanian (1934), Berlin (1936)[14] and Slovak Philharmonics (1937), Berlin

Chamber Orchestra (1936) and the orchestra of the Frankfurt Opera (1938 and in 1940).[15] These facts clearly speak of the changed status of Belgrade on the musical map of Europe.

As to inter-Yugoslav repertoire, the most ambitious mass project was definitely the Symphonic Music Festival held at the Belgrade Fair of 1938. The press of that time reported the turnout of as many as 6000 visitors (!) at two concerts of all three Yugoslav philharmonics: Belgrade, Zagreb and Ljubljana, conducted by Matačić, Baranović and Štritof.[16] It seems that few events could illustrate better the picture of the rise and affirmation of national symphonic music in the period between the two wars!

One of the most prominent roles in the development of chamber music, which made up the greatest part of concert life, was played by orchestra Collegium musicum (1925), led by Miloje Milojević, who was the first doctor of musicology in Serbia, one of the leading composers and certainly the most influential music critic and ideologist of the time. This amateur orchestra, made up almost exclusively of university professors and students, contributed largely to the popularisation of art music and the education of a wider audience. Thanks to Milojević, themed concerts accompanied by introductory lectures presented the numerous listeners with the characteristics of music of earlier epochs and offered a basic knowledge of contemporary trends, especially in Serbia. A contribution to the generic and stylistic variety of Belgrade concert seasons was made by Collegium at concert evenings dedicated to the music of baroque composers (Turlakov 1986).

Speaking of smaller instrumental groups, although musicians frequently gathered *ad hoc* and maintained a high frequency of chamber music concerts, there were not many permanent ensembles: only two duos (Ličar–Tкalčić and sisters Marija and Olga Mihailović), two trios (Slatin and Stojanović–Hajeк–Mokranjac) and two quartets (Zorko–Slatin, from 1921, and Belgrade quartet, from 1928).[17]

Chamber music quite naturally developed more rapidly and efficiently than orchestral: the professional level and refinement of interpretation were a logical consequence of the individual perfection of chamber musicians, many of whom were building a solo career at the same time. Vivid concert activity in the chamber music field particularly stimulated the composers. Although many concert evenings were dedicated to Lied, a comparison of the genres of Serbian music at the beginning of the third and the end of the fourth decades clearly shows that the rise of instrumental practice caused a shift of focus in repertoire from vocal to instrumental forms.

Chamber works by Serbian composers appealed to guest ensembles both from other Yugoslav musical centres and from abroad. The famous Czech Zika Quartet, for example, performed a piece by Milojević, while the Zagreb Quartet performed music by Konjović, Logar, Milojević and Milošević at concerts in Belgrade, demonstrating its sophisticated taste by identifying the very best in the country's quartet production.[18]

Familiarity with the world's chamber scene, particularly the most recent compositions, was also made possible by significant guest ensembles from abroad: the Ševčík, Zika, and Dresden quartets.[19] The most avant-garde tendencies were introduced by Paul Hindemith himself during his visit with Amar-Hindemith Quartet in 1924.[20] Another Hindemith's work was performed by the members of Prague Brass Quintet, who on the same evening (15 December 1931) in Belgrade presented a student work by the gifted Serbian composer Ljubica Marić. Two years later, she was to participate successfully with this very work at the festival of the International Society for Contemporary Music in Amsterdam.

Choral music

The pluralism of music-making during this epoch is perfectly illustrated by another phenomenon. This is the *cult of choral music*. The activities of numerous Serbian singing societies from the 1830s created a solid foundation for the period of Stevan Stojanović Mokranjac (1853–1914), the most important figure of Serbian musical romanticism, during which the quality of certain choirs, Belgrade ones in particular, was recognised on the international scene. However, after World War I, when according to many artists a *new era* for Serbian culture began, the tradition of "good old times" was not abandoned, but on the contrary experienced a full expansion and development.

During the first half of the 20th century the whole of Yugoslavia, including its cultural periphery, saw the creation of the largest musical front in the cultural history of South-Slavic nations. In Belgrade alone, there were a dozen choirs, among which at least three were excellent: the choir of the First Belgrade Singing Society, "*Obilić*" and "*Stanković*". From their rich history it is worth singling out a few facts.

Thanks to the conductor Kosta Manojlović, who during his studies in Oxford developed an affinity for old vocal polyphony, the choir of the First Belgrade Singing Society was among the first to perform works by Palestrina (*Missa papae Marcelli*, 1925) and the English madrigalists (1927, 1929). Their performances of Verdi's *Requiem* (1934) and Handel's oratorio *Messiah* (1937), together with their receiving the first prize at the international competition in Budapest (1937), mark the "golden" moments of the choir's history from the time they worked with Matačić (1932) and Predrag Milošević.

The Academic Singing Society "*Obilić*" was considered right at the "centre of Serbian musical culture" in the period between the two wars. The choir members – enthusiastic and gifted students of the Belgrade University – won the highest awards not only "at home", but throughout Europe as well.[21] Taking into consideration the fact that "*Obilić*" (with Matačić and Bandur), apart from numerous *a capella* concerts, participated in the Belgrade premieres of Mozart's *Coronation Mass* (1926), the oratorio *Oedipus Rex* by Stravinsky, the *Stabat Mater* of Szymanowski (1933), *King David* by Honneger (1928), Bruckner's *Missa* and *Te Deum*, and Wagner's music-drama *Parsifal* (concert performance, 1938), it is perfectly clear why this choir was beyond competition in the country. We might note too that in 1937, at the festival in Munich, the choir won the prize as "the best in the world". "*Obilić*" remained the only choir in Serbian music-history whose interpretation of the most successful works of Serbian choral literature was recorded by the world's famous companies His Master's Voice, and Columbia.[22]

Members of the Academic Singing Society "*Obilić*" on the Acropolis of Athens, November 1936. University Library "Svetozar Marković", Belgrade.

The high quality of Serbian choirs is indicated by the repertoire and international reputation of the choir of the Music Society *"Stanković"*, which is renowned for performing Beethoven's *Missa Solemnis* (1937) and for its successful tours in Czechoslovakia and Romania (1924), France (1927), Bulgaria (1939) and Hungary (1940).[23]

A special, socially-engaged quality was given to the Belgrade choral scene in 1930 by the Workers' Singing Society *"Abrašević"*, which was frequently harassed by the police as the core of the left-wing ideological movement. Apart from the "fighting song genre", *"Abrašević"* was the only one in the country to follow the model of Czech avant-garde satirical theatres and cherish the genre of a *recitation choir* led by composer and musicologist Vojislav Vučković in cooperation with the choreographer Lujo Davičo, aesthetician Pavle Stefanović, composer Josip Slavenski and pianist and musicologist Stana Đurić-Klajn.[24]

With such a large following of admirers and active participants of choral music, it is hardly unusual that after World War I the choirs of the newly-founded Kingdom were given the task of encouraging the expansion of the Yugoslav idea through repertoire and cooperation. They commenced with reciprocal visits; the Belgrade choirs organised Yugoslav tours, while the choirs from Zagreb, Sarajevo, Ljubljana, Maribor, Trbovlje and Skopje visited Belgrade.[25] In 1924 the South Slav Singing Association was founded, setting up its own music sheet publishing activities, and thus stimulating the promotion and production of national music. Mass gatherings and "competitions" of choirs – members of the Association – were held in 1929, while the gathering of academic choirs took place a year later.

Traditional ties with the Czechs were also strengthened: the extraordinary mixed choirs Hlahol (1921) and Smetana; the all-female Prague (1921) and Moravian Teachers (1922); and the male Prague Teachers (1922), established high standards of choral music. By World War II Belgrade had hosted many other foreign guild choirs (Romanian Railway Workers, Lvóv Technicians), but the Russian choir The Don's Cossacks seemed to have been the most popular. Foreign guests tried their best to perform at least one work by Yugoslav composers.[26]

It is, however, indicative that West European choirs rarely appeared: it was not before the mid-1930s that a Magdeburg choir (1935) visited Belgrade, followed by the famous Vienna boys (1937), the choir of the English Journalists (1938) and the choir of Regensburg Cathedral (1940). Englishmen performed the masterpieces of their renaissance tradition, while German signers, apart from compositions by German classicists and romanticists, performed several pieces from the Italian and Flemish renaissance. Those were rare but significant indicators of the vocal repertoire being enriched: "opening windows" to an earlier music past was, after all, as valuable and *new* for the Serbian music scene as the appearance of current novelties! A great excitement was caused by the 1939 visit of the choir and orchestra of Turin radio that performed Verdi's *Requiem* and Beethoven's Ninth Symphony, led by conductor Armando La Rosa Parodi.

Perhaps in no other field did Yugoslav composers have such good preconditions for their work as in choral music, and that goes even for more modern compositional styles. A national repertoire dominated the choral programmes, for, just as in the previous epoch, compositions inspired by folklore prevailed. We can conclude, then, that the *collective spirit* and *Romantic ideology of the national* in Yugoslav musical culture reached its high point between the two wars.

Education problems and progress

The significance of education in the development of a nation's overall culture is well understood. Schools of art and music are not only the seed-bed for future generations of artists but for future audiences as well. Data about educational development help us to "introduce order" into debates about the developmental level of the national culture, while data about the schooling of artists abroad help us to map those European centres from which novelties emanated, in turn resulting in the transformation of the national tradition.

At the end of World War I, Belgrade saw the establishment of two elementary and secondary music schools. Stevan Mokranjac founded the first, the Serbian Music School (later called '*Mokranjac*') in 1899, while Binički inaugurated the second in 1911, from within the Singing Society "*Stanković*". The curricula of the Belgrade music schools were based on European models, but the desire to improve professional standards could really only be fulfilled with more comprehensive music studies.[27] The opening of Belgrade Music Academy had to wait until 1937, when Hristić, Stojanović and, in particular, Kosta Manojlović, managed to provide formal and material conditions for its foundation. However, by the beginning of World War II the Academy had still not succeeded in educating a single generation of graduates!

After acquiring basic knowledge at home, from the end of the 19th century practically all renowned Serbian composers studied abroad. Traditionally, they studied most frequently in Prague, but they also went to Munich, Leipzig, Moscow, Paris, Rome, and London. Among performers, only a few were lucky enough to be granted a state scholarship for studies abroad. Upon their return to the home country, they performed as soloists, played in chamber ensembles and, fortunately, worked as professors. The opinions of the music critics of the time were undivided in their high praise of the violinist Marija Mihailović and her sister, pianist Olga, violinist (and composer) Petar Stojanović, concert singers Ivanka Milojević and Jelka Stamatović-Nikolić, pianists Ljubica Maržinec, Milka Đaja, Alisa Bešević, Jelena Dokić, and cello player Jovan Mokranjac. They were all educated in the West.[28] The greatest number of musicians who went to school "at home" could get only the secondary school certificate. And it was these musicians who had to bear the burden of the overall musical life, particularly of the work of the opera and symphony orchestras!

In such circumstances, the arrival of the Czech pianist Emil Hajek [Hayek][29] at the "*Stanković*" school in 1929 represented a turning point. With Hayek, whose name was widely recognised in Europe, Belgrade got a complete musician, who had already achieved a successful concert career before coming to Belgrade. Hayek had been the Rector of the Saratovo Conservatory for eleven years, where he achieved fame as a piano professor. After taking up a position as head of the piano department in *"Stanković"*, he took several key steps: he founded the Concert Department; harmonised marking criteria with the European ones; introduced obligatory participation in school concerts for all students and professors of that department; and reformed the curriculum, encouraging the introduction of a contemporary Slav and especially national repertoire. Setting a personal example to colleagues, he actively staged solo concerts, accompanied prominent foreign guests and collaborated with other musicians in chamber music concerts.[30] As a critic, he set new standards in writing on music; when assessing the concerts of foreign pianists, he used expert terminology and made comments that revealed his profound knowledge of all aspects of pianism and his familiarity with the finer points of piano literature interpretation.[31] In order to lay the foundations for the development of Belgrade piano playing and piano pedagogy, it was crucial to have Hayek as early as possible as the head of the piano department in the secondary school which was later to become the Music Academy.

The figure of Emil Hayek has merited special attention because I want to emphasise the importance of establishing professional criteria not only in the work of pedagogical institutions but also on the concert stage and in music criticism. For the progress of national performance standards, it was not enough for Belgrade musicians simply to attend concerts by leading soloists, some of whom will be soon given space here; it was also necessary to meet them and to work with them in their own environment on a daily basis.

The greatest energy in building professional musical life, however, had to be devoted to two parallel fronts: the *struggle for quality* and the *struggle for an audience*.

Struggle for quality and struggle for an audience

Advancement on both these fronts was encouraged and spurred on by numerous foreign guests to Belgrade: the above-mentioned orchestras, choirs, chamber ensembles and conductors, but also world-famous soloists, whose concert itineraries after World War I included Belgrade as an important venue. Belgrade was visited often and with pleasure by the pianists Paul Weingarten, Eugene d'Albert, Alfred Cortot, Nikolai Orlov, Alexander Borowsky, Arthur Rubinstein, Joseph Lhevinne, Maurycy Rosenthal, Claudio Arrau, Carlo Zecchi, Lazare Levy, Nikita Magaloff, Frederic Lamond, and Alexander Uninski; by the violinists Jan Kubelík, Váša Příhoda, Bronislaw Hubermann, Nathan Milstein, Joszef Szigeti, and Jacques Thibaut; and by the cellists Enrico Mainardi, Pierre Fournier, and Gaspar Cassado.[32] Besides Paul Hindemith, Belgrade audiences listened to Albert Roussel and Sergei Prokofiev performing their own compositions![33]

It is obvious that among the guests the most numerous were pianists, but also that artists with a world reputation rarely introduced significant repertoire novelties in the musical life of the Yugoslav capital. On the contrary! Exactly as with the symphony concerts, their repertoire was dominated by popular Beethoven sonatas and sentimental and popular virtuoso pieces from the Romantic era. As time passed, Debussy and Ravel appeared frequently on the repertoire of western pianists, while the Russians liked to play attractive pieces by Stravinsky and Prokofiev.[34] If the famous guests did not come to Belgrade intending to introduce repertoire novelties that would "disturb" the long-established taste of the audience, they no doubt introduced new "rules of the game" in the field of winning over the professional quality of musical life.

Audience tastes were also marked by the atmosphere of "old times". Since the greatest number of visitors attending music performances possessed no basic knowledge of the history of music, the practice of having introductory lectures before concerts was an efficient propaganda remedy "discovered" in the period between the two wars. The form, however, was old, having been taken over from the epoch of romanticism, but it proved useful in Belgrade. All those well-attended "Music lessons" at the Kolarac People's University,[35] at the concerts of the chamber orchestra, Collegium musicum, and at chamber evenings in the Art Pavilion "Cvijeta Zuzorić" (so-called "People's Conservatory"), were based on that model.

The expansion of choral music was also based, as we have seen, on "old" cultural patterns. The Society of the Friends of Slavic Music (from 1939), where Konjović and Vučković in particular actively participated, continued to spread the spirit of pan-Slavism, confirming the loyalty of Serbian musicians to the old romantic idea of the unity of all Slavic nations. Dedication to the Slavic circle before World War II was also enhanced by the support of a group of Serbian artists who showed sympathies for communist ideas from the Soviet Union. As we demonstrated with the example of the anti-establishment Singing society "Abrašević", which promoted ideological struggle through its artistic activities, the frontline of the struggle for an audience for Serbian music was equally influenced by political ideas and political struggle in the inter-war period.

The overall effect of the methods applied in propagandising for art music in Belgrade is best exemplified by activities at the end of the 1930s. "Our composers have a richer agenda in the music programmes […] Music performances are visited not only by 2000 students of music schools but also by other school youth sitting in the upper circle" wrote Milojević in 1938 on the pages of the renowned *Srpski književni glasnik* [Serbian Literary Magazine] (M. [Milojević] 1938: 640).

At first sight the struggle for an audience seemed to have been won!

However, the data about the phenomenon of *mass culture* spreading in Belgrade with the onset of new media will show that the situation was quite complex and that the taste of the audience at the beginning of the 1930s was difficult to channel and control.

Radio

The introduction of new media proved to be an irreplaceable catalyst in the modernisation processes in the field of music as well. The official beginning of Radio Belgrade broadcasts (24 March 1929) was marked by art music and heralded the future orientation towards a national Yugoslav repertoire, in accordance with the official state cultural policy.[36] Professional musicians invested heavily in the radio promotion of art music: a great number of concerts, mostly chamber but also symphonic, were directly broadcast, while a competition for new works (1935) stimulated the creation of new (primarily orchestral) works.

Integrating music into the global media space was also important. During the first year, seven concerts from Prague and Vienna were broadcast, and in the following year as many as fifty concerts, including those from Munich, Berlin and the Salzburg festival. After 1931, which saw the beginning of Belgrade concert broadcasts, an opportunity was created for the promotion of Yugoslav music abroad. The effects were felt in performance quality as well: the very idea that they were listened to by "the whole world" encouraged musicians to do their best. The so-called "Yugoslav" concert of the Radio Symphony Orchestra (June 1938) was broadcast by as many as fifty radio stations from fourteen European countries![37] Taking into account the fact that soon there were several other broadcasts with similar programmes,[38] we may conclude that the compositions that had proved popular in Belgrade were welcomed by international audiences too.

Despite many attempts to promote artistic genres, so-called "light music" was still the most popular on the radio programme. It was cultivated in the salon orchestra repertoire and in broadcasts of recorded popular music from the West. It was one of the significant results of the spread of so-called 'mass culture'. However, like elsewhere in the world, the process of differentiation soon invaded the sphere of mass taste, with older listeners remaining loyal to stylised folk songs, Vienna waltzes and operetta arias, while the younger audiences followed contemporary trends, especially from America, which were brought to Belgrade together with film, musical and jazz.[39] Changes affected the sphere of private life, too. At parties given by the Belgrade middle class traditional *kolo* dancing completely disappeared, while previously popular European dances – polka, waltz, quadrille and lance – were in the 1930s replaced by the American Charleston, andalus, blackbottom and banana-slade.

Most professional musicians stood out against the breakthrough of "light" genres, but their struggle to influence the tastes of audiences was ineffectual; one attempt to organise a public listening to recordings of art music was, for example, a total failure. Just as the beginning of industrialisation caused protests among craftsmen, so the appearance of the radio and the record player as new technological media initiated social unrest in the music guild. Fearing that the concerts as a medium for classical music would completely disappear, musicians angrily stood up against these "mechanical instruments", pointing out their harm in forming the taste of the audience.[40] In order to understand the phenomenon completely, it is necessary to know that the new media were available only to the well-off, whose interest was of vital significance for the survival and further progress of art music.[41] It should also be noted that concerts given by famous artists from abroad, despite their very expensive tickets, were, as a rule, much better attended than the more reasonably priced concerts of Yugoslav performers.[42]

The development of musical life in Serbia during the first half of the 20th century presents us with a colourful and dynamic picture, but it is just one piece in the mosaic of all those changes which intensively and profoundly changed the course of our national culture, especially after World War I, bringing it closer to West European models. A specific concept of work patterns in artistic institutions laid the foundations, quite solid for that time, for the development of a cultural model of the civic type. On these foundations there gradually emerged the contours of the future building of a modern civic Serbian art, before new political conflicts intervened. A strong surge of cultural development was virtually blocked during World War II and – after the war and the victory of socialist revolutionary forces – much of the valuable heritage of the civic society were questioned and exposed to doubt. However, once established, the major institutions of musical life – the Opera and ballet, Philharmonic, the excellent choirs, the music schools and the Academy, and Radio-Belgrade – were far from being undermined. It was their work that provided the foundation for the overall musical life and for the further development of Serbian music in the second half of the 20th century.

Notes

1. For overall aspects of the development of Serbian music in the period between the two wars, see in detail: Tomašević 2009.
2. About the contribution of the Russian music immigrants see Mosusova 1994 and 1995; Milin 2003.
3. Shalyapin performed in the operas *Boris Godunov* and *Don Quixote* (*Jedan vek…*, 1968: 634–641; Turlakov 1994: 136).
4. While visiting Athens (17–19. Jan. 1933), the troupe performed Cherepnyn's *Secret of the Pyramid*, *Swan's Lake* by Tchaikovsky, *Sheherazade*, music by Rimsky-Korsakov, Krešimir Baranović's ballet *Cvijeće male Ide* [Little Ida's Flowers], ballet from the opera *Prince Igor* by Borodin and Baranović's ballet *Licitarsko srce* [The Gingerbread Heart]. The following tours were in Romania (1936), Czechoslovakia (1938) and Bulgaria (1938).
5. Until the opening of Kolarac Foundation, rehearsals and concerts were given in National Theatre and in the hall of the Hotel Kasina.
6. Until 1941, many conductors, e.g. I. Brezovšek, K. Baranović, L, Matačić, J. Bandur, M. Vukdragović, P. Milošević, P. Stojanović, M. Živković, appeared with the Philharmonic.
7. They culminated in 1936; Hristić was shortly replaced by Brezovšek and Vukdragović, until 1937, when Lovro Matačić took the leading position.
8. Famous artists performed with the Philharmonic: pianists Alfred Cortot (1926), Carlo Zecchi (1932), Alexandar Borowsky (1936), Nikolai Orlov (1939), violinist Váša Příhoda (1933), cello players Enrico Mainardi (1933, 1934, 1937, and 1940) and Pierre Fournier (1935) (Turlakov 1994).
9. By World War II, Mainardi had performed in Belgrade eight times, every year from 1932 (Pejović 2004: 225).
10. Shostakovich's *First Symphony* was performed in Belgrade in 1934.
11. By affirming the Yugoslav idea, the concert program in Romania (February 1937) included the works of Slovenian and Croatian composers, Albini and Gotovac. The Yugoslav program was also presented in Bulgaria (October 1937): besides orchestral works performed by the Philharmonic, Zagreb quartet presented string quartets by Jarnović, Odak and Konjović, and singers M. Bugarinović and Ž. Cvejić – songs by Yugoslav authors (Pejović 2004: 141).

12. The premiere of the First Symphony by Stanojlo Rajičić (23 December 1938) lasted twice as long! See Rajičić's memories in: Veselinović 1983: 299.

13. Bernhard Paumgartner conducted the "*Obilić*" choir and Philharmonic at the Belgrade premiere of Bruckner's *Mass* and *Te Deum* (28 February 1931); Dimitri Mitropoulos, as a soloist and conductor, performed Prokofiev's Piano Concerto no. 3 (14 October 1933); Grzegorz Fitelberg dedicated the whole concert to more recent Polish music (23 November 1933), while Rhené Baton – to French composers (Franck's Symphony and Berlioz, *La Damnation de Faust*) (16 March 1937) (Turlakov 1994).

14. Conducted by Hermann Abendroth, the Berlin Philharmonic performed (28 February 1931) Bach's *Brandenburg Concerto* no. 3, Beethoven's Symphony no. 7, R. Strauss's poem *Tod und Verklärung*, Wagner's Overture for *Meistersingers* and the *Symphonic Dance* from the opera *Ero s'onog svijeta* [Ero from the Other World] by Jakov Gotovac, a composer from Zagreb (Turlakov 1994).

15. This orchestra performed (9 March 1940) Bruckner's Second and Fourth Symphony and Weber's overture *Oberon*, as well as the premiere of *Rhapsody* by the young Serbian composer S. Rajičić.

16. Two festival evenings (10 and 11 April 1938) had a rich program: Tchaikovsky Symphony no. 5, Dvořak Symphony no. 9, Wagner Overtures for the operas *Tannhäuser* and *Meistersinger*, Mussorgsky *Night on the Bare Mountain*, Smetana symphonic poems *Vltava* and *Vyšehrad*, Konjović *Symphonic Triptich* from the opera *Koštana*, Baranović, Overture for the opera *Striženo košeno* [Sheared or Mown], Bravničar *Himnus slavicus* (Turlakov 1994: 196; Pejović 2004: 142).

17. The cellist Juro Tkalčić and pianist Ciril Ličar performed as a duo immediately after the war, while the violinist Marija and pianist Olga performed from the 1930s; the Trio Slatin gathered the Russian musicians, violinist Vladimir, cellist Aleksandar and pianist Ilija, who sometimes performed in a Quartet with Jovan Zorko. The Trio Stojanović–Хајек–Мокрањац, consisting of violinist Petar, pianist Emil and cello player Jovan, performed together from the beginning of the 1930s; M. Mihailović, Ličar, Tkalčić and Zorko performed in the Belgrade Quartet.

18. The Zika Quartet performed (10 May 1930) Milojević's *Quartet* in C-minor; the Zagreb Quartet played quartets by Konjović (First, *Muzika skrivenih slutnji* [Music of Hidden Presentiments], 15 March 1920 and 10 May 1931), Mihovil Logar (Second, *Kvartet sa uspavankom* [Quartet with a Lullaby]), Milojević (in E-minor) and Milošević (3 May 1930).

19. The Ševčík Quartet, who performed with Hajek (Hayek) in Czechoslovakia, visited in 1924; in 1932, together with Borodin's and Dvořak's quartets, the Zika Quartet performed the *Lirski kvartet* [Lyric Quartet] by Slavenski; in 1935 the Zika quartet was joined by Hayek: they performed quintets by Dvořak, Janáček and Suk; the Dresden Quartet in 1936 performed works by Beethoven, Brahms and Debussy.

20. The Amar–Hindemith Quartet (Licco Amar, Walter Caspar, Paul and Rudolf Hindemith) visited on 21 December 1924; besides compositions by Mozart and Ravel, they performed Hindemith's *Quartet* op. 32 and the quarter-tone *Quartet* by Alois Hába.

21. Foreign tours: Poland (1926), Greece (1927), Austria (1928), Czechoslovakia (1929, 1933), Switzerland and Germany (1934), Bulgaria, Romania and Poland (1935), Turkey (1936), Romania, Poland and Germany (1937), France (1938), Bulgaria (1939), Romania (1940) and Hungary (1941) (*Akademsko…*2005).

22. His Master's Voice (1928): Josif Marinković – *Narodni zbor* [The People's Meeting] (anthem of the Society), Matačić – *Motto of Obilić*, Mokranjac – fragment from *The Liturgy* [Njest svjat] and *Rukovet* [Garland] no. 10, Hristić – fragment from *Opelo* [The Requiem]: Svjati Bože [Holy God]; Columbia (1928): the same compositions by Mokranjac and Hristić (*Akademsko…* 2005: 139).

23. There were other active choirs, with varying results: Choir of Serbian-Jewish Society (premieres of oratorios *Elias* by Mendelssohn (1905), *Judas Maccabaeus* (1926) and *Samson* (1932) by Handel)

and Vocal Ensemble of Russian Immigrants /Mihail Glinka (premieres of significant works of Russian sacred music – *Liturgies* by Tchaikovsky and Rachmaninov, in 1928).

24. The most successful drama-music-ballet visions were based on principles derived from Émile Jacques-Dalcroze's concept of rhythm, visual sensations and film projections, with the poetry of Neruda, Chinese and Latin American poets and texts of J. Wolker. In 1937, eighty members of the Society took part in the project *Hej, kuli* [Hey, кули], based on Louis Aragon's text and with Slavenski's music (Pejović 2004: 209).

25. From Zagreb: Kolo, Lisinski, Balkan, Mladost, Serbian Singing Society (1920–4, 1926, 1927, 1930); from Sarajevo: Serbian Singing Society *"Sloga* [Concord]*"* (1926); from Ljubljana: Academic Singing Society (1930); from Maribor: Choir of Glazbena Matica (1922, 1925); from Trbovlje: Trbovlje's slavček [Nightingale] (1934, 1936), from Skoplje: Obilić (1936–40).

26. The famous Czech Hlahol performed, for example, (2 May 1932), the choral works by Konjović (*Za gorom* [Behind the Mountain] and *Vragolan* [Mischievous Boy]) and by Slavenski (*Voda zvira* [Water rises]).

27. When he became the schoolmaster in 1925, P. Stojanović reformed the syllabus according to the Prague and Vienna conservatories (*Muzička enciklopedija* 1973, III: 442).

28. M. Mihailović graduated at the High Music School in Vienna (1927) and specialised, with Enescu, in *Cours d'interpretation* in Paris (1928–29); O. Mihailović graduated at *L'École normale de musique* in Paris (Levy, Cortot); J. Mokranjac graduated at the High School in Munich; J. Stamatović-Nikolić studied both singing (Morfova) and piano (Veselý) in Prague; I. Milojević studied singing in Munich (1907–1910) (*Muzička enciklopedija* 1973).

29. Emil Hayek (1886–1974) graduated in piano (Jiránek, 1908) and composition (Dvořak, 1903) in Prague. He specialised with Ansorge in Berlin (1908–9). From 1909 to 1921 he worked as a piano teacher and as Rector of the Conservatoire in Saratovo. He performed with the conductor V. Talich, cellist Fingerland and Ševčík quartet, as well as with the famous violinist Jan Kubelík (1923–1928). Later he was a member of the jury at prestigious international competitions: F. Chopin in Warsaw (1955 and 1960), Smetana – Prague spring (1948 and 1957) and George Enescu in Bucarest 1964. For the first and the only time in the history of Belgrade piano music, he performed (in a direct radio broadcast) Beethoven's 32 sonatas and the 48 preludes and fugues from Bach's *Das Wohltemperierte Klavier* (*Muzička enciklopedija* 1973 II: 60; Hajek 1993: 102–103).

30. He accompanied, for example, the cellist Pierre Fournier (1935).

31. He usually published reviews in the music periodicals *Zvuk* [Sound] and *Muzički glasnik* [Serbian Literary Magazine] (Hajek 1993: 45–69; Pejović 1999: 162–165).

32. Pianists: Weingarten: 1923 (four concerts), 1924–1925, 1932–1933; d'Albert: 1924; Cortot: 1924, 1926, 1933, 1935, 1937–1938; Orlov: 1925, 1932–1934, 1936, 1938–1939; Borowsky: 1925, 1933, 1936–1939; Rubinstein: 1927 (four concerts, at the first concert: Stravinsky, *Petrushka* – N.B. Stravinsky dedicated the piano version of the suite to Rubinstein – at the third and the fourth – Prokofiev, Albéniz, De Falla, Szymanowski), 1929 (two concerts), 1932 (two concerts). This equals eight performances during five years! Lhevinne: 1928; Rosenthal: 1928, 1935; Arrau: 1931 (three concerts), 1932; Zecchi: 1932–1933; Levy: 1933–1934, 1937; Magaloff: 1937, 1939–1940; Lamond: 1937 (N.B. During three concert evenings in 1937 he performed twelve Beethoven sonatas, the "great" *Variations* in C-minor etc.); Uninski: 1938; violinists: Kubelík: 1926; Příhoda: 1923, 1926, 1928, 1930, 1932–1933, 1935, 1937; Hubermann: 1928, 1934, 1939; Milstein: 1931–1932, 1938; Szigeti: 1937 (N.B. Accompanied by Magaloff who then performed for the first time in Belgrade); Thibaut: 1938; cello players: Mainardi: 1932–1934, 1937–1940; Fournier: 1935 (N.B. Accompanied by Hayek); Cassado: 1936.

33. At a "French modern music" concert (6 April 1933) there were the *Second Sonata* for Violin, *String Quartet* op. 45 and *Five Melodies* for soprano and piano by A. Roussel, who accompanied on the piano M. Mihailović and B. Nuri-Hadžić. Prokofiev played, on 16 January, *Sonata* op. 14 no. 2, *Ten Visions* op. 22, *Three Gavottes* op. 12, 24 and 32, *Toccata, Three Grand Ma's Fairy Tales, Landscape* op. 35 and *Etudes*; encores: *Prelude in Spanish Style, March* from *Three Oranges* and *Diabolic Visions* (Turlakov 1994: 168).

34. On 19th February, 1935 Soulima Stravinsky (Igor's son) visited Belgrade, where (with the Philharmonic Orchestra) he performed his father's *Concerto for Piano, Winds and Contrabass*. As E. Hajek wrote: "Almost in each movement his memory failed. As the widely advertised son of the famous father, he was a major disappointment" (Hajek 1993: 60).

35. At the "Music lessons", the audience could learn about the most contemporary tendencies. Vučković and Slavenski, for example, fully dedicated "Fourth public lesson" (15 December 1935) to quartertone music (Dragutinović 1935).

36. Orchestra and soloists of the opera performed fragments of ballet music by Hristić (future *The Legend of Ohrid*) and Baranović (suite from ballet *The Gingerbread Heart*), as well as the arias from hit-opera *Zulumćar* [The Oppressor] by P. Krstić (Simić-Mitrović 1988: 17).

37. Conductor Vukdragović; the programme included the works by Milojević, Baranović, Gotovac and Konjović.

38. In the programme broadcast in the USA (27 November 1938), apart from Hristić's suite from ballet *The Legend of Ohrid*, there was also a brilliant choral scherzo *Kozar* [The Goat herd] by Mokranjac and Milojević's solo-song *La chanson du vent de mer*. There were broadcasts in England (7 December 1938 and 2 July 1939), as well as the broadcast of the joint Paris-Belgrade concert (18 May 1939) (Pejović 2004: 225).

39. Silent and (from the beginning of the 1930s) sound movies became the favourite entertainment in Belgrade (Marković 1992: 87). American jazz artists were rare in Belgrade at that time: apart from the vocal quintet Black Revelers (1928) only one jazz opera troupe Louisiana (1931) visited Belgrade (Turlakov 1994: 128, 135). However, on the eve of World War II the radio broadcasts included top jazz musicians: Goodman, Ellington, and Whiteman (Marković 1992: 82).

40. Here is one such commentary: "Mechanical instruments come to the hands of musically uneducated elements playing with no control. [...] All of us know what comes from the record players in rooms with open windows. There are but a few who use the record-player as a noble music instrument" (Švarc 1931: 78–87).

41. In 1929, the price of the cheapest radio was 2750 dinars (two average salaries!), while five times as much money should be put aside for the purchase of a new piano.

42. Despite the sky-high price of the ticket (1000 dinars), Belgrade people queued all night in front of the box-office in order to see Anna Pavlova, the "earth goddess of dance". See Đurić-Klajn 1974: 401. On the other hand, the price of the tickets at the People's University was symbolic (1 and 2 dinars), just like those for Collegium musicum concerts (5 and 10 dinars) (Turlakov 1986: 114).

References

Dragutinović, B., "1/4 stepena muzika na IV času Kolarčevog narodnog univerziteta" [1/4-tone Music at the Forth Public Lesson of Kolarac's People University], *Pravda*, 16 December, 1935.

Đurić-Klajn, S., "Muzički život u gradu između dva svetska rata" [Musical Life in the Town between the Two World Wars] in *Istorija Beograda, 3, Dvadeseti vek* [History of Belgrade, 3, 20th Century], Belgrade, SANU, Odeljenje istorijskih nauka & Prosveta, 1974, pp. 398–409.

——, "Orkestri u Srbiji do osnivanja Filharmonije" [Orchestras in Serbia before the Foundation of Philharmonic] in *Akordi prošlosti* [Chords of the Past Times], Belgrade, Prosveta, 1981, pp. 128–154.

Hajek, E., *O muzici i muzičarima* [On Music and Musicians], (ed.), Priredila Olga Jovanović, Belgrade, Univerzitet umetnosti & Fakultet muzičke umetnosti, 1993.

Jedan vek Narodnog pozorišta u Beogradu [One Century of National Theatre in Belgrade], Belgrade, Narodno pozorište & Nolit, 1968.

M. [Milojević, M.], "Ekspanzija muzičkog života" [Expansion of Musical Life], *Srpski književni glasnik* XXX, Belgrade, 1938, pp. 640.

Magazinović, M., *Moj život* [My Life], (ed.), Jelena Šantić, Belgrade, Clio, 2000.

Majdanac, B. & Radojčić, M. (eds), *Akademsko pevačko društvo "Obilić". 1884–1941* [Academic Singing Society "Obilić". 1884–1941], Belgrade, Istorijski arhiv Beograda, 2005.

Marković, P. J., *Beograd i Evropa. 1918–1941. Evropski uticaji na proces modernizacije Beograda* [Belgrade and Europe. 1918–1941. European Influences on the Process of Modernization of Belgrade], Belgrade, Savremena administracija d.d., 1992.

Milin, M., "The Russian Musical Emigration in Yugoslavia after 1917", *Muzikologija*, 3, 2003, pp. 65–79.

Mosusova, N., "Ruska umetnička emigracija i muzičko pozorište u Jugoslaviji između dva svetska rata" [The Russian Art Emigration and Music Theatre in Yugoslavia between the Two World Wars], in *Ruska emigracija u srpskoj kulturi XX veka* [The Russian Emigration in Serbian Culture of the 20th Century], Belgrade, Filološki fakultet, 1994, pp. 139–149.

——, "Srpska muzička scena (125 godina Narodnog pozorišta)" [Serbian Music Stage (125 Years of National Theatre)] in *Srpska muzička scena* [Serbian Music Stage], Belgrade, Muzikološki institut SANU, 1995, pp. 5–36.

Muzička enciklopedija, I-III [Music Encyclopaedia, I-III], (ed.), Krešimir Kovačević, Zagreb, Jugoslavenski leksikografski zavod, 1973.

Pejović, R., *Muzička kritika i esejistika u Beogradu (1919–1941)* [Music Criticism and Essays on Music in Belgrade (1919–1941)], Belgrade, Fakultet muzičke umetnosti, 1999.

——, *Koncertni život u Belgradu (1919–1941)* [Concert Life in Belgrade (1919– 1941)], Belgrade, Fakultet muzičke umetnosti, 2004.

Simić-Mitrović, D., *Da capo all'infinito. Pola veka od osnivanja Simfonijskog orkestra i hora Radio-televizije Beograd* [Da capo all'infinito. The Half Century of the Symphonic Orchestra of Radio-TV Belgrade], Belgrade, Biblioteka Radio Beograda, 1988.

Švarc, R., "Muzika u domu" [Music at Home], *Muzički glasnik*, IV: 3–4, 1931, pp. 78–87.

Tomašević, K., *Na raskršću Istoka i Zapada? O dijalogu tradicionalnog i modernog u srpskoj muzici između dva svetska rata* [Serbian Music on the Cross-roads between East and West? On Dialogue of the Traditional and the Modern in Serbian Music between the Two World Wars], Belgrade and Novi Sad, Muzikološki institut SANU and Matica srpska, 2009.

Turlakov, S., "*Collegium musicum* i Miloje Milojević" [*Collegium musicum* and Miloje Milojević], *Godišnjak grada Beograda* XXXIII, 1986, pp. 93–122.

——, *Letopis muzičkog života u Beogradu. 1840–1941* [Chronicle of Music Life in Belgrade. 1840–1941], Belgrade, Muzej pozorišne umetnosti Srbije, 1994.

Veselinović-Hofman, M., *Stvaralačka prisutnost evropske avangarde u nas* [Creative Presence of European Avant-garde in Serbian Music], Belgrade, Univerzitet umetnosti, 1983.

Chapter 3

Features of the Serbian Symphony in the First Half of the 20th Century

Biljana Milanović

Petar Konjović (1883–1970).

The complex processes of modernisation in Serbia at the beginning of the 20th century took the form of a revival in almost all material and spiritual fields of life. They marked the gradual infiltration of modern thought into Serbian music from 1906 onwards, but going into full swing in the period between the two wars, and during the fourth decade culminating in a polyphony of different attitudes and tendencies, and in a variety of stylistic directions that interact and blend, from the late romanticism of the oldest generation via impressionism to the expressionism and constructivism associated with the youngest composers.

The constant changes and multiple co-existing styles suggest interaction with contemporary streams in the wider European context, but it simultaneously testifies to the contradictions inherent in the local tradition, which derived from very different (older and younger) cultural models that overlapped and constantly expressed themselves within all aspects of cultural practice in Serbia in the first half of the century. There were disproportionate developments as between different art forms, as well as between composition, performance and reception in the field of music itself. They represent an important context for researches into the output of Serbian music and for the problems associated with specific genres, especially those such as symphonic music that were marked by their short-lived tradition, and burdened by difficulties of institutionalisation and lack of technical-material support.[1] Composers adopted many different approaches when tackling the long-term difficulties associated with musical culture as a whole, but their responses can be measured in terms of regularities specifically imposed by the demands of the symphony.

There are two very different stages in the development of the Serbian symphony in the first half of the century. In the first phase, a small number of works appeared: Symphony in C minor by Petar Konjović (1907), two *Yugoslav Symphonies* by Milenko Paunović (1914–20; 1924), Symphony in D major by Svetolik Pašćan (1920) and the symphony *Spiritual Impressions* by Sava Selesković (1928).[2] Their composers do not adopt equivalent approaches in terms of traditional and modern tendencies, but they do share a similar foundation in Romantic aesthetics and in their view of Serbian folk music.[3] The second stage started with the Sinfonietta by Predrag Milošević (1930), leading to works by the then youngest Serbian composers.[4] Among these, Stanojlo Rajičić, Milan Ristić and Vojislav Vučković were dedicated to symphonic music.

The first Serbian modernists, particularly noteworthy for genre premieres and for the modernisation of an existing local heritage, had been striving to achieve some measure of inner continuity and a gradual expansion of audiences' horizons of expectations. Therefore, the use of stylistic novelties was more marked and more frequent within those genres that had already established their own tradition in the national context. Composing symphonies in Serbia emerged only with the work of these composers, and it did not represent a solid framework for the introduction of stylistic innovations. Moreover, among all modernists, as well as those who worked with a more traditional musical language, there were only a few symphonists; moreover the symphonic genre remained a rarity thanks to the emergence of avant-gardists. However, the absence of major symphonic achievements in an earlier period was compensated for by other orchestral works (e.g. overtures, symphonic suites, variations, symphonic poems) where extra-musical, programmatic components often played an important role. Also, certain symphonies were located at the border of other genres. Whereas, for example, Seleskovic's work *Spiritual Impressions* is closer to a symphonic poem, one of the most important achievements of Serbian music, the seven-movement *Symphony of the Orient* by Josip Slavenski (1934), belongs rather to a symphonic cantata genre and can only be described symbolically as a "symphony".[5]

Avant-gardists had a different attitude towards their national heritage, advocating an anti-tradition and anti-folklore attitude more-or-less from the start. Their avant-gardism, however, was fully expressed in works for various chamber ensembles, which were the ideal medium for preserving a sense of distance from romanticism, and, for applying atonal, athematic, quartertone or dodecaphonic techniques. Symphonic achievements, where they aspire to make an abrupt breakthrough into the new, as with the first symphonies of Vučković (1933) and Rajičić (1935), and Ristić's *Sinfonietta* (1939), were usually early works, composed at the end of the respective composers' studies. And although these works demonstrate great talent, technical skill and artistic quality, the fact that they are still youthful, not yet fully-mature, compositions should not be neglected. Whereas, then, Ristić's First Symphony (1941) represents the peak of the author's expressionist phase, it is symptomatic that this genre again became important for Rajičić and Vučković at the very moment when they were losing interest in the most advanced contemporary techniques.[6] Symphonic composition thus remained a field in which the avant-garde, which was a short-lived phenomenon in Serbian music until World War II anyway, was much less of a presence than in the majority of other musical genres.

It is obvious that this genre was not at the centre of Serbian musical creativity. Those that were composed had no possibility for further creative dissemination: by the middle of the century none of the works had been published and the only ones performed in Belgrade were Paunović's *First* (1925), Vučković's *First* (1939), Rajičić's *First* (1939) and *Fourth* (1946), and Seleskovic's programmatic symphony (1935).[7] Apart from the disincentives of the local institutional context, this lack of interest in the genre can be related to more general attitudes at that time. The symphony had a centuries-long history in art music, so many Serbian authors, too, considered it to be an exhausted genre. Some older composers addressed it at the beginning of their career but never returned to it later on. Therefore, the two successive stages in its development were clearly separated. This, in itself, was an unusual feature for Serbian music between the wars, since it was more often characterised by parallel approaches

Stanojlo Rajičić (1910–2000).

to the same genres by composers belonging to different generations, and bringing to bear very different perspectives on those genres.

The symphonies of older composers can be viewed in the context of features associated with the German symphonic tradition, inherited directly in the case of Paunović and Selesković, and indirectly, through Czech music, in Konjović.[8] The composers aimed for an epic quality, and sought to unify their works through strong thematic connections between the movements on the cyclic principle. Paunović, Pašćan and Selesković inclined toward a rich, late-Romantic orchestral palette, additionally emphasised in Selesković's symphony with a large Wagnerian orchestra including organs in the Finale. Apart from Pašćan, whose work exhibits a highly condensed thematic working, and rapidly shifting orchestral textures, rhapsodic forms are conspicuous. In Selesković's work, this is the result of non-periodic melody of the Wagnerian type, as well as a treatment of the programme that leads at times to extravagant emotionality and occasional structural ambiguity. In the symphonies of Konjović and Paunović, on the other hand, it was the consequence of applying variation procedures to the musical material, rather than more conventional thematic development (Blagojević-Milin 1986: 26-47; Peričić 1973: 478; Milanović 2002: 85–96).

Although Konjović wrote his best orchestra works in the period between the wars, when he was a leading figure in Serbian music, already in the symphony he strongly inclines toward Slavonic music. The complex stylistic profile we would later associate with him is already here, albeit concealed by the traditional framework of the symphony, which is close to the romanticism of the Czech and Russian national schools. At the same time, Konjović's symphony enters into an impressive dialogue with an existing Serbian choral heritage, using the well-known folk melodies from Stevan Mokranjac's popular *Garlands* (*Lele, Stano Mori* from the Fifth Garland and *Cvekje Cafnalo* from the Twelfth Garland). And while these songs appear as the main themes of the sonata-form first movement and as important cyclic material in all four movements, the first of them is, in comparison with Mokranjac's work, from its very beginning noticeably re-shaped and adjusted to the new, symphonic context, already announcing Konjović's deeply personal and creative attitude to folk material (Milin 1989: 46–48).

Music folklore plays an important role in Paunović's symphonies too, but it is here part of a wider philosophical and poetical aspiration that affects certain late-Romantic compositional idioms, approaching in particular the transcendental qualities associated with Mahler's symphonic output. Paunović in his first symphony gives us a literal programme with autobiographical moments and philosophical dimensions thematising alienation, destiny and peace under the general umbrella of nature. Like Mahler, he uses stereotypical illustrative elements (imitations of the cuckoo) and turns these into abstract music material that is given the role of a monothematic nucleus, incorporating it thus into the very structure of the work. He similarly engages in musical quotation, drawing this into a process of thematic transformation characteristic of late-Romantic symphonism. Serbian folk music in his symphonies goes through various stages of transformation between folk-sounding and abstract, between dance character and powerful drama, so that it comes to represent a potent tool of the musical dramaturgy. Analogies with Mahler's works can also be found in the expansion of inner "subjective" form and in the colouristic approach to the orchestra. In the second symphony, they are further evident in a more complex monothematic approach, in a more powerful process of atomisation of the music material, and in the important role assigned to self quotation. Thanks to the imaginative and highly individual selection of folklore elements, Paunović reaches his own, recognisable type of symphonism. He is the first true symphonist in Serbian music (Milanović 2002: 85–96).

A new chapter not only in the symphony, but in Serbian music more generally, begins with Milošević's *Sinfonietta*, which inaugurated the developing interest of Serbian composers in Schoenberg's atonality and Hindemith's neoclassicism. One can only discern the Romantic and impressionist heritage in the occasional tonal references and sporadic lyricism of this work, but the objectivity, grotesquery, mobility, linear atonality, neo-Baroque cut of the melodic lines, together with an orchestra whose corpus of brass instruments has been reduced to trumpets, all mark the essential distance from Romantic prototypes and the proximity to the most recent tendencies in European music at that time (Blagojević-Milin 1986: 48–53).

Milenko Paunović (1889–1924).

Although the youngest composers were enthralled with the avant-garde spirit of Prague, their personal artistic sensibilities can already be noticed in their early works. For Rajičić, the application of a radical expressionist framework meant fighting against his own, primarily emotional, musical nature that imposed itself even when the composer sought to renounce it conscientiously. On the other hand, objectivism, rationality and construction suited Ristić's temperament, and the idiom of his early works, especially those for chamber ensembles, can be considered as the rigorous result of adopting and combining Schöenberg's, Hába's and Hindemith's theoretical postulates. Vučković, however, had different artistic motives. From the beginning he composed in accordance with a Marxist ideology, first in the form of a radical musical language, but at the end of the fourth decade, under the strong influence of ideas on the accessibility and social role of art, in the context of a greatly simplified style. Emotionality was part of his physiognomy, but always subordinated to theoretical stands on the social engagement of art.

In this context, we may also consider the first symphonies of these composers. Rajičić almost explicitly demonstrates the dualism indicated above: the orchestral sonority of the

Milan Ristić (1908–1982).

slow movement and the harmonic focus of the scherzo suggest the older tradition, whereas atonality and a two-voiced dissonant polyphony in the outer movements indicate the early style of Hindemith, pointing towards Rajičić's chosen creative path for the few next years (Peričić 1977: 17-18).

Vučković's *First Symphony* can be related to the theoretical orientation developed during his first phase, but it is not typical of the kind of expressionism that exists in an atonal-athematic form in his other works dating from the mid-1930s. The formal aspects of the symphony and the quest for unification of its three-movement cycle led the composer to place atonality, linearity, lack of thematic development and sparse orchestration within neoclassical frameworks that maintain their contact with sonata-form design and thematically-linked movements (Peričić 1968: 99–103).

This work, along with Milošević's earlier work, can be compared to the Sinfonietta, which displays the most radical style in the context of these early symphonic works. It was written in a normal semitonal scale system unlike the quartertone and six-tone systems of Ristić's other works from that period. With its athematicism, atonality, linearity, neo-Baroque motorics and free, one-movement structure divided into four different sections distinguished by character, tempo and contrapuntal working, it demonstrates Ristić's unique approach to musical construction. Basic materials, with a sense of coherent line or with a generative motivic cell, alternate with dynamic linking sections, rich in counterpoint and with dense "verticals" that have the importance of thematic material. Basic sections then seem like a series of plateaus, giving the impression of a static "moments" within their surroundings (Bergamo 1977: 32–35).

These procedures have already developed into a method in the First Symphony. It represents the most complete symbol of Ristić's expressionistic phase and the highlight of his interest in the transformation of classical form in the context of atonality. The composer rigorously implements Schöenberg's atonality and uses free dodecaphony. He does not adopt an attitude that the series works equally well in vertical and horizontal layout, because for Ristić chords have harmonic meaning and are therefore not part of the dodecaphonic structure. Also, the composer incorporates elements of Hindemith's thematic work, so he is more relaxed in his application of athematic procedures. When dealing with form, he relies on the most general characteristics of established formal archetypes, organising the musical flow by replacing "expositions" and "developments" with alternating static moments and dynamic paragraphs (Bergamo 1977: 40–49).

Previous interpretations of Serbian symphonies created during World War II stress the influence of the war on the music, discussing how the various composers react to wartime events. The dramatic and heroic tone of Ristić's first and Rajičić's third symphonies are experienced as personal creative responses to war (Bergamo 1977: 43; Peričić 1977: 38–40).

Rajičić's second and fourth symphonies can lead us towards similar conclusions, because they are close to his third, if we judge by the character, conception and time of their appearance. But if these interpretations could be assessed comparatively, then they are at their clearest in the context of Vučković's second and third symphonies, where programmatic aspects represent part of an explicit ideological orientation but are equally marked, not least through the sudden simplification of music language, by the war.[9]

The concept of the Second Symphony – from a slow, dark movement, with one of the melodies intoning Russian folklore, by way of the modified, conflict-driven sonata form of the central movement to the heroic march of the Finale with fugato and fanfare ending in the major – implies a dramatic plot with an optimistic outcome. Similarly, the dramaturgical foreground of the Third Symphony is, according to its poetic and musical components, made almost in the "(socialist)-realist" manner (Peričić 1968: 123-127). The composer clearly employs tonality, using not only pedals and fulcra tones in the horizontal stream, but also chords built of superimposed thirds. But the intensive thematic development, the orchestral polyphony and the contrasts in the larger symphonic dynamic reveal some new creative qualities that are either non-existent or suppressed in his earlier works.

If Vučković's creativity at this time is marked as the only pre-war representative of "socialist realism", it has to be assumed that the change of style was also influenced by the composer's personal experience which assured him that the wider audience he cared for most was not about to equate a progressive ideology with radical forms of musical expression. This is to some extent confirmed by the case of Rajičić where a gradual stylistic appeasement stems not from ideology but from the aspiration to reach wider audiences. Finally, it should not be forgotten that the simplification of style, conceived sooner or later by all the composers of this generation, overlapped in time with so-called neoclassicism which, after 1936, also affected European music more generally. Younger composers in Europe at that time also developed a model of contemporary musical classicism but with fewer dilemmas and less need for radical shifts of direction. This generation, starting with Orff, Britten and Messiaen, and on to Dallapiccola and Petrassi, was close in age to the young Belgrade composers.

In Rajičić's symphonies there are none of the stylistic dilemmas typical for his early works. The composer employs an accessible tonal idiom and often uses the colour of the 'Balkan' minor mode with sharpened fourth degree. He does not avoid folkloristic elements in the melodic material, classical thematic work with sequential transpositions, nor a clear formal layout. His cyclic principle is based on the preparation for the outer movements by an introduction that forms the monothematic source of the entire work, especially apparent in the Third Symphony. Rajičić demonstrates this peculiar neo-Romantic procedure in a bleak orchestral structure of two-voice polyphony with doubled lines and sporadic chord blocks without any more extensive harmonic fill-in. Although he gradually moderated such methods after the Second Symphony, they still provoked criticism of his Fourth Symphony of 1946. The reasons for these negative opinions were, above all, to do with the ideological climate of the first post-war years, "when the ill-defined term *formalism* has already started playing the part of bugbear given to it by the famous Ždanov principles" (Peričić 1977: 62, original emphasis).

Rajičić then suffered something of a crisis. He started writing tonally and polytonally, and constructed his forms and instrumentation according to all classical postulates. This sudden stylistic simplification, provoked by external circumstances, was also, however, in his case an immediate liberation from his earlier suppressed emotional expressivity, and therefore a specific investment in the stylistic synthesis he achieved from the mid-1950s. Without it, there might not have been the complex personal symphonism this author was about to achieve in the post-war decades. Moreover, expressive and significant symphonic works of the second half of the century were also created by Milan Ristić. Therefore if the path taking us from the emergence of the Serbian Romantic symphony to this simplification of more radical developments, was short and accelerated (and thus full of difficulties as well as omissions and 'leaps' across insufficiently developed stages), it could not, in the very nature of artistic creativity, move backwards. Certain highly-valued pieces are adequate testimonies to the quality of both older and younger composers at this time, and these are joined by key works from the second half of the century – when, besides composers of the new generation, two pre-war symphonists were still composing, and in a style based on highly personal responses to their own, and a collective, past.

Notes

1. Symphonic music in Serbia had its roots in the second half of the 19th century. The first symphony in Belgrade was performed in 1899, and a special role here was played by the concerts given by the Royal Guard Orchestra. However, the Philharmonic Orchestra was not established until 1920, and by the second half of the 1930s it encountered serious financial-organisational difficulties of survival and unresolved membership status, which influenced the number of concerts, their quality and programme policy in general.

2. The genre was previously addressed by Robert Tolinger (*Symphony for big orchestra*), Hugo Doubek (*Serbian Symphony*) and Isidor Bajić. Their works have not been preserved. Miloje Milojević composed the symphony *Vsegord and Divna* (1903) while still a student; it is a semi-amateur work which only has historical importance.

3. Petar Konjović, together with Miloje Milojević and Stevan Hristić, belonged to the first generation of Serbian modernists born by the middle of the eighties. They were joined by slightly younger composers: Josip Slavenski as an emphatic modernist on one side, and on the other side Milenko Paunović, Kosta Manojlović, Svetolik Pašćan and Sava Selesković, more traditionally-minded composers. The most significant representatives of the second generation of the modernists, born at the beginning of the century, were Marko Tajčević, Mihailo Vukdragović and Milenko Živković, as well as Predrag Milošević, who was, by his age and in certain works, closer to the youngest, avant-garde group of composers.

4. Mihovil Logar, Dragutin Čolić, Stanojlo Rajičić, Milan Ristić and Ljubica Marić belong to the group of composers born in the first decade of the 20th century. As the representatives of the second generation of modernists and like some older students, they also studied in Prague.

5. In the work of Slavenski, these procedures are part of a broader poetics directed to relativism and to the rejection of well-established canons of West-European practice. They form recognisable elements of the modernistic profile of Serbian music but they depart from the conventional genre frames of the symphony.

6. Rajičić, *Second and Third Symphony* (1941; 1944), Vučković, *Second* and *Third Symphony* (1942). Vučković died in war. Ristić and Rajičić emerged as significant symphonists of post-war Serbian music.

7. It is a fact that almost all the earliest symphonic works of the avant-gardists were immediately performed in Prague. Some of their compositions in other genres were then performed at international festivals, so that the music of this generation, as well as some of Slavenski's works, achieved successful but short appearances on the international music scene in the period between the wars.

8. The nature of their composition studies partly dictated these directions (Paunović – Leipzig, Selesković – Stuttgart, Münich; Konjović – Prague). Pašćan, who studied in Zagreb, could not have had role models in local tradition, as the Croatian symphony was not yet born at that time, but the German repertoire significantly marked the concert life of the then Austro-Hungarian province, which probably influenced the young composer.

9. The initial movement of the Second Symphony is named "Victory". The Third Symphony, for soloists, choir and orchestra, is marked as "Heroic Oratorio" and it includes textual fragments from folk poetry and from *The Mountain Wreath* by Petar P. Njegoš. The other orchestral works of Vučković at this time also had poetic guidelines (e.g. *Beaming path, Herald of Tempest, Legacy of Modest Mussorgsky*). Most of them he composed while in hiding, and at the same time that he was writing war songs for propaganda purposes, sent to the Partisans by way of secret channels.

References

Bergamo, M., *Delo kompozitora. Stvaralački put Milana Ristića od prve do šeste simfonije* [The Work of the Composer. The Creative Course of Milan Ristić], Belgrade, Univerzitet u Beogradu, 1977.

——, *Elementi ekspresionističke orijentacije u srpskoj muzici do 1945* [Elements of Expressionistic Orientation in Serbian Music Until 1945], Belgrade, Srpska akademija nauka i umetnosti, 1980.

Blagojević-Milin, M., *Simfonije prve polovine XX veka u Srbiji* [Symphonies in Serbia in the First Half of 20th Century], unpublished thesis submitted to the History of Music Department at the Faculty of Music of Belgrade, for the master degree, 1986.

Jakšić, Đ., "Konjovićeva simfonija" [Konjović's Symphony], *Zvuk,* 58, 1963, pp. 361–373.

Koren, M., "Simfonija u stvaralačkom opusu Milana Ristića" [The Symphony in the Creative Output of Milan Ristić], *Zvuk,* 69, 1966, pp. 494–504.

Milanović, B., "Milenko Paunović i srpska muzička tradicija" [Milenko Paunović and the Serbian Musical Tradition] in *Josif Marinković (1851–1931). Muzika na raskršću dva veka* [Josif Marinković (1851–1931). Music at the Crossroads of the Two Centuries], Novi Bečej, Radnički dom "Jovan Veselinov Žarko", 2002, pp. 85–96.

——, "Recepcija *Prve jugoslovenske simfonije* Milenka Paunovića" [The Reception of the *First Yugoslavian Symphony* of Milenko Paunović], in *Istorija i misterija muzike. U čast Roksande Pejović* [History and Mystery of Music. In Honour of Roksanda Pejović], Belgrade, Fakultet muzičke umetnosti, 2006, pp. 337–346.

Milin, M., "Stilski profil Konjovićeve orkestarske muzike" [A Stylistic Profile of Konjović's Orchestral Output], in *Život i Delo Petra Konjovića* [The Life and Work of Petar Konjović], Belgrade, Srpska akademija nauka i umetnosti, 1989, pp. 46–50.

Milojević, M., "Koncert Beogradske filharmonije" [Concert of Belgrade Philharmonic Orchestra], in *Vojislav Vučković, umetnik i borac* [Artist and Fighter Vojislav Vučković], Belgrade, Nolit, 1968, pp. 283–285.

Pejović, R., "Pedeset godina Beogradske filharmonije" [50th Anniversary of Belgrade Philharmonic Orchestra], in *Београдска филхармонија 1923/1973* [Belgrade Philharmonic Orchestra 1923/1973], Belgrade, Beogradska filharmonija, 1973, pp. 31–72.

Peričić, Vl., "Stvaralački lik Vojislava Vučkovića" [A Creative Profile of Vojislav Vučković], in *Vojislav Vučković, umetnik i borac* [Artist and Fighter Vojislav Vučković], Belgrade, Nolit, 1968, pp. 94–128.

——, *Muzički stvaraoci u Srbiji* [Composers in Serbia], Belgrade, Prosveta, 1973.

——, *Stvaralački put Stanojla Rajičića* [The Creative Development of Stanojlo Rajičić], Belgrade, Umetnička akademija, 1977.

Veselinović-Hofman, M., *Stvaralačka prisutnost evropske avangarde u nas* [The Creative Presence of the European Avant-Garde with us], Belgrade, Umetnička akademija, 1983.

Chapter 4

The Music of Ljubica Marić: The National and the Universal in Harmony

Melita Milin

S everal important criteria were decisive for singling out the output of Ljubica Marić[1] as one of the most outstanding contributions to Serbian music of the 20th century. Not only was account taken of the individuality and artistic value of her works and their successful continuation of the Serbian and European music traditions, but also the fact that some of those works have already achieved an international reception (although by far weaker than deserved).

We shall try to approach the oeuvre of Ljubica Marić (1909–2003) from different angles. Data from her private life will be introduced cautiously, always with the aim of better understanding her compositional work. In her case, the links between her professional and private life were very close.

Ljubica Marić (1909–2003).

Basic principles of composition

Ljubica Marić never explicitly exposed her aesthetics of composition. She gave some important interviews for music journals and appeared in several radio and television broadcasts, so that a certain number of her thoughts (precious for researchers of her works) have been preserved. In them, however, she made no concrete statements concerning her aesthetics of music, neither of the technical compositional means she used. All those who had the chance to communicate with her know that she avoided such conversation; the evidence for this can be found in a statement during an interview, namely that "all living reality [...] eludes strict definitions" (Makević 1993: 9–11). She obviously thought that it was more appropriate that others (critics, colleagues, and people from the audience) discuss those matters and create freely their own views about her works. She preferred to talk about the effects of her (or someone else's) music on the listeners, their poetic and transcendental dimensions, her experience of time, or the invisible threads that link people to their ancestors from ancient times. She left evocative poetic/philosophical short texts, which she photocopied, making little notebooks (*Tablice / Tablets, Bajka / Fairy Tale*). Most important for her was the ability of music *to move* listeners, to have an *artistic impact* on them. In all music she valued most the power of expression and personal imprint. She was ready to accept different interpretations of her works, within reasonable limits.

The earliest preserved piece by Ljubica Marić is *Sonata-Phantasy* for violin solo (1929), a work for her final exam at Music School in Josip Slavenski's class. Like a molecule, it possesses some features that indicate the composer's later output: spontaneity of expression; suggestion of improvisation; a marked individuality of expression devoid of Romantic exaggeration and mannerisms; a kind of controlled incandescence; and an atmosphere that is tranquil and ecstatic at the same time. Idioms inspired by Baroque music are discreetly present: the form has an arch design.

Continuing her studies in Prague, Ljubica Marić was able to learn much more about different contemporary developments in musical thinking, since the city (with its long cultural tradition and rich musical life) was open to many innovative trends in composition. Exposed thus to different influences, she absorbed ideas that corresponded to her basic anti-Romantic attitude, to her striving for freedom and novelty of expression. She found that the ways to new horizons could be opened by atonality, athematism and quartertone music, so that Arnold Schoenberg and Alois Hába – the protagonist and his creative follower – can be recognised as vitally important for her development as a composer. *Wind Quintet* (1931) and *Music for Orchestra* (1932), her only two existing works from her "Prague period", are atonal and based on a linearity that presupposes independence of parts. The athematic concept is applied through variation of several basic motif cells, so that the form is coherent enough (Bergamo 1980: 96–105). Ljubica Marić referred to this procedure in *Music for Orchestra* (and the same applies to *Wind Quintet*) by writing that there occurred "a spontaneous transition from the thematic to the athematic way of formal conception."[2]

On the way to Marić's most mature works there are also several compositions from the socialist realism period, after World War II. Although they do not count as being among her most accomplished, some of them do possess real artistic value, such as several pieces for piano (*Etude, Preludes*), *Sonata for Violin and Piano* and *Stihovi iz Gorskog vijenca / Verses from the Mountain Wreath* for voice and piano (1949). That period of her work was marked by her discovery of the possibilities offered by tradition, so she managed to discipline herself to compose a classically organised and moderately modernist three-movement *Sonata for Violin and Piano*. She also rediscovered the wealth of Serbian folk music – rediscovered, because as a child, although growing up in urban surroundings, she used to have contact with musical folklore – and she often stated later that she had learnt everything from folk music. It should be reminded here that her first professor of composition was Josip Slavenski, who was fascinated by traditional folk music from the whole Balkan Peninsula.

Although there are successful works among those composed before her cantata *Pesme prostora / Songs of Space* (1956), they cannot compare with it in mastery and personal stamp. It was the first of a series of her works that ensured her a reputation as an outstanding composer. Her greatest, though not voluminous, output was produced from 1956 to 1996, when she finished her last work (leaving some more unfinished). The common characteristics of her work include: a sensitive and individually-coloured approach to the ancient past, resulting in the successful crossing of ancient and modernist expression; melodies permeated with elements of church or folk singing; monistic principle of building a whole work from a basic motif; harmonic language with modal features deriving from church chant and with sharp dissonances (resulting either from heterophonic motion in the parts or the need to heighten dramatic accents and achieve robust sound); and a special tone colour (she used the notion of *snop / bundle* to designate the surrounding of important tones with seconds above and below). She also often used a metro-rhythmic dimension with two main aspects – even and ostinato-like, with unexpected accents (suggesting a feeling of timelessness disturbed by interventions of the "subject"), or free-improvisational, fluid, with "levelled" metrical accents, associated with singing (rubato character) – and evolving form with gradations and thematic rounding-up at the end. However, there are examples of stricter organisation; instrumentation with exposed sounds of piano and brass instruments, especially of the trumpet, and with imaginative evocation of the ringing of bells, creating an archaic atmosphere.

Biography. Being a woman composer

Ljubica Marić thought that her belonging to the female gender was not to be discussed in relation to her creativity because she was convinced that such a fact did not influence at all the character and value of her work. She liked to retell how letters she received from abroad were sometimes addressed to "Mr Ljubica Marić", which was a sign that, at that time, her works were considered "equal to a man's". She simply believed that there was no specific difference between musical thought and compositional gifts regarding men and women.

Having lost her father at an early age, Ljubica Marić grew up under the intensified care of her mother, who devoted her life to providing financial means by which her daughter got as good a musical education as possible and could build a successful career afterwards. In the first decades of the 20th century life in Serbia was still basically patriarchal, but, as far as is known, Ljubica Marić had never suffered any prejudice as a woman.

She began to take private violin lessons when she was eleven, and very soon after she began to attend courses at the Music School in Belgrade, which had the level of a conservatory. Lessons from Josip Slavenski were very stimulating for her musical development. At the time he was already internationally renowned as a composer and was happy to transmit his enthusiasm for traditional music and modernist exploration of novel sounds to his talented pupil. She continued her studies at the Prague conservatory, in Josef Suk's class at the Master School department (1929–32), where she also took courses in violin and conducting. Her *Wind Quintet* (1931) was selected for performance at the festival of the International Society for Contemporary Music (ISCM) in Amsterdam in 1933, where it received a very warm reception. Her composition for the final exam at the Prague conservatory, *Music for Orchestra,* was also performed with success at the music-dramatic course, organised by Hermann Scherchen in Strasbourg that same year. She was fortunate that Josef Suk was a very tolerant pedagogue, with an understanding for music different from that which he composed, so that he allowed her to apply some avant-garde techniques such as atonality and athematism. He also advised her to contact his colleague Alois Hába who was very much engaged in getting recognition for avant-garde ideas, especially his own. There are indications that as early as the autumn of 1932 Ljubica Marić began to attend his class for quartertone music (Koren (= Bergamo) 1968: 35), but it seems that she stayed there only for a short time, as she found herself in Berlin next spring,[3] probably with an aim to study conducting – though we still do not possess concrete data concerning that period of her life. She returned to Prague to join Hába's class in 1936 and she stayed there for two terms. It is known that she conducted a concert in Belgrade in 1934, when she performed, among other pieces, her *Music for Orchestra*. She finally returned to live in Belgrade in 1938 and became professor of theoretical subjects in the "Stanković" Music School. After the war she continued her pedagogical career at the Belgrade Music Academy (1945–1968) where she again taught music theory, never initiating a compositional class of her own.

The first performance of her cantata *Songs of Space* (1956) in Belgrade was received in an exceptionally warm way. The works she composed in the following years are also among her best, and some of them, such as *Vizantijski koncert / Byzantine Concerto* (1959) and *Prag sna / Threshold of Dreams* (1963), including the *Songs of Space,* have quickly acquired recognition not only in Serbia, but also in the whole of Yugoslavia. Her late works possessed freshness of ideas, intense and compressed expressivity, and a specific tone obtained by the sounds of ancient church melodies (*Iz tmine pojanje / Chants from Darkness,* recitative cantata for voice and piano, 1984; *Monodija Oktoiha / Monody of the Octoechos* for violoncello solo, 1984; *Čudesni miligram / The Prodigious Milligram* for voice and flute, 1992; *Torso* for piano trio, 1996).

Ljubica Marić was elected corresponding member of the Serbian Academy of Sciences and Arts in 1963, and full member in 1981. Although she was very close to the communist movement during her stay in Prague, after the war she never adhered to the League of Communists (the only party in the country). Confronted with the true character of the regime, its dogmatism and hypocrisy, she abandoned her idealistic views on socialism as a just political system. She never took part in any political activities, with the exception of her joining the protest in the anti-regime demonstrations of 1996–1997, when she was quite advanced in age. She was gifted also for literature and the visual arts, but only a small fraction of those activities of hers became known to the wider public.

When we contemplate Ljubica Marić's creative biography as outlined above, it is difficult to perceive any trait that would indicate that she had to suffer frustration on account of her being a woman. The fact that she never married, and that she lived with her mother, cannot and should not be interpreted otherwise than it would be in the case of a male artist. This might only be seen as a sign of her unconventional attitudes in life (which she was known for) and as an expression of her need to dedicate herself to composition as much as possible.

An effort to find features in Ljubica Marić's works that could be linked to her being a woman composer would almost certainly prove to be an unfruitful endeavour. She was able to create refined and delicate moods and climates of meditative inwardness – which should not, of course, be attributed to some "female writing" – but her works are also robust, energetic and highly dramatic – again, qualities not just "reserved" for male composers.

Ljubica Marić and her elder contemporaries

Similar to most other composers, Ljubica Marić was subject to a number of influences, early ones different from later ones.[4] The ideas and music of Arnold Schoenberg were certainly of great importance for her during her studies in Prague in the 1930s. Alois Hába's ideas (more than his works) also influenced her musical thinking at the time. She assimilated easily the tendencies widespread in those years towards objectification of expression, and to creating emotional distance. She was strongly opposed to Romantic confessional tone and the hypertrophy of the "I". The athematic technique found resonance with her primarily because she sought freedom in the building of form and wished to let the whole evolve from one motif, and also because she highly valued an intuitive approach to composition.

In the pre-war works of Ljubica Marić there are no traces of neoclassicism or twelve-tone technique, but it should not be excluded that she experimented with both. It seems plausible that she was inclined especially to twelve-tone technique, since in her later period we find a work, *Byzantine Concerto,* whose first movement owes something to that type of constructing.

It is hard to point to influences in Ljubica Marić's works created from 1945–1949, when she turned to tradition. It is probably just to say that nothing concrete or non-mediated found its way into her music, but that she made use of all of her knowledge of Serbian and Yugoslav music and pre-20th century music of Europe. Her opening to tradition resulted in a sublimated Romantic gesture and the accompanying formal organisation.

In Ljubica Marić's mature works, starting with *The Songs of Space* (1956), to her last completed composition – *Torso* (1996), could be noticed certain influences coming from some of the greatest composers of modernist music, Stravinsky and Bartók, but those elements are masterfully transformed into something new, that bears the stamp of her own authorship. The traces of her admiration for the oeuvre of the great Russian can be detected in her creative application of polymetry (both horizontal and vertical) and chord building (e.g. in using fifths and fourths), whereas Bartók's influence is noticeable in the art of blending her own and the folk (including church) idiom, and in the application of some formal-constructive procedures deriving mainly from the study of J.S. Bach's music.

Value of the early works

Only four works of Ljubica Marić written before World War II have been preserved, two from her earliest, Belgrade period (*Sonata-Phantasy* for violin solo, 1929, and the mixed choral *Tuga za djevojkom / Lament for a Girl*, 1929), and two from her Prague years (*Wind Quintet*, 1931, and *Music for Orchestra*, 1932). The fate of her other pre-war works is not quite clear. It is known that she also composed *Canon* for quartertone piano (1936–7), *Quarter-tone Trio* for clarinet, trombone and double-bass (1936–7) and *Music for orchestra no. 2* (1937).[5] Ljubica Marić may have destroyed those works, as she did with her *String Quartet* (1931), although it was selected by her professor, Josef Suk, for performance at the concert of the final year students at the Prague conservatory, which was remarkable as she had still not completed her studies. There were very affirmative critiques of her *Wind Quintet* in the Czech, Dutch and British press, and the same can be said of her *Music for Orchestra*.[6]

We can only try to guess when and why Ljubica Marić destroyed most of her early scores. The probable answer is that she did that after 1945, when the spirit of new times must have put some doubts into her mind, so that she began to regard those works as just experimental in character.

Although they do not belong to the most valuable part of her oeuvre, the preserved works show that their author was an extraordinarily gifted young composer who sought to discipline her musical thinking, while retaining spontaneity and freedom of expression. Although Josef Suk's student, she was attracted more by the musical ideas of Alois Hába, and it was a happy circumstance that those two excellent composers and colleagues had a mutual respect for each other and readily directed their students to each other in order to offer them wider perspectives. For researchers of her output, her recollection of her Prague period could be important. She remembered how Hába made an observation concerning one of her pieces regarding its inconsistence in athematicism, as there was a reminiscence of a certain motif at the end. The answer she gave shows how self-assured and resolute she was: she said that she had felt the need to do just that and so further discussion was prevented. She had indeed always been indisposed to follow any kind of dogmatic thinking. The composition in question was probably the *Wind Quintet* or *Music for Orchestra*. In the fourth, final movement of the *Quintet,* part of the introductory material is repeated in the recapitulation, and the same thing can be noticed in the middle part of *Music for Orchestra*, which also brings back a thematic fragment from the introduction.[7]

Attitude towards socialist realism

Not inclined to speak about her private life or the technical aspects of her works, Ljubica Marić did not wish to comment on works she created during the socialist realism period (1945–1948). Since pre-war times she had felt sympathy for the communist ideology, so she must have had positive sentiments for Tito's regime and all the promises he gave. When she began to work as a professor at the Music Academy in 1945, she left behind the many years marked by privation – in Prague and Berlin during the 1930s and after that in Belgrade during the German Nazi occupation.

The dominantly hopeful atmosphere in the country (in spite of many brutal settlings of accounts by the victors upon their class enemies), as well as more or less clear instructions on the need to compose for the "working masses", directed her to compose short and simple pieces for children and also works for piano or mixed choir. Among those compositions, several are more ambitiously conceived, such as *Etude* and *Preludes* for piano (1946) and the *Sonata for Violin and Piano* (1948).

Instructions expressed by the Party officials for cultural politics requested that composers should write in a simpler and "acceptable" vein in order to ideologically influence the public; these instructions were understood, as could be expected, as an invitation to look back at the pre-20th century musical traditions. In that way, similar to the earlier situation in the USSR, the revolutionary claim that the communist regime was "progressive", and would advocate for such art and music, was disregarded. Therefore they proclaimed that composers ought to give up modernist experimentation and instead devote themselves to socialist functionalism. So, Ljubica Marić, like all her colleagues, turned temporarily to the classical-Romantic tradition as a basis upon which to build and to introduce some elements of the music of the early 20th century.

It is difficult, if not impossible, to discuss the inner attitude of an artist towards the ruling political ideology. Therefore we can only suppose that Ljubica Marić renounced her avant-garde views without major dilemma in the years following the end of the war. At the beginning of the 1950s her belief that such an orientation was right certainly began to weaken. She did not compose anything from 1950 to 1956, or at least did not present anything to the public. It is impossible to say anything positive about the reasons for the change in the meantime, bringing a full maturity to her works, starting with *Songs of Space* (1956). It can only be suggested that her creativeness was simply in need of bigger challenges and richer spiritual contents.

Ljubica Marić and musical nationalism

The special relation Marić had with folk and church music could suggest to those who did not know her personally that it was an expression of her Serbian nationalism. A basis for such reasoning might be found in her marked closeness to Serbian church music, and that at a time when the church as an institution was regarded by the ruling power as retrograde, outmoded and still dangerous because of its potential to assemble nationalists dissatisfied with the overall situation in the country.

Ljubica Marić was however not a churchgoer and she spoke of herself as "cosmically religious". The Serbian Orthodox Church appealed to her because it was a source and guardian of the rich Serbian spiritual tradition: a bearer of Serbian identity, which had been endangered many times in the past. In one of her interviews she stated that she had bought a copy of *Osmoglasnik (Oktoechos),* the collection of church melodies, in the early 1940s. The study of those melodies certainly initiated new spiritual states in her.

One of the main features of cultural life in Serbia in the 1950s and 1960s was a conspicuous interest in domestic medieval heritage, religious in essence. This was not received enthusiastically by the authorities, but no remonstration occurred, and the government was all too satisfied to have been invited to organise exhibitions of the medieval art of Yugoslavia abroad (such as one in Paris in 1950). Out of that atmosphere emerged Ljubica Marić's heightened interest in Serbian chant, which had been orally transmitted since the 9th century when the Serbs were Christianised. The chant cannot be seen and understood separately from other forms of medieval art – monastic architecture, fresco painting and religious poetry.

It could be asserted that Ljubica Marić observed Serbian medieval art and chant neither from the aspect of religion, nor out of nationalistic impulse (the absence of which in her mind was witnessed by all who were in contact with her), but as an expression of spirituality in a wider sense (the values of which fascinated her). The fact that she named her important work *Byzantine Concerto,* not a *Serbian* one, could account for that. She spoke likewise of a folk song, which she used as the theme of her *Passacaglia* as originating from Pomoravlje, the region of the river Morava, although she could designate it as Serbian. Similarly, she designated the *stećaks,* tombstones bearing inscriptions that inspired her for one of her most accomplished works, as Bosnian, thus giving priority to historical principles over ethnic ones (the population of medieval Bosnia was dominantly Serbian, before and after its fall under Turkish rule).

She was not only sensitive to the beauty that had endured through long centuries and to the expressivity of ancient poetic texts created on Serbian soil, but also to great achievements of foreign artists, so that among her works one can find the melodic recitation: *Čarobnica / Sorceress,* after Virgil.

On one of her "tables", pieces of thick paper of postcard dimensions, on which she wrote poetico-philosophical short texts, designed in original ways, she inscribed: "To the soil, roots, origins, milk of our spirit, I dedicate." Such dedication of her creative work should not be interpreted as a glorification of the national heritage (it could be noticed that she did not use the adjective "Serbian", but "our"). It is in fact a poetically inspired reflection on creative work as a link in the chain of similar past achievements; as a vision of art that lasts through many epochs, animating, for all time, new generations of creators.

It is not easy to answer the question whether the output of Ljubica Marić belongs to the national branch of Serbian music. On one hand, it really bears some national features, because of the use of selected elements of Serbian folk and church music (though not in all works). She used to say that all she knew she learned from folk music. On the other hand, folk and church music are transformed in such a way in her works that they do not fit into a standard idea of nationally oriented music. It would be nearer to the truth to link her way of musical thinking with that of Béla Bartók, with his art of sublimation of the musical material of folk origins.

Byzantine Concerto for piano and orchestra (1959): the past in the present

More than ten years had passed since Ljubica Marić came into contact with *Osmoglasnik (Octoechos)*, the collection of church melodies written down and edited by Stevan Mokranjac, before she began to compose her *Music of the Octoechos*. The basic idea behind the imagined cycle of works with that title was to use those church melodies as themes of the works according to their typical characteristics, which derived from their belonging to one of the eight modes ("voices") of the *Osmoglasnik*. So, the introductory work, *Oktoicha 1* for orchestra, was based on the first mode, *Byzantine Concerto* on the second, third and fourth mode (each movement upon one), *Ostinato super thema octoicha* for chamber ensemble and the chamber cantata *Prag sna / Threshold of Dreams* on the fifth. The cycle has remained unfinished as the last work, *Symphony of the Octoechos*, that was planned to be built on the remaining three modes, never developed beyond sketches.

Most outstanding among those fine works is the *Byzantine Concerto*. In this "triptych" on Byzantium, the movements bear evocative double titles. When hearing the first – Preludio quasi una toccata. *Zvuk i zvonjava / Sounds and Ringing of Bells* – the listener might experience the atmosphere of a solemn imperial procession in Byzantine times. The empire is presented as powerful and universal, with harmonised concepts of worldliness and Christian orthodoxy. The second movement – an Aria, *U tami i odsjaju / In Obscurity and Reflections* – could provoke associations to numerous Byzantine monasteries in which, without any break for centuries, the chanting of prayers under the glittering light of candles lasts. The sounds of battle in the last movement, (Finale) *Tutnjava i bljesak / Thunder and Glare*, invite an interpretation of being the representation of the final battle for the defense of the empire. Although it collapsed, its spiritual power still radiates upon the contemporary world.

Piano as a solo instrument is integrated into the texture of the work, so that it became an "organic constitutive part of the symphonic orchestra", as Ljubica Marić herself states in the introduction to the printed score of the work. Indeed, there is no "competition" between the soloist and the orchestra, but a complementary relation is created, not only as regards the disposition of the thematic material, but also because of the creation of specific instrumental colours and their blending.

The treatment of the piano was obviously inspired by baroque models and, in a certain measure, mediated through the works of Igor Stravinsky, but with no neo-Baroque effects. The piano writing is linearistic, usually two-part, with marked continuous movement based on a variational spinning from one motif cell. Sometimes those two lines act independently, and sometimes they mingle, interlace and complement each other, like in situations when one line presents a variant of the other, developing simultaneously. When intensification of expression is sought, melodic lines become thicker through the use of different vertical structures, often producing an effect of clusters. In her typical way, Ljubica Marić organises the metro-rhythmical level of the melodic lines. She creates long rows of same rhythmical values, grouped into different metrical units, resulting in irregular accentuation and polymetric pulsation.

The *Byzantine Concerto* is composed for an orchestra without woodwind instruments, so that the effect of bright sound is obtained. The other elements of the sound climate of the works consist of the special treatment of different instruments or groups of instruments: the piano that sounds either sharp and austere, or soft like clavecin, especially when combined with harp; usually discreet strings; and active percussion, especially in the final movement.

In her introductory note for the printed edition of the score, Ljubica Marić stated that "the whole first movement is built upon the hexachord f, g, a, b flat, c, d flat of the IInd mode of the *Osmoglasnik* which has been transposed three times, so that a circle of the tonal trinity f – c sharp – a has been made. In such a way, the tonal basis covers, in polytonal relations, all twelve tones". The application of this principle can be briefly explained in the following way: the basic form of the hexachord (from f) and its two transpositions (from c sharp / d flat and from a) are treated as different modes, which can be used in pure form and in combinations. The first and the third part of the movement are spaces built, for the most part, of just one transposition of the hexachord, while the middle section has a more complex, more dynamic harmonic basis.

The constructing method of the theme of the first movement is similar to those seen in the other works of Ljubica Marić that make use of melodies from the *Osmoglasnik*. The theme of solemn character is built of four fragments belonging to different melodies of the second mode of the *Osmoglasnik*. Thus the theme is "authentic", being wholly based on the chant, and at the same time it is "original" because the composer organised the fragments in her own way.

The gentle, wide-breath and richly melismatic theme of the second movement is supported on three typical melodic formulae of the third mode, and carries inside it the impulse for the development of the whole movement. Like the theme of the previous movement, this theme is made of selected fragments taken from church melodies; the main difference here is that, in the first case, the fragments are taken from different melodies of the same mode, whereas in the second their origin is in the same melody.

In contrast to the meditative and elegiac second movement and its free evolutive development, the beginning of the third movement creates an atmosphere of unrest, with its robust and energetic strikes of the timpani. The finale of the work is its dramatic peak. It seems as if a battle is depicted: unrest in the rhythmic unfolding prevails, creating a sensation of anxiety. The mood gradually changes, so that in the coda a peaceful and vibrating choral theme shines forth filling up all the space. This frequent narrative in music – the path from darkness to light – was interpreted by Ljubica Marić in an inspired and fresh way. The mostly free form of the movement does not follow any traditional model, although it could be defined as a specific type of rondo. Although rhythmically nervous and seemingly without elements of church chant, the piano part is indeed based on it.

The *Byzantine Concerto* occupies a high place in Serbian music. Its value was recognised at its premiere, followed by several very positive reviews in newspapers and journals, one of them with the title "Magnificent Sound Fresco" (B.M.D. (= Dragutinović) 1963: 10). There is no doubt that Ljubica Marić succeeded in achieving her aim: to produce an artistic vision of her presence in her time, and to present her contemporaries' quest not to lose links to their spiritual roots in an epoch too much oriented to the future. She was aware that the works of her mature period do not participate in the avant-garde movements, but she was right when, referring to the *Byzantine Concerto,* she expressed her faith that her works were not "outside of Time – the unique and undivided Time, in which every moment in some far away or very close spot, the Past and the Future meet, creating an at the same time most real and most deceptive part of Time which we call the Present".[8] Her new approach to the past, as exemplified in the works of the cycle *Music of the Octoechos* and a number of other works, has inspired several younger Serbian composers to follow that path.

Notes

1. The name of the composer is pronounced: Lyoubitsa Marich.
2. Ljubica Marić was certainly the author of that sentence taken from an article which she signed together with her colleague in Prague, Vojislav Vučković (Marić and Vučković 1934).
3. The letters she sent to Josip Slavenski from Berlin on March 22 and April 27 have been preserved. The letters are kept in Josip Slavenski's memorial rooms in Belgrade.
4. See more about the influences in Ljubica Marić's works in: Milin 2005: 81–82.
5. These data were obtained from the composer herself.
6. We shall quote a sentence from one of those reviews: "Ljubica Marić, who had already left a very good impression with her work for winds at the music festival in Amsterdam, confirmed that impression with her *Music for Orchestra,* a dazzlingly talented work which she herself conducted" (Dorn 1933).
7. More detail about Ljubica Marić's early works can be found in: Milin 2001: 93–104.
8. Published in the programme of the premiere of the *Byzantine Concerto.*

References

Bergamo, M., *Elementi ekspresionističke orijentacije u srpskoj muzici do 1945 godine* [Elements of Expressionistic Orientation in Serbian Music Before 1945], Belgrade, Srpska akademija nauka i umetnosti, 1980.

B.M.D (= Dragutinović, Br.), "Velelepna zvučna freska" [Magnificent Sound Fresco], *Politika*, 6 July, 1963.

Dorn, Alb. van., [The title of the article is not preserved], *Aornold-Algemeen Handelsblad von Woensdag*, 23 August, Amsterdam, 1933.

Koren (= Bergamo), M., "Chapter on Vojislav Vučković's biography", in (ed.) V. Peričić, *Vojislav Vučković, umetnik i borac* [Vojislav Vučković, Artist and Combatant], Belgrade, Nolit, 1968.

Makević, Z., "Vreme koje nas nosi dalje. Razgovor sa Ljubicom Marić" [The Time Which Carries Us Further. A Conversation With Ljubica Marić], *Novi Zvuk*, 1, 1993, pp. 9–11.

——, "*Torzo*, klavirski trio Ljubice Marić" [*Torso*, a piano trio by Ljubica Marić], *Novi Zvuk*, 8, 1996, pp. 31–32.

Marić, L., and Vučković, V., "O uticaju apsolutne muzike na razvoj umetničke forme. Povodom V simfonijskog koncerta orkestra 'Stanković'" [On the Influence of Absolute Music on the Development of Art Form. On the Occasion of the Fifth Symphonic Concert of the 'Stanković' orchestra], *Politika*, 7–10 April, 1934.

Milin, M., "Transpozicija napeva iz Mokranjčevog Osmoglasnika u Vizantijskom koncertu Ljubice Marić" [The Transposition of the Melodies from Mokranjac's Osmoglasnik in Ljubica Marić's Byzantine Concerto] (The translation of the article into English is given in extenso) in *Folklor i njegova umetnička transpozicija* [Folklore and its Artistic Transposition], Belgrade, 1991, pp. 187–198, 100–212.

——, "Being a Modern Serbian Composer in the 1930s: The Creative Position of Ljubica Marić", *Muzikologija*, 1, 2001, pp. 93–104.

——, "Unutarnja biografija kompozitora. Skica za studiju uticaja u delima Ljubice Marić" [The Inner Biography of a Composer. A Sketch for a Study of Influences in Ljubica Marić's Works"], *Muzikologija*, 4, 2005, pp. 61–82.

Stefanović, A., "Moderno, arhaično, postmoderno. O najnovijoj stvaralačkoj fazi u opusu Ljubice Marić" [The Modern, the Archaic, and the Postmodern. On the New Creative Phase in Ljubica Marić's Work], *Muzički talas*, 1–2, 1997, pp. 10–20.

Chapter 5

Serbian Music of the Second Half of the 20th Century: From Socialist Realism to Postmodernism

Melita Milin

The development of Serbian music after World War II was very similar to that of other East-European countries, especially those situated in the Balkans. There was naturally a very close relationship between Serbian and other national musical cultures within Yugoslavia, notwithstanding many divisions caused by the diverse traditions to which they had belonged before the foundation of the common state in 1918.

The socio-political environment decisively influenced musical life and creativity in Serbia, especially during the first post-war decades. The fate of Serbia, one of the six federal republics of Yugoslavia, was determined by some important events in the political sphere, several of which will be mentioned here. In October 1944 the Communist Partisan Army, led by Josip Broz Tito, together with the Soviet troops, liberated most of Serbia, but the war would last several months more. A serious conflict with the USSR broke out because Tito was not subordinate enough to Stalin and seemed to have wanted to establish himself as a regional communist leader. This resulted in Yugoslavia being expelled from Cominform (1948), the consequence of which was a gradual rapprochement to western countries. In spite of strong opposition among Serbian *intelligentsia*, a new constitution was proclaimed in 1974, introducing confederal elements into the state system. Tito died in May 1980, leaving the country to be governed by a rotating presidency. In spring of the next year, the Albanian minority organised demonstrations demanding that the Serbian autonomous province of Kosovo and Metohija, in which they formed an ethnic majority, obtained the status of an autonomous republic within Yugoslavia. Slobodan Milošević, who had previously become popular due to his willingness to resolve the position of Serbs both in their own republic and in the whole of Yugoslavia, became president of Serbia (1988). The first democratic elections in Yugoslavia after World War II were held in 1990. Two of the six republics, Slovenia and Croatia, proclaimed independence in June 1991, which provoked the outbreak of the wars that would lead to the disintegration of Yugoslavia. NATO forces launched an air strike campaign against Serbia in reaction to the conflict between the Serbian state and the separatist movement of the Albanian minority in Kosovo (March–June 1999). In October 2000 Milošević admitted his defeat at presidential elections and his opponents came to power.

These and other dramatic historical events had a predominantly negative effect on Serbian contemporary musical life and composers' work, particularly during the time of the imposed doctrine of socialist realism and in the long years of cultural isolation both after 1945 and during the 1990s. However, some of those events also had positive consequences, such as the gradual liberalisation of cultural activities following the break with the USSR, so that from the beginning of the 1960s state officials no longer tried to direct musical development in the country. Although there had been efforts to modernise the sphere of musical creativity, it was only after 1960 that there was no longer any ideological control from "above". The last decade of the 20th century showed that wars, however terrible, did not silence the muses, so that composers' production was relatively fruitful, especially among the young.

Although an important year for Serbian music, 1945 did not bring total discontinuity with the previous period. Indeed, with the exception of several pre-war modernists who made some kind of turn towards tradition – it should be remembered that two or three of them had changed their aesthetics in that direction even before the war – the styles of the older generations were not disturbed significantly. Serbian music on the eve of World War II seemed to have been moving in several different but parallel directions. The three most eminent Serbian composers, Petar Konjović (1883–1970), Stevan Hristić (1885–1958) and Miloje Milojević (1884–1946) were then in their most mature creative periods, and the same could be said of Josip Slavenski (1896–1955), a Croat who had settled in Belgrade in 1925. These composers had a central position in the inter-war period, not only in view of their objective importance as composers, but also because of the stylistic features of their works. On one hand their music was rather remote from the anachronistic Romantic nationalism of some older and even some younger colleagues. On the other hand, they could not feel close to young "leftist" modernists who had studied in Prague and had fallen under the influence of Schoenberg and Hába. What connects those four composers could be defined as their similar positions in relation to the aesthetics of national expression and the need for stylistic modernisation. The innovations they introduced into Serbian music consisted in the broadening of late romanticism in the direction of impressionism, and an intensification of expression sometimes close to expressionistic. Their harmonic boldness was most often the effect of linearistic voice-leading (Konjović), but they also used chromaticism that – although quite rarely – reached the limits of tonality (Milojević, Slavenski), as well as bi- and polytonal structures, modality and polymetry (Slavenski). However, they were never too far from late romanticism, sometimes with veristic colouring (Hristić).

Although Serbian music had reached important ascendance during the 1920s and 1930s, mostly due to the works of the above four composers, the overall situation was very unsatisfactory for several young composers who were born around 1910. They pursued different ideals and did so in different European cities where they chose to study, most often in Prague. The composers of the "Prague generation", to which belonged, among others, Ljubica Marić (1909–2003), Stanojlo Rajičić (1910–2000) and Milan Ristić (1908–1982), were enthusiastic about exploring the world of new possibilities. They admired the works of Schoenberg, Hindemith and Hába, rejecting at the same time the works of their elders in Serbia as "conservative" and "outdated" – the more so as the problems of national expression were outside their field of interest.

During the World War II German occupation, concert and opera life continued, though with far lower intensity. The same could be said of the work of composers, who were no longer motivated to compose, since they could not expect to have their works performed in the near future.

Although the post-war development of music in Serbia was marked by a wholly new, ideological pressure to affirm the values promoted by the new communist regime, the year 1945 should not be proclaimed as a "new beginning", or some kind of "year zero". Official policy certainly insisted on establishing discontinuity of every kind with the pre-war period, but composers and other artists usually could not (and sometimes did not want to) accept all the "diktats". It was a time of "imposed serenity and optimism" and of discussions organised by the Union of composers, in which it was recommended that "healthy forces" should compose "accessibly" and use folklore.[1] Luckily, the period of socialist realism did not have especially malign forms, nor did it last too long. The first five post-war years were rather dogmatic, but afterwards came a "decrescendo" phase, lasting until the late 1950s. This period did cause discontinuity with the earlier epoch, but its meaning was not a radical break with the past and the beginning of something totally different, but rather an explicit turn towards the traditional. So a paradoxical situation was seen: the new that arose in the first post-war years (looking for models in the past styles) was really old (already experienced), while the pre-war old (modernism as applied by the "Prague generation") was too novel and "bourgeois" to be acceptable for the new epoch.

The spirit of the new times brought certain simplification in the creative approaches of older composers, such as Konjović (in the opera *Seljaci / The Peasants,* 1951) and Slavenski (*Symphonic Epos,* 1945). Hristić's evening-long ballet *Ohridska legenda / The Legend of Ohrid* (1947) enjoyed general recognition because his folkloric atmosphere, impetus, and directness of expression coincided with some of the main demands of socialist realism.

The position of the younger composers who had had an avant-garde past during the 1930s was different, as they needed to adapt their styles to the new demands. This mainly meant that it was expected that they establish tonal centralisation and build traditional forms. The general source of inspiration was 19th century music, especially that belonging to Slavonic national schools, but reliance on some contemporary composers, usually Prokofiev and Shostakovich, was also sometimes noticeable.

Having privileged "accessible" music, Serbian composers of the time left a great number of works in vocal and vocal-instrumental genres. Revolutionary themes provided bases for mass-songs, cantatas, orchestral suites and poems, while especially voluminous is the heritage of different arrangements of folk songs. The other genres – such as operatic, and to a lesser degree "absolute" music – went through a crisis which lasted until a new generation of composers made their appearance around the middle of the 1950s, showing an inclination for symphonic and chamber music.

From 1950–1960 the course of Serbian music was constantly evolving towards more modern expression. The youngest composers contributed mostly to that process, but members of the "Prague generation" were also very active. Conflicts between representatives of more traditional (basically neo-Romantic) and more modern ideas (basically neoclassical) were rather acute and could be compared to similar clashes of the pre-war period. Although contacts with the outside world were scarce, a feeling was growing that it was necessary to restart the process of modernisation of Serbian music and to make up for lost time, caused this time by the isolation of the country.

Notwithstanding the fact that the *String quartet* of Vladan Radovanović (b. 1932), composed in 1950, worth mentioning as the first dodecaphonic work in Serbia after World War II, was not performed publicly, and thus did not exert any influence, it should be regarded as a composition that anticipated a wave of post-war avant-garde music in Serbia. In contrast, the works of Dušan Radić (b. 1929) and Enriko Josif (1924–2003), then students of composition, attracted a lot of attention. They were performed at a concert that took place in Belgrade on 17 March 1954. It was especially Radić's *Spisak / The List* for two female voices and chamber ensemble that provoked heated discussions because of its anti-romanticism (à la Stravinsky) and its eccentric tone, which in fact matched perfectly the chosen poems of Vasko Popa. It seems, however, that the main event of the 1950s was the performance of Ljubica Marić's cantata *Pesme prostora / Songs of Space* (8 December 1956), a work of exceptionally high expressive power, which encouraged a number of younger composers to produce works that would be modernistic yet, at the same time, possess a distinctively national stamp. Ljubica Marić, who had been a radical avant-gardist before the war, did not wish to renounce the music of the past: "Why should one discard any way given by the past? At any rate they will acquire a new meaning, because they will build new relations and in that way become, more or less, a new way. Of course, it should be applied creatively, not through imitation."[2]

One of the perspectives from which the output of Ljubica Marić composed in the 1950s, and could be observed later, is her fascination with the Medieval Serbian world, closely connected with its Byzantine cultural frame. Such inspiration not only had the connotation of discovering spiritual closeness with creative expressions of ancient ancestors, but also had a symbolic meaning, as an "escape from the present" – the present national and political situation in the country that darkened many horizons, and the present in the music of the world that had given birth to some too-cerebral avant-gardistic tendencies. Both presents were seen as lacking meaningfulness and spiritual content. The orientation towards the archaic was thus motivated by the need to rebuild art through Anteian contact with ancient creations of the human spirit, which could be interpreted as a discovery of a forgotten heritage.

The rich talent of Ljubica Marić, the main representative of this branch of Serbian music and one of the most outstanding Serbian composers in general, found its most important inspiration in the melodies of the Octoechos (a collection of Serbian church chants).[3] Here her cycle of works based on the "voices" (*echoi*) of the Octoechos, *Music of the Octoechos* (1959–1963) and its constituent parts should be mentioned: *Octoicha I* for orchestra, *Byzantine Concerto* for piano and orchestra, chamber cantata *Prag sna / Threshold of Dreams* and *Ostinato super thema octoicha* for instrumental ensemble.

Interestingly, Dušan Radić, twenty years younger than Ljubica Marić and enthusiastically orientated towards new international trends, also became receptive to the medieval Serbian heritage and approached it with a wish to create a synthesis of archaic and modern expression. It is possible that in this he was influenced by Marić's *Songs of Space,* but there are also grounds to believe that the poetry of Vasko Popa, for which he had had a strong inclination even before, provided him with inspiration for it. Like Marić, Radić in his cantata *Ćele-kula / Tower of Sculls* (1957), the chamber cantata *Uspravna zemlja / Earth Erect* (1964) and some other works, uses a basically diatonic language with modal elements and tingling harmonies. Enriko Josif also belongs to this group of composers, considering the archaistic features of some of his key-works, the monumental and neo-Baroque *Sonata antica* (1956) and the "motets" for speaker, soloists, choir and chamber orchestra *Smrt Stevana Dečanskog / The Death of Stevan of Dečani* (1956).

Apart from a trend that could be classified as *poeticised archaisation,* works with *neoclassicist* and *neoexpressionist* stylistic features could also be observed during the 1950s.[4] Those who were attracted by neoclassicism, mostly young composers, aimed for modern, cosmopolitan expression, and took as their starting points the works of Prokofiev, Stravinsky and Hindemith. The *2nd Symphony* (1951) and *Suita giocosa* (1956) of Milan Ristić, *Sinfonietta* (1954) and *Divertimento* (1954) of Dušan Radić, *Symphony* (1955) of Dejan Despić (b. 1930), *Sinfonia concertante* (1956) of Vladan Radovanović and *Concertino* (1958) of Vasilije Mokranjac (1923–1984) represented that orientation.

Although the neoexpressionists developed their variety of modernism on late-Romantic foundations, it is not always easy to make a clear distinction between these two compositional groups, because in some works their main characteristics were combined. There were also composers who contributed to both trends, such as Vasilije Mokranjac. Nevertheless, key composers in the neoexpressionists camp were Stanojlo Rajičić (1910–2000) with his opera *Simonida* (1956) and *Symphony in G* (1959), Rudolf Bruči (1917–2002) with *Sinfonia lesta* (1965), Vasilije Mokranjac with the *1st symphony* (1961), and Aleksandar Obradović (1927–2001) with his cycle of songs for baritone and orchestra *Plameni vjetar / Flaming Wind.*

The work of Vladan Radovanović presents a special case when compared to his contemporaries, who sought different ways to achieve modernist expression during the 1950s. He was also active in other art forms (visual and poetic) but was especially interested in polymedia, in which he achieved innovative results, not only within a local context. In 1956 he created the *Four Chorales,* without indicating which instruments should perform them. These are extremely short pieces in two parts, with all note values in semibreves. When judging their importance one should have in mind that Christian Wolff began to write his minimalist works at about the same time. Before the end of that decade Radovanović composed nine *Polyphonies,* which he based on a serial concept of his own.

During the 1960s, the process of modernisation gained strength, thanks mostly to easier communication with foreign institutions and individuals, made possible by the liberalisation of travel abroad. Of primary importance for the development of Serbian and Yugoslav music was the foundation of the International Biennale of Contemporary Music in Zagreb (1961). The main idea for that initiative, whose *spiritus movens* was Milko Kelemen,

Dejan Despić (1930).

a Croatian composer living in Germany, was to copy the positive experience of the Warsaw Autumn Festival (1956). The Poles had successfully established open communication between eastern and western contemporary composers during this period of the "cold war", and enabled domestic composers to come into direct contact with the most up-to-date avant-garde ideas of the times. The Zagreb Biennale made its appearance at the time of post-serial avant-garde, when the possibilities for the new and unconventional still seemed endless, while composers in Serbia and Yugoslavia as a whole were taking their first steps in the domain of serial thinking. The general impression among domestic composers and professional audiences after the end of the first Biennale could be summarised as evident astonishment at some of the radical avant-garde works they could hear, such as those of John Cage and Karlheinz Stockhausen, as well as a positive reception of composers from the "Polish school". Although the significance of this biennial musical event was enormous, in giving impetus to the development of domestic music, it should be stated that, contrary to the Polish precursor, our modernist music did not succeed in getting recognition on an international level as something original or exceptionally valuable. Perhaps the domestic tendencies in the world. In that context should be mentioned Vladan Radovanović's *Sphaeroön* (1960–1964), an extremely complex work for piano, organ and recitative chorus in which controlled aleatorics was implemented. Only by successive recordings and tape montage can that work be realised, so it can be termed "tape music". In *Sphaeroön* some procedures related to the technique of Ligeti's mass-music could be detected, although in fact the work was created at the period when Radovanović had no chance of coming to know Ligeti's most recent achievements.[6]

Generally speaking, the 1960s saw the beginning of a more resolute rapprochement to the European avant-garde, although intended international recognition was not attained. In that time of late avant-garde, when the excessive and the bizarre too often claimed to represent the truly innovative and authentic, Serbian composers who assimilated the novelties rather cautiously could hardly be observed as interesting or provocative enough.[7] It seems that more time was needed for the maturation of Serbian avant-garde music, but a change of sensitivity towards postmodernism was also beginning to spread at that very time, which came too soon for the majority of our composers. In order to form a fair appreciation of Serbian music of this decade, it should be noted that, even in more advanced musical cultures than Serbia or Yugoslavia, composers who searched for some "third way", in between the traditional and the avant-garde, outnumbered the radical avant-gardists. The decade 1970–1980 brought an enrichment to the existing stylistic pluralism of Serbian music. Composers of older and middle generations were still dominant on the musical scene, those born before World War II, who either kept to tradition (meaning the heritage of the first decades of the century), or gravitated towards the avant-garde. They were then joined by the youngest composers, who also differed a lot from each other.

Among the composers from the first group who did not show inclination for the avant-garde the most outstanding figure was still Vasilije Mokranjac, whose most fruitful years were in the 1970s. In his *4th symphony* (1972), the suite *Odjeci / Echoes* for piano (1973), *Lyric Poem* for orchestra (1975) and *5th symphony* (1978) he used elements of modality, inspired by the works of Messiaen, in a very refined way, creating an overall meditative atmosphere, sometimes disturbed by the eruptions of unrest and anxiety. In the same decade the works of Dejan Despić developed more intense emotion, yet kept their form balanced and clear (*Tryptich* for violin and orchestra, 1978). Dušan Radić, who in the previous decade had lost his earlier avant-garde reputation, having distanced himself from the ideas that had been promoted in Darmstadt and Warsaw, produced a witty and critically intoned musical essay on the contemporary situation in music. In this work, called *Oratorio profano* (1975), he demonstrated an ability to use different avant-garde techniques and procedures such as happening.

Little is known of Ljubica Marić's work during the 1970s, but some younger composers, probably under her influence, explored the possibility of synthesising archaic musical material with modernist means. Well-accomplished works of that type include *Eclogue* for wind quintet and percussion (1974) by Ludmila Frajt (1919–1999) and *Iz tmine pojanje / Chants from Darkness* (1975) for chorus *a cappella* by Rajko Maksimović.

The founding of the Electronic studio at Radio Belgrade in 1972 was an important event for composers willing to enrich their experience in the field of the avant-garde. As director of the studio, Vladan Radovanović created a number of works that used electronic sounds alone or in combination with traditional sound sources (*Audiospatial* for female chorus and electronics, 1978). However, he also continued to compose music for traditional ensembles (*Stringent* for chamber string ensemble, 1973). Although still interested in the avant-garde, Petar Ozgijan also introduced some traditional elements into his works, combining the use of twelve-tone clusters with motif development (*Symphony'75*). Srdjan Hofman (b. 1944) was much more radically oriented and was interested in serial and aleatoric techniques. His cycle *Hexagons* (1974–1978) contains the only strictly serial works in Serbian music.

Vuk Kulenović (b. 1946) and Vlastimir Trajković (b. 1947), both a little younger than Hofman, developed in different directions. Whereas Kulenović found inspiration in sound-mass technique and in Schoenberg's "Klangfarbenmelodie" (*Icarus* for orchestra, 1978), Trajković was, in the main, attracted by 20th century French music, the works of Debussy, Ravel and Messiaen. His *Arion – le nuove musiche per chitarra ed archi* (1979) with its references to Renaissance monody and refined interpretation of minimalism and repetition, could be regarded as one of the first postmodern works in Serbian music.[8]

During the second half of the 1970s a group of very young composers, still students (b. around 1950), provoked a series of scandals, being dissatisfied with traditional teaching at the Belgrade Music Academy. The members of the group whose name was first "Opus 4", then "The New Generation" – Miodrag Lazarov-Pashu, Miroslav Savić, Milimir Drašković, Vladimir Tošić and Miloš Petrović – created works and events that would have been considered novel in the world at the beginning of the previous decade. In doing this they relied heavily on the works of John Cage and the American minimalists.

During the next ten years, the 1980s, Serbian music was characterised by widening space for postmodernism in its different aspects. One of the features of this orientation was the idea of communicating with a broader audience, and of stepping out of the isolation brought by avant-garde ideology. The new music thus assimilated impulses from the spheres of jazz and rock music, which influenced the creation of works with elements of repetition and minimalism, with special attention devoted to sound quality. Although there were composers who were too occupied with the new world of popular music so that their works lost the necessary complexity of musical thoughts, such was not the case with Vuk Kulenović's *Raskovnik*[9] for string orchestra (1981) and Zoran Erić's (b. 1950) *Off* for double bass and thirteen strings (1982), *Cartoon* for thirteen strings and harpsichord (1984) and *Talea Konzertstück* for violin and orchestra (1989).

During the 1980s the number of women composers, already relatively high, continued to rise. New generations of women were certainly encouraged by the success of Ljubica Marić,[10] who returned to composing after a longish break. She created several chamber works that make a magnificent coda for her whole output: *Chants from Darkness*, recitative cantata for voice and piano (1984), *Monody of the Octoechos* for solo cello (1984), *Asymptote* for violin and string orchestra (1986), *Archaya* for wind trio (1993), *Torso* for piano trio

(1996). Among the most creative successors of Ljubica Marić was Ivana Stefanović (b. 1948), who provided evidence of this when still a young composer with *Kuda sa pticom na dlanu / Whither with the Bird on the Palm,* for percussion and tape, made at Ircam in Paris, 1980. Another female composer whose talent was quickly recognised was Katarina Miljković (b. 1959). She created a subtle atmosphere, mixing sound and noise in her minimalist and repetitive works (*E silentio* for voice, prepared piano, strings and tape, 1987). In *Sequenza 6* for amplified alto-saxophone and prepared piano (1989) she used a motif from Byzantine music as a basis for the work, probably inspired by Marić's example.

During the same decade, Milan Mihajlović (b. 1945) achieved full recognition for his music, characterised by a distinct lyric sensitivity and refined use of orchestral colours. He was among the first Serbian composers to introduce quotations from other works into their music (*Mala žalobna muzika / Eine kleine Trauermusik* for chamber ensemble, 1990). In that context Srdjan Hofman should also be mentioned for his use of collage in his electro-acoustic work *Déja vu* (1985).

Two very different composers, Dejan Despić and Vladan Radovanović, who had resolutely defended their artistic identities throughout the turbulant post-war decades (marked by frequent changes of musical-ideological leading ideas), continued to compose along their firmly grounded paths. Especially valuable works produced in this period were Despić's *Three Meditations* for cello and strings (1989) and Radovanović's radiophonic work *Malo večno jezero / Little Eternal Lake* (1984).

The jubilee celebration of an important event from Serbian history, six hundred years since the Battle of Kosovo (1389), inspired several composers to contribute to events. Here will be mentioned two of the works that were composed in a rather conventional vein, but whose significance was not just occasional: *The Passion of St. Prince Lasarus* for chorus and orchestra (1989) by Rajko Maksimović and *Zadužbine Kosova / Legacy of Kosovo* for chorus and orchestra (1989) by Ivan Jevtić (b. 1947).

By the end of the 1980s a group of very young, talented composers, some of them still students, made its appearance on the Serbian art music scene. They called themselves auto-ironically "The magnificent seven" and organised their first concert in 1988. Their members were: Vladimir Jovanović (b. 1956), Srdjan Jaćimović (1960–2006), Ognjen Bogdanović (b. 1965), Nataša Bogojević (b. 1966), Igor Gostuški (b. 1966), Isidora Žebeljan (b. 1967), and Ana Mihajlović (b. 1968). They were ambitious and impatient to get recognition for their works, into which they introduced elements of popular music. Among their first works to gain attention was Nataša Bogojević's *Različite forme zvučanja Ruže i Krsta / Different Forms of Sounding of the Rose and Cross.* This work, for piano, prepared piano and harpsichord (1989), complex in all its dimensions, especially the rhythmic, was successfully performed at a festival of young composers in France in 1990. Preoccupied by their music, these young composers hardly noticed that their country was nearing some big events – not only the end of the communist era, but also the break-out of secessionist wars that would change dramatically the map of their country and the fate of millions of people.

It is understandable why consideration of Serbian music of the last decade of the 20th century usually invites questions about the marks left on it by wars and other turbulent events in the country.[11] Conditions for creative work – like life itself – were almost unbearable. Apart from the war, sanctions imposed by international organisations in the field of cultural exchange threatened any dedication to composition. There were anti-war protests by composers and other musicians, but they could not, of course, influence the tragic events. An individual gesture of protest was made by Enriko Josif: he decided not to let his works be performed as long as the war lasted. A few middle-aged composers emigrated to the United States of America, Canada or Western Europe (Vuk Kulenović, Svetlana Maksimović), but most emigrants belonged to younger generations (Katarina Miljković, Ognjen Bogdanović, Nataša Bogojević, Ana Mihajlović, Igor Gostuški, Milica Paranosić).

There is no doubt that the several-year-long pressure of the war atmosphere had negative effects on composers' work (although before the NATO campaign in 1999 the war had not been fought in Serbia, but in the neighbouring Croatia and Bosnia-Hercegovina where the Serbian population was involved), but those influences were, on the whole, deeply transformed in their music. In works produced during those years, the ethical position of their authors was not generally stated, either by composition titles or by some kind of programme. Even when there were some indications of the composer's views, this was done indirectly, without pathos. Dejan Despić reacted to the brutal events in two ways. He successively composed works such as *Dies irae* for oboe, violin, viola, cello and piano (1992), with musically transposed symbols of death and hate, and works that ignored such a reality (*Concerto sereno* for piano and orchestra, 1993).[12] When listening to Vuk Kulenović's *Boogie* for piano and orchestra, the Belgrade public understood its ecstatic mood and explosive repetitive rhythmic energy as "music of despair".[13] Much more direct was Ivana Stefanović's message in *Lacrimosa* for tape (1993). She had made a moving work constructed with quotations from "lacrimosae" of Mozart, Pergolesi, Verdi, Britten, Penderecki, and also fragments from the "opelos" (requiems) of Mokranjac and Hristić. By using radiophonic techniques these quotations were used as music material and intertwined with recordings of sounds from the streets of Sarajevo and Belgrade on the eve of the war and afterwards.

The majority of Serbian works from the 1990s, however, are works that appear to have been composed in normal circumstances. Their dominant feature is postmodernism in its different meanings: from a technological variant that makes vast use of computers, to that which is closer to "new simplicity". The emphasis is on works with quotations, fragmentation of form, usage of popular genres, repetitive technique, and exploring the possibilities of electronic and computer technologies. In his *Musica concertante* for piano, strings and electronic devices (1993), Srdjan Hofman introduced rock music pulsations and paraphrased the concerto as a genre belonging to the past. At the same time he did not renounce the complex structures that characterise all works by this essentially modernist composer. Zoran Erić problematised the sense of creation and communication in "stable chaos", as he called the self-organising system, which feeds itself with order from the sea of disorder (*Slike haosa / Images of Chaos, I–IV,* 1990–1995).

During the 1990s composers of the youngest generation continued to work in the area of connecting "high" and "low" music, aiming at more direct communication with the audience. Such general tendencies did not prevent their works from differing one from another in their relation towards form, genre, and level of synthesis of different material, which could be seen for instance in some typical works of the period: *Scarabeus* for electronics, 1994, by Milica Paranosić (b. 1968), *Speed* for orchestra, 1996, by Goran Kapetanović (b. 1969) and *Rukovet / Bouquet of Songs* for female voice and orchestra, 2000, by Isidora Žebeljan.

Vladan Radovanović remained a significant figure in Serbian music during that decade. He continued his works in the domain of multimedia, which he defined more precisely as "synthesic", stressing that in those works all media should be of equal importance and at the same time mutually dependant. A characteristric example of that can be seen in *Sazvežđa / Constellations* (1997), a complex work for mixed electronics, in which three components belonging to different media are active: the sound, visual and kinetic.

One of the phenomena that characterised this period was the turning to a genre that had been completely neglected during communist times – church music. Since the majority of composers lacked the necessary knowledge of theology and Serbian church tradition, a lot of works were produced that were more or less imitations of earlier works of the genre composed before World War II, with many mannerisms which they took over. There were, however, some composers who showed more invention, but there were no especially novel or fresh approaches.

This review of five decades of Serbian music testifies to the existence of a dynamic, stylistically diverse and fruitful scene, vigorous in spite of many obstacles such as unfavourable socio-political climate and inadequate financial support from the state. The highly professional and artistic standard that was attained should be respected, all the more when it is born in mind that the tradition of Serbian art music is so short that its first symphonies and operas were composed only at the beginning of the 20th century. Although during the last decades domestic composers did not produce works of such significance and originality that would situate Serbian music as a whole on an especially important and distinctive place on the map of contemporary art music of the world, it has however shown that our composers were able to contribute to the international scene with valuable individual works.

Notes

1. See Jevtić 2003: 22–23.
2. See Ljubica 1957: 517.
3. The Serbian Octoechos differs from those of other Orthodox chants.
4. See Milin 1998, and Milin 2006: 89–112.
5. See Radovanović 1963: 497.
6. See Radovanović 2006: 164–171.
7. In Serbian musicology, however, it is generally assumed that the Serbian musical avant-garde of that time possessed a significant stamp of distinction, which was characterised by modifications of established norms. See Popović-Mladjenović (1995,1996)

8. On Serbian musical avant-garde and postmodernism see for instance: Veselinović-Hofman (1983 and 1997).
9. Name of the plant believed to have magical powers.
10. Among those who deserve mentioning are: Mirjana Živkovic (b. 1935), Svetlana Maksimović (b. 1948) and Vera Milanković (b. 1953).
11. See more about Serbian and East European music in general at the end of the century in: Milin 1999: 109–118.
12. See Despić 1994: 3–4.
13. See Premate 1993: 127.

References

Despić, Dejan. "Pečat (ne)vremena" [The Stamp of Stormy Times], *Muzički talas,*1, 1994, pp. 81–82.

Jevtić, Miloš, *Svet muzike. Razgovori sa Dušanom Radićem* [The World of Music. Conversations with Dušan Radić], Belgrade: Beogradska knjiga and Kej-Valjevo, 2003.

Marić, Ljubica, "Izmedju zvuka i logosa (Muzičari o muzici) " [Between Sound and Logos (Musicians on music)], *Delo,* 1957, pp. 3–517.

Milin, Melita, *Tradicionalno i novo u srpskoj muzici posle Drugog svetskog rata (1945–1965)* [The Traditional and the New in Serbian Music after World War II (1945–1965)], Belgrade, Muzikološki institut SANU, 1998.

Milin, Melita, "Überleben mit Klängen – Osteuropa nach der Wende" [Surviving With Sounds – Eastern Europe After the Turn], *Jahrbuch Polyaisthesis. Polyaisthesis angesichts eines neuen Jahrtausends* [Polyesthetics Observing the New Millenium], 3, München-Salzburg, 1999, pp. 109–118.

Milin, Melita, "Etape modernizma u srpskoj muzici" [Stages of Modernism in Serbian Music], *Muzikologija,* 6, 2006, pp. 89–112.

Peričić, Vlastimir, "Tendencije razvoja srpske muzike posle 1945. godine" [Tendencies in the Development of Serbian Music After 1945], *Muzički talas,* 26, 2000, pp. 64–80.

Popović-Mladjenović, Tijana, "Differentia specifica. Iz kompozitorske prakse u Beogradu" [Differentia specifica. The Practice of Composition in Belgrade], *Muzički talas,* 1995, 1996, 1: 4–6, pp. 28–40, 2: 1–3, pp. 36–52, 3: 4, pp. 18–49.

Premate, Zorica, "Blistavi fetiš očajanja" [Dazzling Fetish of Despair], *Novi Zvuk,* 2, 1993, pp. 119–127.

Radovanović, Vladan, "Bitni faktori razvoja naše muzike" [Essential Factors in the Development of Our Music], *Zvuk,* 59, 1963, pp. 494–497.

Radovanović, Vladan, "Srpska avangarda u odlasku od muzike (1955–1980)" [Serbian Avant-garde in the Process of Leaving Music (1955–1980)], *Gradina,* 10, 1984, pp. 5–37.

Radovanović, Vladan, "Muzikološki radovi – komentar" [Musicological Works – Commentary], *Koraci,* 3-4, 2006, pp. 164–171.

Veselinović-Hofman, Mirjana, *Stvaralačko prisustvo evropske avangarde u nas* [The Creative Presence of the European Avant-Garde in Serbian Music], Belgrade, Univerzitet umetnosti, 1983.

Veselinović-Hofman, Mirjana, *Fragment o muzičkoj postmoderni* [Fragment on Musical Postmodernism], Novi Sad, Matica srpska, 1997.

Veselinović-Hofman, Mirjana, "Problems and Paradoxes of Yugoslav Avant-garde Music (Outlines for a Reinterpretation)", *Impossible Histories – Historical Avant-gardes – Neo-avant-gardes, and Post-avant-gardes in Yugoslavia, 1918–1991,* Cambridge, MA-London, The MIT Press, 2003.

Part II: Art Music in Greece

Chapter 6

The Ionian Islands

Katy Romanou

Iōannēs Aristeidēs' autograph of a church hymn with figured bass (c. 1825). Archives of Corfú Philharmonic Society.

The ideology of the Enlightenment entered Greece both through the West and the East.[1] The western passage was the Ionian Islands that, except for a few cases, had been of Venetian dominion since the 13th century and maintained close contacts with Italy even after its falling under subsequent non-Italian rulers (French *liberators* in 1797, Russian *mediators* in 1799 and English *protectors* in 1814 until 1864, the year of the Islands' incorporation to Greece). The cultural Renaissance that commenced on the Islands during the first few years of the 18th century coincides with the last sparks of the tradition of classical Greek studies and Humanism that had been transfused in Venice by Greek refugees who had fled their Latin-dominated islands at the imminence of the Ottoman occupation (Chios 1566, Cyprus 1571, Crete 1669). The contact of those refugees with members of the Greek aristocracy of the Ionian Islands proved decisive in the maintenance of national conscience and the study of the Greek language. The enlightened Greek aristocrats[2] would thus play a primary role in the preparation of the Greek Revolution. Venetian settlers and subsequent rulers offered them attendance to the administration, as a shield from local citizens' discontent. Greeks of this class kept close contact with educational institutions of Italy, where they studied and taught. They also gained free access to Academies founded on the Islands, initially for Venetians only.[3] Towards the end of the 18th century the number of educated Greeks grew larger since many were leaving Venice in order to settle on the Ionian Islands as well as other parts of Western Greece (Kitromēlidēs [Κιτρομηλίδης] 1996: 73).

Music education

Whether any kind of music instruction was connected with the Academies mentioned previously is not known. However, it is an established fact that, prior to the founding of the first music school in 1824, music had been taught privately by foreigners primarily of Italian origin.[4]

The first music school for the Greek inhabitants of the Islands was founded in Corfú in 1824 by Frederick North, 5th Earl of Guilford (1766–1827)[5] (known simply as 'Guilford' in Greece). This English nobleman spent years of hard work and a great part of his wealth on the establishment of the Ionian Academy (1824–1864), the first Greek University that was founded after the fall of Constantinople. With the desire to create a genuinely Greek institution, Guilford travelled to all the places that were known for their Greek schools and teachers and managed to get feedback from every successful Greek school (in Bucharest, Chios, Constantinople,

Ioannina, Athens, etc.). He also visited European cities with prosperous Greek communities (Paris, various Italian, Austrian, as well as Russian cities). He chose promising youngsters, whom he sent to study in Europe at his own expense. Despite his admiration for ancient Greek civilisation, he was extremely careful not to offend people's religious feelings. In 1818 he visited Russia to get information on the education of Russian clergy and use it as a model for the education of Greek clergy, which he considered to be of great importance (Angelomatē-Tsougarakē [Αγγελομάτη-Τσουγκαράκη] 1997: 38). Guilford realised how delicately he should act in order not to be accused of proselytism, since Christian communities of the ailing Ottoman empire were flooded with missionaries of western churches.[6] Guilford's restrictive measures affected the university's Music Department to a great extent since it offered instruction solely on Greek church music.

Greek church music was taught by Iōannēs Aristeidēs (1786–1828), a deacon from Ioannina who was sent by Guilford to study music and ancient Greek literature in Naples. The subject matter of his music lessons greatly disappointed musically inclined citizens who, immersed as they were in Italian operatic culture, were looking forward to studying the *bel canto*. It seems that a lot of talented young people, who wished to study music, were rejected. Church chanters on the other hand, were being put under a lot of pressure to attend (Typaldos Iakōvatos [Τυπάλδος Ιακωβάτος] 1982: 47).

Convergence of the "academic" and the "popular"

The outcome was that Iōannēs Aristeidēs stopped teaching music lessons long before his death (1828) due to very poor attendance. Thereafter, philharmonic societies undertook music education, where instruction was more practical than theoretical, while church music constituted only a small part of the repertory taught and performed.

The Philharmonic Society of Corfú was founded in 1840 and is in operation up to the present day. The society's ensembles made good use of Aristeidēs' teaching manuscripts; some among them were copied out, while others were completed and perfected by the society's music teachers. This important body of manuscripts was lying intact remaining unexploited for almost a century until August 1999, when it was retrieved by a team affiliated to the Music Department of the University of Athens, during a research project in the Music Library of The Philharmonic Society of Corfú.[7] A close look at these manuscripts gives a satisfactory account of Aristeidēs' teaching repertory and the way it was developed and applied by subsequent generations (Rōmanou [Ρωμανού] 2000: 175–188; Rōmanou, Zōtos [Ρωμανού, Ζώτος] 2004: 85–102).

To what extent Aristeidēs' work is connected to the local popular tradition is not easy to decide. For instance, one cannot say whether Aristeidēs wrote down what he had heard by local chanters or if he applied the music theory he had studied in Naples to harmonise melodies of the Constantinopolitan tradition that he already knew from the time he was a chanter. Titles on some manuscripts such as "On the style of the people of Corfú", "On the

Nicolò Calichiopoulo Manzaro (1795–1872). Probably the unique photo. Archives of Corfú Reading Society, with the courtesy of Cōstas Kardamēs.

style of Holy Mount" or "On Eastern style" suggest that he might have done both. What is evident however is that, before leaving for Naples he had certainly been trained in the New Method.[8] Another established fact is that subsequent local musicians and members of the clergy used his manuscripts for teaching and public performances, and that his teaching got assimilated in local culture.

The manuscripts are all in staff notation on Greek ecclesiastic texts. The modes (*echoi*) of the chants are usually indicated on the front pages. Iōannēs Aristeidēs' name appears on a great number of them, while the names of subsequent musicians (El. Palatianos, Theoph. Karydēs, Cypriōtēs and Nicolò Chalikiopoulo Manzaro) appear on manuscripts written from the 1830s onwards.

Older manuscripts, written by Aristeidēs, are almost all on a double stave; on the upper one the chant's melody is written in the soprano C clef while on the lower stave there is a harmonic bass (at times, figured) in F clef. Later manuscripts have from four to six staves where all clefs are being used and all parts are written out. Many have a piano or organ

G.7 518/1840   (13)   Num. 518

ΑΓΓΕΛΙΑ.

Η ΦΙΛΑΡΜΟΝΙΚΗ ΕΤΑΙΡΕΙΑ ΤΗΣ ΚΕΡΚΥΡΑΣ.

Εχουσα σκοπὸν νὰ διοργανίσῃ μίαν ΑΣΤΥΚΗΝ ΜΟΥΣΙΚΗΝ προσκαλεῖ νὰ παρουσιασθῶσιν εἰς τὰς αἰθούσας τῆς ΕΤΕΡΕΙΑΣ ὅσοι τῶν νέων Ἑλλήνων, ἡλικίας ἐτῶν 15 καὶ ὑπεράνω, ἔχοντες χλίσιν νὰ διδαχθῶσιν ὄργανόν τι ὑπαγόμενον εἰς αὐτήν, ἐπιθυμοῦν ν' ἀποτελέσουν μέρος τῆς ἰδίας.

Δὲν φέρει ἐμπόδιον κανὲν ἄν τις ἐξ αὐτῶν δὲν ἡξεύρῃ νὰ ἀναγνώσῃ καὶ νὰ γράψῃ, καθότι ἡ ΕΤΑΙΡΕΙΑ θέλει καὶ περὶ τούτου προβλέψει.

Αἱ Αἴθουσαι τῆς ΕΤΑΙΡΕΙΑΣ, αἱ εἰς τὸ πρῶτον Πάτωμα τῆς ἐν τῇ Πίνζα Οἰκίας Πολυλᾶ ἀριθ. 1295, θέλουν ἐκ τῆς σήμερον εἶσθαι ἀνοικταὶ ἀπὸ τὰς ὥρας 10 τῆς αὐγῆς ὡς τὰς 2 μ. μ. καὶ ἀπὸ τὰς 5 μ. μ. ὡς τὰς 8 τῆς ἑσπέρας καθ' ὅλας τὰς ἡμέρας τῆς Ἑβδομάδος, διὰ νὰ καταγραφθῶσιν οἱ ἐπιθυμοῦντες καὶ νὰ λάβωσιν γνῶσιν τῶν ἀναφορικῶν ὑποχρεώσεων.

ΚΕΡΚΥΡΑΙ, τῇ 14/26 Νοεμβρίου 1840.

AVVISO.

LA SOCIETA' FILARMONICA DI CORFU',

Desiderando instituire una BANDA CIVILE, invita tutti quei giovani nativi Greci, dai 15 Anni in su, che trovandosi disposti ad apprendere un Istrumento relativo alla medesima, volessero prestare l'opera loro, di presentarsi nelle Sale della SOCIETA'.

Non è ostacolo che taluno non sappia nè leggere nè scrivere, dappoichè la SOCIETA' provederà ancora a questo.

Le Sale della SOCIETA', *in Casa Polillà alla Pigna N.o* 1295 *primo Piano*, saranno aperte per ricevere i nomi de' concorrenti, e far loro note le relative obbligazioni, dalle ore *Dieci* fino alle *Due* della mattina, e dalle *Cinque* alle *Otto* della sera, in tutti i giorni della settimana, cominciando da oggi.

CORFU', *li 14/26 Novembre* 1840.

Billingual announcement inviting young Greeks to join Corfú Philharmonic Society's wind band (14/26 November 1840). Archives of Corfú Philharmonic Society.

accompaniment. The layout clearly shows the way in which Aristeidēs' adaptation of the chants to Italian *partimenti* practice was further developed by The Philharmonic Society's musicians in a mode that was gradually minimising improvisation.

Similarly to the culture of contemporary Italian music, the local culture was generally characterised by a convergence of the "academic" and the "popular". More specifically, just like in Southern Italy, what seems to be the dominant style in Corfú until around the mid-19th century is a combination of a popular tradition of improvised polyphonic singing with the semi-practical teaching of counterpoint in South Italian conservatories through Fedele Fenaroli's method of *partimenti*.

Italians call *falsobordone* a popular tradition of improvising the doubling (or tripling) of a melody in parallel thirds primarily.[9] Western sources describe a similar singing practiced by Greeks in Venice and in the Greek islands, where the interval of a fourth is prominent. In an attempt to contradict those who consider the interval of a fourth as dissonant, Gioseffo Zarlino writes in his *Institutioni Harmoniche*: "If it were truly dissonant, as they say, we would not use it in our compositions, nor would modern Greeks have it in their sacred part-songs which are heard here in Venice on every feast day, in which the diatessaron is in the lowest part without any other consonance as a base" (Zarlino 1968: 14).[10]

Two centuries later Charles Burney makes reference to Zarlino's passage when the Abate Cirillo Martini informed him that

> Greeks in Passion Week sing several tropes or modes which they now term ἤχοι, in four parts, in the style of Palestrina; and this kind of music they call Cretan, but why, is not easy to divine […]
>
> The Abate says that he often heard the common people of Greece sing in concert, and observed that they made frequent use of the fourth: della consonanza che noi chiamiamo oggi quarta. By this he must mean that they used it as a concord in two parts, or if there were more than two parts, in positions where our harmony forbids the use of it; otherwise it would not have affected his ear as a singularity.
>
> The fact is curious; and I find it confirmed by Zarlino, who observed the same practice in the Greek church at Venice. (Burney 1782: 52–53)[11]

The Abate Cirillo Martini (often confused in Greek texts with Giovanni Battista Martini, known as Padre Martini) travelled to Greece in order to learn about modern Greek civilisation. He gave a lot of his manuscripts to Charles Burney who visited him in Venice on the 8–9 August, 1770, and used them in the second volume of his *History of Music*. After Burney's visit, Cirillo Martini also sent information to Padre Martini on Greek music, for the fourth, unfinished, volume of his *History of Music*. This information, together with all information that Padre Martini had prepared to use in this volume, has been collected and put in order in a manuscript book by Gaetano Gaspari (1807–1881). The book (ms. I.36), entitled *Materiali valudati dal P. Martini per la continuazione della Storia della musica in occidente dai primi tempi della chiesa fino a Guido Aretino. Possi nel miglior ordine possible da G.Gaspari*, is kept in Civico Museo Bibliografico Musicale of Bologna, which supplied us with a microfilm copy of the fragment on Greek music (cc.156r–169r).[12] The fragment deals mostly with music notation and monophonic chanting, but towards the end, reference is also made to polyphonic singing:

> He [the Abate Martini] remembers having heard that non-ecclesiastical Greeks singing in choir at night in the city use in their harmonies the diatessaron. He also remembers […] that he had heard certain troparia in Greek, and among others the *Velum Templi scisus est*, composed in four parts according to the tradition of Cretan music, that was apparently established in the 15th and 16th centuries, when harmonic music flourished in Flanders and Italy, and were written in the style of Palestrina or Marco da Gagliano […]

A Greek source conforming to most of the above is a text by the musician Panagiōtēs Gritsanēs (1835–1896), originating from Zante, speaking on Cretan Music as practised by his contemporaries. What is understood from Gritsanēs' description is a practice of parallel chords in second inversion, which agrees with Zarlino's remark that "the diatessaron is in the lowest part without any other consonance as a base".

Gritsanēs' research on Cretan music (Gritsanēs [Γριτσάνης] 1908) was commissioned by the Ecclesiastic Music Association of Constantinople in 1867, in an attempt to show that the Orthodox tradition in the Ionian Islands was not alienated from the tradition of Constantinople. Cretan music is called polyphonic chanting in the Ionian Islands, a tradition that was supposedly introduced by Cretan immigrants who settled there when the Ottomans captured Crete in 1669. It is reasonable to assume, however, that it is not harmony and polyphony that the Cretans introduced in the Ionian Islands (where they were certainly practiced before), but that they brought a revival of Byzantine chant, that, in turn (in the 15th century), was brought into Crete by immigrants from Constantinople who settled on the island (among them, the famous church musicians Iōannēs Laskarēs and Manouēl Doukas Chrysaphēs).

Harmony had been assimilated in the Ionian tradition to such a degree that it was considered a natural element of all music. In fact, Gritsanēs, as well as other Ionian musicians trying to show the connections of Ionian church music with Constantinopolitan tradition, bypass the fact that church music was sung with harmony, and compare the melodies only.

Looking back at such efforts – a common feature towards the end of the 19th century – to defend Ionian church music by presenting it as oriental, they seem as if moving in retrograde amid the overall venture for westernisation in the more oriental parts of Greece!

Like an Italian provincial city

In fact, music culture in the Ionian Islands *was* western during the entire 19th century. Corfú's musical life was that of a provincial Italian city.

Despite their isolation from the developments beyond the Alps up to about the 1850s, Italian musical centres were fully equipped with the infrastructure used throughout centuries of Italian supremacy in music. In every city, no matter how big or small, there was an uninterrupted function of dramatic and lyric theatres, conservatories, philharmonic academies or societies, as natural components of daily urban life. They functioned regularly and traditionally, keeping numerous anonymous musicians and related professionals under their employment, and maintaining amateurism in high vitality among the people.

The dominant genre is, undoubtedly, opera. Opera was produced in Italy in rhythms and numbers of ephemeral artistic genres by innumerable composers, all of whom –including the ones penetrating anonymity– were connected to the great public with ephemeral art's bonds of familiarity. Opera, available to paraphrasing, transcribing, and all kinds of adaptations, circulated fragmented, in various metamorphoses. This mode of transmission had multidimensional impacts: it preserved the melody as the dominant element, undermining that of orchestration, and created a flow of music that was springing from the theatre to all neighbours and citizens of the city; it brought successful productions to bourgeois homes –through piano transcriptions– and to the people in the streets – through wind band's open air performances – thereby building cultural channels between the classes. Its fragmentation reflects the absence, yet, of any notion concerning the integrity of a *work of art*.

San Giacomo and Italian musicians

In Corfú there was only one theatre, so antagonism did not leave its imprints the way it did all over Italy (strong and wealthy printing houses and highly developed advertising nets). Nonetheless, the town's theatre, San Giacomo, operated like all Italian opera houses, for two seasons during the year, at a frequency of about five performances per week.

The theatre's audience was the island's foreign dignitaries and the Greek nobility, who rented a loge for the entire year. Rich civilians watched the performance from the parterre. Opera performances were seen as social gatherings. Descriptions of the atmosphere that reigned in San Giacomo are almost identical to those of any Italian theatre (Burney 1969: 192): flirting, eating and drinking, playing cards, visiting one's neighbouring balcony would only be interrupted for the attentive listening of the work's famous arias. In 1800 the French consul André-Grasset Saint Sauver wrote:

La plus grande liberté regnoit dans le théâtre; on y jouoit, on y mangeoit. Tantôt une partie des loges ressembloit à autant de cabinets de restaurateur; tantôt à des cabinets de jeux ; on juge qu'on ne pouvoit jouir du spectacle ; aussi personne ne s'en occupoit guerre qu au moment où, dans une pièce, un morceau de musique avoit fait le plus d'impression. (Saint Sauver 22.9.1799–22.9.1800: 208)[13]

We have a fairly clear idea of the operas produced in San Giacomo during the 19th century.[14] Information is also at hand concerning musicians that collaborated with The Philharmonic Society of Corfú and participated in the theatre's performances.

Some interesting points are: the belated impact on the repertoire by the events deriving from Greek Revolution; the gradual creation of a permanent orchestral core by local musicians (Greeks and Italians); the communication that was being developed between the theatre and The Philharmonic Society; and the enrichment of the repertory towards the 1850s with operas by French and especially by Greek composers (initially produced in Italian, and later on in French or Greek).

Italians and patriotic libretti

The impact of the Greek Revolution on San Giacomo's repertoire was belated in comparison with what happened in the West, especially in Paris, during the philhellenic movement, but also in comparison with Italy, where the heroes and the events of the Greek Revolution were presented in a number of operas or *balli* since the 1830s – with the intention to inspire the Italian cause while deceiving official censorship. In 1832–1833 the ballo eroico *L' ultimo giorno di Missolungi*, with music composed by Luigi Viviani, was produced in Venice. In 1836 another ballo eroico tragico spettacoloso *La caduta d'Ipsara*, of an unknown composer, was performed in Alexandria. The ballo tragico *La caduta di Suli* was produced in Genoa in 1838; the opera *La Battaglia di Navarino* by Giuseppe Staffa was produced in Naples in 1837; another opera, entitled *Ultimi Giorni di Suli*, by Giovanni Battista Ferrari was staged in Venice in 1843 (the performance of this opera in San Giacomo was announced in 1867). Also, the Maltese composer Vicenzo Napoleone Mifsud wrote the opera *Il giuramento di Germanos ovvero La liberazione della Grecia*, the performance of which was to take place in Rome in 1849 but got cancelled because of political troubles (Sessa 2003: 322–323). The same composer's grande scena *Marco Bozzari* was published in Trieste in 1849 with a Greek translation of the libretto (Ladas [Λαδάς] 1976: 101).

The earliest opera by a Greek composer (but on an Italian libretto), on a subject related to the Greek Revolution, is Francesco Domenegini's *Marco Bozzari*, produced in Zante in 1849. Under the same title there is another work by Paolo Carrer (also from Zante) which happened to be most popular in Greece; this was performed for the first time in Patras in 1861 and afterwards, up to the first decades of the 20th century, in most cities in Greece as well as abroad, in places with Greek communities.[15]

Italians and Greek orchestras

Italian musicians formed the first core of a local orchestra in the theatre, where initially theatrical pieces "du bas comique" were performed. By the 18th century theatre had already been replaced by opera and ballet because

Le goût de la musique, qui s'etoit singulièrement accru dans Corfou, rendit bientôt ce genre de spectacle insipide; et les comédiens furent remplacées par les opere buffe (opéras comiques); on y ajouta, dans la suite, la divertissement de la danse. […] Les musiciens attachés au provediteur-general et aux divers chefs des armées navale composoient l'orchestre: les amateurs y etoient aussi admis. (Saint Sauveur 22.9.1799–22.9.1800: 207)[16]

In the 1820s the Italian musicians who formed the permanent core of the opera's orchestra were prominent figures of the city's musical life (Kapadochos [Καπαδόχος] 1991: 118). Giuseppe Castignace had been *maestro al cembalo* or *maestro e direttore della musica* of at least 44 performances in San Giacomo, from 1817 to 1855. Nicolò Manzaro makes reference to this musician in 1859 as being one of his oldest friends and a *maestro concertatore* for over 32 years in San Giacomo. He says that he had been a student of Fenaroli in the Neapolitan conservatory where he had also studied, and that he had composed operas for Naples's Teatro Nuovo, among which, *Le metamorfosi di Pulcinella* was the most successful (Manzaro 1851: 20).

Another Italian, Luigi Trippa, played *contrabasso al cembalo* regularly in San Giacomo, from 1827 to 1832. Marco Battagel had been *primo vl. e direttore d'orchestra* in twelve opera performances from 1824 to 1830. This musician (rendered in Greek as Μάρκος Μπατάγιας) came to Corfú from Zante, where in 1816 he had founded the first philharmonic society of all Ionian Islands, organising an orchestra (initially a wind orchestra and later on a mixed one) with instrumentalists he had invited from Italy. Only two concerts of that orchestra are known – both directed by Battagel: one in 1817 and the other in 1823 (Motsenigos [Μοτσενίγος] 1958: 166; Tzerbinos [Τζερμπίνος] 1996: 25).

Models of music education

The philharmonic societies that were founded on the Ionian Islands during the 19th century were modelled on the Italian conservatories and philharmonic academies. They also shared the aims of the Conservatoire de Paris in the first years of its founding: that of providing musicians for the army's ensembles and for the celebrations of national feasts.[17] Consequently, the philharmonic societies of the Islands acquired a popular, philanthropic and nationalistic character.[18]

In particular The Philharmonic Society of Corfú, on the initiative of its life-president Nicolò Chalikiopoulo Manzaro, operated also like an Italian academy, as a gathering point of intellectuals discussing theoretical topics but also issues connected to the Greek Revolution and the politics of the new Greek state. Though it has not been confirmed, the connection of The Philharmonic Society of Corfú with Freemasonry is something quite possible.

The first Heptanesian Philharmonic Society was founded, as said, by Marco Battagel in Zante, in 1816. From that moment, a number of short living societies were off-handedly being founded (and repeatedly re-founded)[19] by Italian and Greek musicians. The foundation of The Philharmonic Society of Corfú was well planned and legally secured. Since 1840, and up to the present day, it has played a leading role in the music education and musical life of the island.

The influence of Neapolitan conservatories specifically on the Society's function was great. Manzaro himself, who shared a warm friendship with Zingarelli, the director of the *Collegio Musicale Real of San Pietro a Majella*,[20] was given the chance to spend some time in the institution, and so did many of his students.[21]

The character of the Islands' philharmonics described above is well demonstrated in the events that led to the establishment of The Philharmonic Society of Corfú. The occasion was given in the procession of Saint Spyridon – the island's protector Saint – of August 11–23 1839, and was carried through in total absence of music, in compliance with Queen Victoria's orders prohibiting English military bands to play for their subjects' feasts in all colonies and protectorates. The humiliation experienced on that occasion led a group of young educated aristocrats to decide upon the founding of The Philharmonic Society of Corfú. The enthusiastic crowds greeted the first appearance of a band of some forty Greek children during the procession of Saint Spyridon in 1841 with pride. The inhabitants of Corfú would claim, years after the event, that the island's unification with the rest of Greece in 1864 was realised thanks to the church bells and the sounds of the philharmonic (Motsenigos [Μοτσενίγος] 1958: 149). Among the decisions taken during one of the first meetings of the society's members was to speak in Greek and not in Italian during their assemblies and to celebrate annually on 25 March (the date of the Greek Revolution).

According to the programme of studies laid out by Manzaro, the music school had a composition and a performance department. The subjects being taught in the first were: harmony, counterpoint (according to the method of the *partimenti*) and composition; while in the latter, what was being taught was mainly wind instruments participating in the society's band, strings (quite often in decline), singing, and piano. Boys over fifteen years old were accepted as internal or external students and as members of the band; while amateurs, including girls, were also trained.

Girls were normally taught the *partimenti* and the piano. An announcement of a "Trattenimento Accademico che avra luogo nello Stabilimento Filarmonico delle Signorine Corciresi, la sera di Giovedi 31 Marzio 1859", gives a programme of various salon pieces, including a Polka-Mazurka by Charpentier "a 18 mani, su 3 piani ed organum melodium".[22]

Female composers

Being the first music schools that were not restricted to church music, philharmonic societies of the Ionian Islands produced a number of female composers. In the music library of The Philharmonic Society of Corfú one may find piano pieces composed by Manzaro's female students, Amalia Genata and Souzana Nerantzē. There is also a polka for piano entitled *La Primavera*, which was composed by Françoise Courage, a student of Spyridōn Xyndas, who, himself, had been a student of Manzaro. Actually, in 1875 Courage won a prize for this composition in the competition of the 3rd Olympiad that took place in Athens.[23] Her name appeared in this competition and was rendered in Greek as *Φραγκίσκη Κοράγιου*, while the same year the work was published in Corfú with her name in French, followed by a dedication "à son Maitre Spiridon Xinda".

Souzana Nerantzē happened to be the most accomplished composer of the three female students. She had been a child prodigy and her compositions were published in Italy as well as in the Greek periodical *Musikē* of Constantinople in the years 1912 and 1913. She was among Manzaro's favourite students.[24]

Corfú's Philharmonic Society music library

A catalogue, published in 2004 under the title *The music library of Corfú's Philharmonic Society* (Rōmanou, Zōtos [Ρωμανού, Ζώτος] 2004),[25] that lists 19th century musical texts kept in the library of The Philharmonic Society of Corfú, presents a great amount of information concerning details as well as general aspects of the island's music culture in that century. We get information on musicians working in a vivid everyday routine, on the various ways the Society was connected to San Giacomo theatre, and on the repertories applied for various uses.

The music library of the society traditionally has a practical use, that of providing music for instruction and for frequent public appearances of the society's ensembles. Many of the 19th century scores kept at the library are still used today in class and in public celebrations around the city.

Not all periods of the society's life in the 19th century are presented with equal persistence within the library's texts; this is because, on the one hand, the island suffered various disasters and on the other, as implied, the library was not regarded as a historic archive, and no special care had been taken for the preservation of its contents.

The texts of the Corfú Philharmonic Society music library are, for the biggest part, manuscript copies. The highly developed art of manuscript copying ensured the vivid rhythms of daily musical activity, where time between music creation and music performance might be minimal. The copyist is one among the most essential artisans of the institution.

Reflected in the manuscript copies of this catalogue is multilingualism, a distinct peculiarity of Corfú's bourgeois culture. Calligraphers of ordinary education copied the titles on the cover of musical scores in Italian, Greek, sometimes French, English and German, and very rarely, in other languages as well. Mistakes and mixing up of languages are frequent. Multilingualism is very striking in music terminology, particularly in the case of instruments that are indicated in scores of wind band transcriptions.

Printed texts that are kept in the library are mainly operas and didactic vocal and instrumental methods published in Italy, while manuscripts are mainly works and band transcriptions by local composers, the majority of whom were music teachers of the society and band conductors.

Conforming to the character of Italian music described above, and the functional use of the library, are a great number of music books, all of which are collections of pieces for similar use, suitable for one occasion. For instance, there are books with funeral marches, books with lively marches, books with salon pieces, with transcriptions of some opera's highlights, with works dedicated to The Philharmonic Society and so on. They contain bound together printed texts and manuscripts, autographs and copies, prototypes and transcriptions, works by Greek and Italian composers written in different periods. At a given occasion, any piece would be chosen, transcribed for the instruments available and performed before the community.

Nicolò Calichiopulo (or Chalikiopoulo)[26] Manzaro

Nicolò Chalikiopoulo Manzaro's (1795–1872) work and activity have contributed highly to the formation of Greek art music. A large part of his work, combining strict technique with melodic naturalness, was integrated in Corfú's popular culture and assimilated by the people. His teaching, which he offered for free all his life, moulded a whole generation of heptanesian composers; during the last four decades of the 19th century, his students have taken their art to Athens and other cities of the new Greek state, establishing therein institutions of western musical culture. The influence of Manzaro and, through him, of Italian music to modern Greek music will start to be overturned in the first decade of the 20th century, when primarily Manōlis Kalomoirēs, another strong and influential personality, will disseminate in the country the aesthetics, ideas, morals, repertory and technique of German (Romantic) music that, through music historiography, will be conceived as universal, inherent in all music.

The fact that in Italy – isolated during the first half of the 19th century from the European centres – music life was based on different principles, morals and ideas, seems to have escaped Greek researchers for quite a time, leading them to fruitless search for heptanesian works on German Romantic forms (symphonies, string quartets, piano sonatas etc.), that gave rise to ungrounded theories about conspiracies against heptanesian musicians, and caused a number of misinterpretations of the surviving documents.

Only recently was it realised that all developments within 19th century German culture were not adopted in Italy and the Ionian Islands until a lot later: sonata form, four-movement symphonies and string quartets were not composed in Italy or in Corfú during the first half of the 19th century. Instead orchestration was underdeveloped and the great 19th century symphonists (including Beethoven) were unknown,[27] as was the veneration of music and composers, theories on the unity of a work of art, on artistic inspiration and originality. The entire net of education, promotion and performance of symphonic music was not yet shaped.[28]

Two personalities whose influence contributed in shaping Manzaro's work were Dionysios Solōmos and Nicolò Zingarelli.

Dionysios Solōmos (1798–1857) is the first important poet of modern Greece. He was born in Zante. Like Manzaro, he was from a noble family and was educated in Italy; his early poems are in Italian language. Gradually from 1822, inspired by the Greek Revolution and the great expectancies on the foundation of the Greek state, he began to write in Greek, indeed, in a popular language (in contrast to contemporary poets who had studied in Greece and applied the official language, the *katharevousa*). In his poems Solōmos relates the heroism and sacrifices of those Greeks who fought against the Ottomans, as well as events from the life of people in the Ionian Islands. Many among his verses were sung in Zante and the other Ionian Islands, as local popular music, on tunes of unknown provenance. In Corfú, many were sung on tunes written by Manzaro in a popular style.

In 1823 Solōmos wrote his *Hymn to Liberty*, a long poem of 158 four-line verses, relating heroic and dramatic events of the Greek Revolution, commenting on political aspects of Greece's liberation and "answering" to Byron's despair from the passivity of the enslaved Greeks (in his *Don Juan*). *Hymn to Liberty* was published in Messolongi in 1824, the year of Lord Byron's death in that town.[29]

In 1828 Solōmos settled in Corfú and became connected to Manzaro with a tight friendship that was inspiring for both.

Manzaro wrote the music to a great number of Solōmos' poems, all in the popular style of improvised harmony, mentioned earlier. Their most famous collaboration is *Hymn to Liberty*, the first verses of which have been, since 1864, the Greek National Anthem. *Hymn to Liberty* was the only work on a Greek text by Manzaro to be published. All the rest exist in manuscript.

Nicolò Zingarelli was teacher and director, since 1813, of the famous Neapolitan *Real Collegio di Musica di San Sebastiano* (which in 1826 was named *Real Collegio di Musica di San Pietro a Majella*). According to Francesco Florimo, he was a proud patriot who denied serving Napoleon (Florimo [1882] 2000: 409–411),[30] while according to Spyros Motsenigos, a philhellene (Motsenigos [Μοτσενίγος] 1958: 166).

In a trip to Greece in 1822, Zingarelli was closely associated with Manzaro who, in turn, spent several years in the Neapolitan conservatorio directed by Zingarelli, perfecting his art in counterpoint and harmony, through Fenaroli's method of *partimenti*, taught in that institution[31] – and elsewhere in Southern Italy.

Manzaro's compositions are distinctly in two styles, written for two different audiences: one is that of Italian contemporary music, addressed to the nobility and the foreigners of Corfú; the other is in the style of local popular music, addressed to the people and aiming to instigate national conscience and cultivate its musicality. The differences are in the tonal structure and the form of the melodies, in the harmonic elaboration and in the overall form of the pieces. The more sophisticated Italian style has good modulations, strictly "correct" harmony and contrasting melodies. Much of what is written in the popular style is in parallel thirds and sixths; modulations are rare and the form is more often strophic.

The composer's father, Iakovos Chalikiopoulo Manzaro (1769–1843) was member of the judiciary during the Venetian and the English rule, and a member of the Ionian Parliament as well as of various academies. Iakovos' uncle was Geōrgios Chalikiopoulo Manzaro, high priest during the later years of the Venetian rule (1795–1799), who became elected for the metropolitan throne that the Russians had re-established in 1799 – but died on the day of his enthronement (Motsenigos [Μοτσενίγος] 1958: 82). Moreover, Nicolò Manzaro was married to the countess Marianna Giustiniani "of the noble family of Komnēnos Ioustinianos of Genoa" (Motsenigos [Μοτσενίγος] 1958: 100).

Manzaro's noble family and his father's position appear to be the reasons why he did not purport to be a professional musician and why he did not publish any of his popular and patriotic works – at least not until his father's death in 1843. All his printed works up to that date do not reflect the influence of major national events. Remarkable is the fact that one of the earliest publications by Manzaro is the Italian canzonetta with piano accompaniment *Ninetta Vezzosa* (on a light love poem) that was printed in Paris by Antonio Francesco Gaetano Saverio Pacini. Pacini published and sold in his printing house a large number of philhellenic works, including his own *Mères, endormez vos enfants. Chant de Missolonghi* (1828). The only Greek work published by him was Manzaro's canzonetta, at a time that the Greek Revolution inspired a great number of compositions performed primarily in Paris – by Rossini, Berlioz, Momigny, Herold and others.[32]

It is due to the reasons mentioned above that the information we have on Manzaro's studies – his relationship to Zingarelli and his supposed teaching in Naples – happens to be quite incoherent.

According to the composer's own statement regarding his stay in Naples, he became closely related to Zingarelli "at the conservatorium of San Sebastiano where he was the director" and, took delight in being taught a lot of things that he was previously not aware of ("apprendendo per mio diletto molto di ciò ch'io non sapeva") (Manzaro 1851: 10).

In that same text Manzaro offers an insight on the kind of study he did in Naples, saying that in 1826 he copied from Durante's autograph his "marvellous" *Messa di morti* in C minor for eight voices, where he was astonished to find "more than few mistakes" (Manzaro 1851: 20).

It is not easy to estimate how Manzaro was received in Naples or elsewhere in Italy. Information about him teaching at the conservatory, directed by Zingarelli, comes from his students and acquaintances; it has been used by his early biographers and repeated thereafter. In many early texts the effort to present Manzaro as a Greek Padre Martini, a theoretician whose opinion is much sought after, even in Italy, is very obvious.[33] His name is not once mentioned in Francesco Florimo's four-volume work, giving plenty of information on Neapolitan conservatories and lists of their teachers (but it should be remembered that Manzaro would not have taught professionally, because of his nobility).

In letters sent to him from Italy, his students and friends convey manifestations of admiration or respect from famous musicians, such as Saverio Mercadante, Giovanni Paccini, Luigi Vecchiotti, Giovanni Grassoni, Francesco Ruggi, and so on (Papageōrgiou [Παπαγεωργίου] 1890: 15). However, we only have proof of such manifestations from the following publications by lesser musicians dedicated to Manzaro, found in Italian libraries:[34]

Gaetano Masini's *Il pentimento della monaca,* published in Milan in 1865 with the dedication "Al N.U. illustre Cav. Nicola Manzaro, celeberrimo contrapuntista"; Antonio Vigentini's *Quarta raccolta di romanze e canzoni,* also published in Milan (undated) with the dedication "al cavaliere Niccolo C. Manzaro"; the piano caprice *La campana di st. Spyridione* by the pianist Alphonse Holstein, who gave recitals at various cities around Greece,[35] which was similarly released in Milan (undated) with the dedication "Al chiaris.[mo] cav.[re] Nicolò C. Manzaro".

The most flattering and grounded declaration of admiration regarding Manzaro's music attributes comes from Zingarelli himself. It is a letter, with the date 12 July 1835 inscribed, in which he invites Manzaro to become his successor in the direction of the conservatory and the teaching of composition (Motsenigos [Μοτσενίγος] 1958: 102–103).[36]

Works for the dominators

During the first decades of the 19th century San Giacomo's audience had listened to quite a few of Manzaro's works, such as the azione comica *Don Crepuscolo,* a one act opera, in 1815, arias,[37] duetti,[38] the cantatas *L'Aurora* in 1818 and *La gratitudine* in 1821, the ballo eroico *L'arrivo d'Ulisse alla isola de' Feaci* in 1819.[39]

Such works continued to be produced by Manzaro in the following decades but at a slower pace and for very special occasions. In January 1827 the cantata *Minerva nell'isola di Corfú* was sung by Elisabetta Pinotti in a *beneficiata* concert, together with an aria in Greek, written by Manzaro for the occasion, as a way of gratitude to the audience of Corfú (Marco Battagel, playing from the first violin desk, conducted the orchestra), (Kentrōtēs [Κεντρωτής] 2003: 26–27).

In March 1832, during a reception ceremony held for Frederic Adam who had returned from Naples, Manzaro's work *La festa delle fontane* was performed to celebrate the introduction of fresh water in the city (thanks to Adam's actions). Part of the celebrations held for Adam were also a theatrical performance of Metastasio's play *La Clemenza di Tito*[40] that included chorals, an orchestral introduction and a march, all composed by Manzaro.[41]

Among Manzaro's published works (printed in Italy), the following are extant today in Italian and Greek libraries:[42]

Otto ariete e due madrigali, for voice and piano or cembalo, *opera terza,* (edition: Luigi Bertuzzi, Milan). This unique work of Manzaro, which happens to be numbered, is in Italian lyrics and is dedicated to "miledi Hankey" (probably the wife of Friedrich Hankey, governor of Zante in 1821). To that same lady Manzaro has also dedicated his unpublished cantata *La Gratitudine,* presented at San Giacomo in 1821.

A *Sinfonia,* for piano, dedicated to sig. Marianna Campione, of the family Du Parc de Cormand, "an honorary member of various philharmonic academies". She was probably the singer that performed in 1818 in San Giacomo, the cantata *L' Aurora* that the composer dedicated to his father (Leōtsakos [Λεωτσάκος] 1987: 236).

Tre ariette for alto or mezzo, dedicated to "madama la contessa Elena Pollila Bulgari" (published by Giovanni Ricordi).

Dodici fughe in four and five parts, with piano accompaniment, dedicated to "al s. m. Nicolò Zingarelli" (Calcografia Negri of Naples). Motsenigos presents the dedication of this work to Zingarelli with the date August 8th 1826 inscribed, wherein it is being clarified that the fugues are based to Zingarelli's *partimenti* (Motsenigos [Μοτσενίγος] 1958: 135).

A *Grande sinfonia militare,* for piano, dedicated to "miledi Adam" (published by Luigi Bertuzzi in Milan). This was written in 1832 on the occasion of the return of the English Commissary Frederic Adam and was regularly played by the English band until its abolition in 1840. Adam's wife, Adamantinē, of the Greek family Palatianos, to whom it is dedicated, was the godmother of Manzaro's son, Spyridon, a talented musician who died prematurely (1821–1847). For Milady Adam, Manzaro had also written a piano transcription of a cavatina from G. Paccini's opera *Arabi nelle Gallie,* which is extant in manuscript (Rōmanou, Zōtos [Ρωμανού, Ζώτος] 2004: 70).

A number of Manzaro's works were published after his death, by his family at the publishing company G. Venturini (Rome and Florence), when the Greek Parliament decided upon the funding of the edition. However, the project stopped, since, of the 10000 drachmas that had been voted for, only 1200 were actually granted (Kentrōtēs [Κεντρωτής] 2003: 200, 226). The publications that took place at the time were: *Redowa mazurka* for piano, *Raccolta di sinfonie per pianoforte* (wherein two symphonies are included), *Pensieri musicali: Levommi il mio pensier/sulle parole del sonetto di Mr. Francesco Petrarca* for voice and piano, as well as part of his contrapuntal composition of the *Hymn to Liberty,* with the text being both in Greek and Italian, translated in Italian by N. Gonemi. The score consists of twenty-three pages and is entitled: *Inno alla liberta posto in musica dal Cav. N.C. Manzaro voltato in versi italiani dal Dr. N. Gonemi.*[43]

Works for the Greek people

The *Hymn to Liberty* is the longer composition Manzaro wrote on the poems of his close friend, the poet Dionysios Solōmos. In this work the two men express their admiration for the heroic events of the Greek Revolution, their belief in the continuation of Greek civilisation and their perception of a high art inspired by popular art and which is accessible to the people.

In fact, Manzaro composed at least two versions of Solōmos' *Hymn to Liberty*. What is considered the *first version* was published in London in 1873, despite the composer's initial refusal. In order to convince him, his relatives claimed that the English asked it for through the Greek Embassy. Eventually, the publication of 1873 was done from the manuscript of his twenty-four-year-old student, Spyros De Biasi, who describes the semi-successful effort it took to convince Manzaro to correct and complete his score. Another of Manzaro's students, Stylianos Prosalendēs, wrote part of the piano accompaniment. The edition includes mistakes that at times become a lot more than superficial, like that of the key signature of three sharps in an extract that clearly is in B flat major (Solōmos [Σολωμός] [1873] 2000: 77).

The work was composed in between the years 1829–1830 at Solōmos' presence – who was also musical. It is written for a four-part male choir and piano,[44] in twenty-four numbers. All, except the last, which is a *fuga reale*, are homophonic, with melodic purity (reminiscent of Zante's popular urban songs) and simple, effective details that highlight the meanings and the musicality of the poem.

The hymn's so-called *second version*, in 46 numbers, is contrapuntal. Manzaro dedicated it to King Otto (5 December 1844). It is not an established fact that this version was composed *after* the "popular" setting (whose completion did not, after all, take place by Manzaro).[45] Nonetheless, the very existence of the work was not known to anyone except Dionysios Solōmos, until 5 February 1844. It was then that Manzaro showed it to friends, who convinced him to dedicate it to King Otto. The actual time that Manzaro chose to reveal his unique completed work on the *Hymn to Liberty* cannot be accidental: in May 1843 his father had died and Manzaro was on a trip to Naples that must be relevant to this death.[46] This composition is still unpublished in its whole.

Another patriotic composition by Manzaro is the setting of Rēgas Velestinlēs *Thourios* (a revolutionary song that was very popular across Greece).[47] It is the thirteenth song of a manuscript collection (most likely Manzaro's autographs) that on its cover bears the title *16 Arie Greche dal dilettante Corcirese il Nobil signor Nicolŏ Calichiopulo Manzaro, 1830*. Besides the sixteen numbered songs there are two more that are unnumbered. All of them are for piano; on the upper staff (both for the right hand and for two voices) the melody is in parallel thirds and sixths. This version of Rēgas' poem is original, differing from the most popular melodies around Greece[48] but also from the version that is widely known to the people of Zante.[49] The lyrics of the other songs are about love.

Misinterpretations

Manzaro's image has been seriously misinterpreted. A text written at his death by his close friend and collaborator Domenico Padovan[i], entitled "Poche parole sopra gli scritti del cav. Nicol C. Manzaro",[50] which is, in essence, the first catalogue of the composer's works, has created hopeful expectancies to researchers eager to discover great Greek 19th century symphonies and string quartets. In that text Manzaro's compositions are classified into three categories:

1. stile da Chiesa
2. genere da Camera
3. genere Teatrale

There is also a fourth category, 'opere scholastiche', which consists of theoretical works.

In the first category (namely the works in church style) there is a fragment that – to those researchers – stands as proof that Manzaro had composed symphonies similar to Beethoven's.[51] Padovan deals with Manzaro's music for the Orthodox Church,[52] and afterwards he mentions that he had also composed two Masses for the occidental rite (one of which was performed in Naples in the church of Saint Ferdinand). Further on, he says that in 1830 Manzaro wrote a *Te Deum* for the celebrations of the arrival at Corfú of Monsignor Nostrano, who was consecrated Archbishop of the island's Latin Church. Right at that point in Padovan's text lays the important fragment being quoted below:

> scrisse un grandioso Te Deum, a quattro voci, con Cori, ed una magnifica Sinfonia alla tedesca in stile grave proprio del Tempio del Signore, dove splendevano la squisitezza delle armonie e delle modulazioni, e non stava certamente niente al di sotto delle celebri sinfonie di Beethoven.[53]

Regarding this information, it should be reminded that Beethoven's symphonies were not performed in Italy until the middle of the century and Italian symphonies (sinfonias) were actually single-movement orchestral works, usually in the form of Rossini's overtures (Rostagno 2003).

The fact that Padovan does not have a category for orchestral music is very telling. Yet, when coming to speak of the theatrical genre, the meaning of the above fragment becomes clear. In this category Padovan includes stage works together with all secular vocal works for a large instrumental ensemble (operas, scenes, arias, as well as cantatas), and all the symphonies that Manzaro had composed in the form of independent, autonomous works.

In describing Manzaro's twenty-four symphonies (listed under "genere teatrale"), Padovan highlights the composer's melodic inventiveness in the following words: "queste sinfonie sono tutte di magnifico effeto, piene di bellissime cantilene originali".[54]

Comparing what Padovan values in each category, it becomes obvious that harmonic inventiveness and boldness in modulations was related, to his mind, with serious, German and Beethovenian style, while inventiveness in singable melodies (*cantilene*) were suitable for the theatrical stage.

The inclusion of autonomous symphonies in the theatrical genre seems natural as it so happened that symphonic music, symphonic orchestras or even orchestral houses for the performance of symphonic music did not exist in Corfú (nor in Italy until the 1850s) and orchestral music was being performed in the opera house by the opera's orchestra.

Conclusively, the meaning of Padovan's text is that Manzaro's symphony (single-movement overture)[55] of the *Te Deum* was suitable for the church, being serious music, harmonically interesting, and bold. This was also the case with German music – in contrast to light, melodious and theatrical Italian music.

Another misinterpretation concerns Manzaro's chamber music and the misleading term *quartetto*. *Partimenti* exercises in four parts (called *quartetto* by Italians at the time) written by Manzaro have actually been announced as the earliest Greek string quartets and were in fact performed and recorded as such.

In the category of "genere da Camera" Padovan has pieces for voice (or voices) and piano (very seldom, other instruments) included under various names such as arias, ariettas, melodies, serenades, pensieri, dramatic scenes, (on verses by Petrarcha, Vittorelli and Politiano) that all belonged to the genre of "romanza vocale da camera" (Morabito 1997), as the Italians call it. Many of those Italian romanzas are closely related, in terms of style, to canzonettes, the popular urban songs of Naples. This is one of the reasons why, in spite many of these works belonging to famous opera composers like Donizetti or Bellini (Morabito 1997: 3), it is only recently that they have attracted musicological research. This type of composition, along with its corresponding kinship to local urban popular music, was also produced by Manzaro and other heptanesian musicians in great numbers.

Notes

1. Through the tight connections with the Greek communities of the cosmopolitan cities of Asia Minor, and the great numbers of Greeks from those areas who came to the mainland.
2. No other group of Greek nationals has claimed aristocratic descent since the fall of Byzantium.
3. The *Academia degli Assicurati* (1656), *Academia dei Fertili* (circa 1660), *Academia degli Errantes* (1732) were established in Corfú.
4. Primary source on music in the Ionian Islands is: Motsenigos [Μοτσενίγος] 1958.
5. He was the son of Frederick North, second Earl of Guilford and Prime Minister of Great Britain in 1770–1782, when the kingdom lost America.
6. According to a dubious source, Guilford was baptised an orthodox Christian in 1791 (Vrokinēs [Βροκίνης] 1973: 1–108).
7. Project no. 70/4/4116, sponsored by the University of Athens.
8. The reform of neumatic notation introduced in 1814 by Chrysanthos from Madytos and applied since by Greek Orthodox chanters.
9. See various definitions of the term *falsobordone* in the dictionary Gianelli 1830. For a recent study on this oral and written tradition in Italy, refer to Macchiarella n.d.
10. Beyond the technical information that it includes, this passage is important since it is a non-Greek source that indicates how vivid the presence of the Greeks was in 16th century Venice.
11. Burney is aware that polyphonic singing is exceptional in Greece in his days: "As many travellers assert that the modern Greeks have no music in parts, we may suppose, that in those places where it was heard by the Abate Martini, it had been brought thither by the Venetians, during the time that they had possessions in the Archipelago" (Burney 1782: 53).
12. A translation of this important text was published in: Rōmanou [Ρωμανού] 2006a: 126–140.
13. The greatest liberty reigned in the theatre; they played, they ate. At one moment a part of the loges resembled to as many restaurants; at another moment, to card playing societies; it is assumed that they could not enjoy the spectacle; indeed no one was occupied with it except at the moment when in one play, a piece of music had left the greatest impression.
14. A list of works produced in 1815–1878 in San Giacomo is published in: Rōmanou [Ρωμανού] 2006: 91–98. This list was based on a collection of San Giacomo's announcements of performances kept

in Corfú Reading Society, on two catalogues published in: Kapadochos [Καπαδόχος] 1991 and Chytērēs [Χυτήρης] 1994, on Greek bibliographic works and on Italian catalogues of libretti.

15. On those performances, see Xepapadakou [Ξεπαπαδάκου] 2003: 27–63.

16. Music fondness, which is singularly increased in Corfú, made soon this kind of spectacle insipid; and the comedians were replaced by the opere buffe (comic operas); following, the entertainment of dance was added [...] The musicians attached to the general proveditor and to various naval armies composed the orchestra: amateurs were also admitted.

17. A vivid description of the foundation of the Parisian Conservatoire and the first years of its operation is given in the article "Conservatoire de Paris" (Choron [1810] 1971).

18. That however did not significantly weaken the authority of church, since, until the first decade of the 20th century, Orthodoxy was considered to be among the important parameters that constituted the Greek national identity. The state, in turn, was particularly favourable to this projection, as it was exploiting politically this conservation; especially into areas like the Ionian Islands (where religious feelings were not as strong as elsewhere) it encouraged its fortification. Thus, in the case of Greece one may observe the co-existence of a number of factors that only appeared successively in other parts of Europe.

19. For instance The Philharmonic Society of Zante was re-founded in 1843, 1871, 1883, 1890 and 1900!

20. In 1796, when Napoleon took possession of Italy, most conservatories were shut down due to their association with the church. Among the ones that re-operated under Napoleon, in 1807, there were four Neapolitan conservatories that got unified into the *Collegio Musicale Real* of San Sebastiano. In 1826 the *collegio* was housed in the monastery of San Pietro a Majella (where it is situated up to the present day), and got the second half of its name altered. In 1813 Niccolo Zingarelli succeeded the triumvirate of Fenaroli, Trito and Paisiello, on the conservatory's directorship.

21. Among others, Antonio (1814–1842) and Giuseppe Liberalli (1820–1899), Spyridōn Xyndas (1814–1896), Dēmētrios Digenēs (d.1880), Edouardos Lambelet (1820–1903) and his sons Napoleon (1864–1932) and Geōrgios (1875–1945), Dionysios Rodotheatos (1849–1892), Dēmētrios Andrōnēs (1866–after 1918), Nikolaos Tzannēs Metaxas (1825–1907), Geōrgios Lambirēs (1833–1889), Dionysios Lavrangas (1864–1941).

22. Music concert of Corfú's young ladies, which will take place in the Philharmonic society's building the evening of Thursday 31 March 1859 [...] 18 hands on three pianos and one organum melodium. See, item no 78/β/57 of the Motsenigian archive (National Library of Athens).

23. The Olympiads, inspired by ancient Olympic Games and world exhibitions of western capitals, combined expositions of Greek products (including artistic products) with athletic and artistic competitions. They were planned to take place every four years in Athens, but eventually occurred in the years 1858, 1870, 1875 and 1888. The Zappas brothers, who were successful businessmen in Russia, sponsored the Olympiads. One of the most beautiful neoclassic buildings in Athens, Zappeion, was built to accommodate the Olympiads (Rōmanou, Barbakē, Mousoulidēs [Ρωμανού, Μπαρμπάκη, Μουσουλίδης] 2004).

24. It is very likely that Manzaro is the author of a short biography of Nerantzē published in the Greek daily of Corfú *Τα Καθημερινά* (21 September 1857), signed with the letter "M."

25. This is the result of the research project no. 70/4/4116, mentioned above (footnote 7).

26. In most texts written in Corfú, the name is written Chalikiopoulo[s], in most texts written or published in Italy, it is written Calichiopulo. As for the Greek ending -os, this begun to be added late in the 19th century. Recently, the name appears as Halikiopoulos Mantzaros (see for example

Kalavrytinos-Irmgard 2006) which is the transliteration of the Greek Χαλικιόπουλος Μάντζαρος, a transliteration of the original Italian spelling.

27. Mozart's music was performed – though only in the court – during the Napoleonic reign in Naples (1806–1815) (Maione 2006).

28. Details on the Italian (and Heptanesian) music culture during the first half of the 19th century are given in Rōmanou [Ρωμανού] 2004. The Italian works mainly consulted for this article are De Martino 2003, Morabito 1997 and Rostagno 2003.

29. On that occasion Solōmos wrote his *On the Death of Lord Byron,* a poem of 166 four-line verses.

30. Francesco Florimo (1800–1888) was librarian in that conservatory from 1826 to his death. In the four volumes of his work cited, he gives plenty of information (including many lists of names and of titles) on the Neapolitan conservatories and opera houses.

31. Fenaroli, together with Tritto and Paisiello, was director of this conservatory before Zingarelli.

32. For a reference to music inspired by the philhellenic movement, see Rōmanou [Ρωμανού] 2006: 28–33. See also, "1826. 'Les Grecs sont français': musical philhellenism in Paris", in Walton 2007: 108–153. For a detailed catalogue of philhellenic literary and musical works, see Droulia [Δρούλια] 1974.

33. Some researchers saw this fact as a conspiracy against Manzaro (an effort to undervalue his importance as a composer), being unconceivable that a theoretician might be considered more important than a composer (which was the case in early 19th century Italy).

34. Istituto central per il catalogo unico. Indice SBN, http: //opac.it.

35. A recital in Zante on 27 May 1884 has been recorded.

36. Laurentios Vrokinēs gives a much similar letter, dated in 1825 (Vrokinēs [Βροκίνης] 1972: 30). A possible interpretation of the fact, in: Rōmanou [Ρωμανού] 2006: 71.

37. A scene and aria *Sono inquieto ed agitato,* a recitative and aria *Bella speme lusinghiera* performed in 1815; an *Aria cantata dall' ombre di Patroclo nell sogno di Achille* performed in 1821. The two arias of 1815 together with a third entitled *Come augelin che canta* have been published in the first volume of the series *Monuments of Neo-Hellenic Music,* founded by the Department of Music of the Ionian University (Kalavrytinos-Irmgard 2006).

38. The duet *Si te credo amato bene* was performed in 1818.

39. On the year of this work's performance, in: Rōmanou [Ρωμανού] 2006: 73.

40. Mozart's opera on that libretto was performed in 1809, at the San Carlo theatre for the celebrations of Joseph Bonaparte's arrival in Naples (Maione 2006: 122)

41. There is some dubious information about more works by Manzaro, such as the one written in the Hellenic-French newspaper *L'Observateur Grec* (30 September 1842) of Athens, where it is stated that he had composed the "Greek opera *Aeas flagelliferous*" (Kentrōtēs [Κεντρωτής] 2003: 29).

42. The former were found in: *Istituto centrale per il catalogo unico.* Indice SBN, http: //opac.it; the latter, in: Leōtsakos [Λεωτσάκος] 1987.

43. *Istituto centrale per il catalogo unico.* Indice SBN, http: //opac.it.

44. Works (such as symphonies, cantatas etc.) written "for the piano" by Manzaro and other Heptanesian composers, were not meant to be performed on the piano. Piano scores served as the standard form of music to be performed by varied ensembles, according to instrumentalists available in each occasion.

45. See also Kentrōtēs [Κεντρωτής] 2003: 225

46. "In the year 1843, when Manzaro urgently left for Naples for a while due to a family misfortune", says Spyros Papageōrgiou (Kentrōtēs [Κεντρωτής] 2003: 106–107).

47. See the music in: Rōmanou [Ρωμανού] 2006: 81–82

48. Regarding *Thourios'* melodic settings in various areas of Greece, see Stathēs [Στάθης] 1998.
49. See its music in: Rautopoulos [Ραυτόπουλος] 1996: 65.
50. The text was published in two successive volumes of the periodical of Corfú *Η Φωνή* [The Voice], year 8, no. 361 (12 April 1872) pp. 2–3, and no. 362 (April 20), p. 3. It is also published in its entirety in: Kentrōtēs [Κεντρωτής] 2003: 69–76.
51. See for example, Siōpsē [Σιώψη] 2005: 293, where reference is also made to other musicologists supporting the same.
52. He lists works belonging to the tradition initiated by Iōannēs Aristeidēs, mentioned above, and discovered in the music library of the Philharmonic Society.
53. He wrote a grandiose *Te Deum* for four voices, with choruses and a magnificent Sinfonia alla tedesca in serious style that was appropriate for the Lord's Temple, which consists of exquisite harmonies and modulations and which was certainly not in the least inferior to the celebrated symphonies of Beethoven (Kentrōtēs [Κεντρωτής] 2003: 71). It should be noted that "alla tedesca" may either mean in triple meter or "in German style" and that the text has been corrected by the editor: Beethoven's name is written in the original: *Bettoven*.
54. Those symphonies are all of a magnificent effect, full with most beautiful, original melodies.
55. That it was a one movement overture to the *Te Deum* is further confirmed in a text by Spyros Papageorgiou who writes in 1875, based on the above text by Padovan: "He [Manzaro] wrote a great doxology (*Te Deum*) for a four part choir with an introductory symphony, on the genre of German school, serious and suitable to God's temple, comparable to Beethoven's brilliant symphonies" (Kentrōtēs [Κεντρωτής] 2003: 105).

References

[Angelomatē-Tsougarakē] Αγγελομάτη-Τσουγκαράκη, Ε., *Η Ιόνιος Ακαδημία. Το χρονικό της ίδρυσης του πρώτου ελληνικού πανεπιστημίου (1811-1914)* [The Ionian Academy. The chronicle of the establishment of the first Greek university (1811-1914)], Athens, Ο Μ[ικρός] Ρωμηός, 1997.

Burney, Ch., *A general history of music from the earliest ages to the present period*, II, London, Printed for the Author, 1782.

——, *Music, men and manners in France and Italy 1770*, London, Eulenburg, 1969.

Choron, A. E. & F. J. Fayolle, *Dictionnaire Historique des Musiciens, Artistes et Amateurs, morts ou vivans, qui se sont illustrés en une partie quelconque de la musique et des arts qui y sont relatifs [...] avec des renseignemens sur les Théâtres, Conservatoires, et autres établissemens dont cet art est l'objet. Précédé d'un Sommaire de l'Histoire de la Musique*, I [A-L], Paris, R., Hildesheim, New York, Georg Olms, [1810] 1971.

[Chytērēs] Χυτήρης, Γ., *Η όπερα στο θέατρο του Σαντζιάκομο της Κέρκυρας. Ένας μακρύς κατάλογος* [Opera in the San Giacomo theatre in Corfú. A long catalogue], Corfú, published by the author, 1994.

De Martino, P. P., *Le parafrasi pianistiche verdiane nell'editoria italiana dell'Ottocento*, Firenze, Leo Olschki, 2003.

Droulia, L., *Philhellénisme. Ouvrages inspirés par la guerre de l'indépendance grecque, 1821–1833. Répertoire bibliographique*, Athènes, Centre de recherches Néo-Helléniques de la fondation nationale de la recherche (no. 17), 1974.

Florimo, Fr., *La scuola musicale di Napoli e i suoi conservatori*, II, Napoli, R., Morano, Bologna, Arnaldo Forni, [1882] 2000.

Gianelli , P., "falso bordone" in *Dizionario della Musica Sacra e Profana*, 3rd edition, vol. 1. Venezia, G. Picotti, 1830.

[Gritsanēs] Γριτσάνης, Π., "Περί της των Ιονίων νήσων εκκλησιαστικής μουσικής" [Concerning the Ionian Islands church music], *Φόρμιγξ*, 4: 7–8 (1908), pp. 2–3.

Kalavrytinos-Irmgard, L. (ed.), *Nikolaos Halikiopoulos Mantzaros 1795–1872. Early works for voice and orchesra I. Three arias of 1815*, Corfú, Ionian University / Department of Music / Hellenic Music Research Lab, 2006.

[Kapadochos] Καπαδόχος, Δ., *Το θέατρο της Κέρκυρας στα μέσα του Ιθ΄ αιώνα* [The theatre in Corfu during mid-19th century], Athens, Σύλλογος των εν Αθήναις Κάτω Γαρουνιατών, 1991.

[Kentrotēs] Κεντρωτής, Γ. (ed.), *Νικόλαος Χαλικιόπουλος Μάντζαρος* [Nikolaos Chalikiopoulos Manzaros], Κέρκυρα, Φιλαρμονική Εταιρεία Κέρκυρας, 2003.

[Kitromēlidēs] Κητρομηλίδης Π., *Νεοελληνικός διαφωτισμός* [Neohellenic enlightment], trans., Στέλλα Νικολούδη, Athens, Μορφωτικό Ίδρυμα Εθνικής Τραπέζης, 1996.

[Ladas] Λαδάς, Γ. Ι., *Συνοπτική ιστορία του Ελληνισμού της Τεργέστης. ΙΙ. Βιβλιογραφία των εντύπων που εκδόθηκαν από τους Έλληνες της Τεργέστης* [A concise history of Greeks in Trieste. II. A bibliography of editions that were published by Greeks of Trieste], Athens, Κουλτούρα, 1976.

[Leōtsakos, G.] Λεωτσάκος, Γ., "Νικόλαος Χαλικιόπουλος-Μάντζαρος (1795–1872). Για ένα μικρό του εγκόλπιο…" [Nikolaos Chalikiopoulos-Manzaros (1795–1872). For a small encolpion…], *Μουσικολογία*, 5–6 (1987), pp. 229–272.

Macchiarella, Ign., *Il falsobordone fra tradizione orale e tradizione scritta*, Lucca, Libreria Musicale Italiana, no date.

Maione, P., "Organizzazione e repertorio musicale della corte nel decennio francese a Napoli (1806–1815)", *Fonti Musicali Italiani,* 11, 2006, pp. 119–173.

Manzaro, Cav. N. C., *Rapporto relativo al dono di alcune opere di Monsigny e Grétry*, Corfú, Scheria, 1851.

Morabito, F., *La romanza vocale da camera in Italia*, Brescia, Brepols, 1997.

[Motsenigos] Μοτσενίγος, Σπ. Γ., *Νεοελληνική Μουσική* [Neohellenic Music], Athens, published by the author, 1958.

[Papageōrgiou] Παπαγεωργίου, Σπ., *Τα κατά την Φιλαρμονική Εταιρίαν από της συστάσεως μέχρι σήμερον 1840-1890* [All about the Philharmonic Society from its establishment till today 1840–1890], Athens, Ανέστης Κωνσταντινίδης, 1890.

["Phaeax"] "Φαίαξ", "Εκκλησιαστική μουσική εν Κερκύρα" [Church music in Corfú], *Φόρμιγξ* [Phorminx], 3: 11–12, 1907, p. 6.

[Rautopoulos] Ραυτόπουλος, Γ. Ε., *Ο ριζοσπαστισμός στη μουσική και την ποίηση* [Radicalism in music and poetry], Athens, Έκδοση των σύγχρονων εκδόσεων Κορυφή, 1996.

[Rōmanou] Ρωμανού, Κ., "Ένα αρχείο 'κρητικής μουσικής' στην Φιλαρμονική Εταιρεία Κέρκυρας" [An archive of 'cretan music' in Corfú Philharmonic Society], *Μουσικολογία*, 12–13, 2000, pp. 175–188.

——, *Έντεχνη ελληνική μουσική στους νεότερους χρόνους* [Greek art music in modern times], Athens, Κουλτούρα, 2006.

——, "Απόσπασμα από το *Storia della musica* του Giovanni Battista Martini" [An extract from *Storia della musica* by Giovanni Battista Martini], *Πολυφωνία*, 9, 2006a, pp. 126–140.

[Rōmanou, K., M. Barbakē, Ph. Mousoulidēs] Ρωμανού, Κ., Μ. Μπαρμπάκη, Φ. Μουσουλίδης, *Η Ελληνική Μουσική στους Ολυμπιακούς Αγώνες και τις Ολυμπιάδες (1858–1896)* [Greek Music in the Olympic Games and the Olympiads (1858–1896)], Athens, Γενική Γραμματεία Ολυμπιακών Αγώνων, Υπουργείο Πολιτισμού/Κουλτούρα, 2004.

[Rōmanou, K., I. Zōtos et al.] Ρωμανού, Κ., Ί. Ζώτος κ.ά, *Η μουσική βιβλιοθήκη της Φιλαρμονικής Εταιρείας Κέρκυρας* [The music library of the Corfú Philharmonic Society], Athens, Κουλτούρα, 2004.

Rostagno, Ant., *La musica Italiana per orchestra nell'Ottocento*, Firenze, Leo Olschki, 2003.

Saint Sauveur, J. A.-Gr., *Voyage historique, littéraire et pittoresque dans les isles et possessions ci-devant Venetiennes du Levant, savoir : Corfou, Paxo, Bucintro, Parga, Prevesa, Vonizza, Sainte-Maure, Thiaqui, Cephalonie, Zante, Strophades, Cerico et Cerigotte…*, Paris, Tavernier, an VIII [de la république française = 22.9.1799–22.9.1800].

Sessa, And., *Il Melodrama Italiano 1861–1900*, Firenze, Leo S. Olschki, 2003.

[Siōpsē] Σιώψη, Α. Α., *Η μουσική στην Ευρώπη του Δέκατου Ένατου Αιώνα* [Music in Nineteenth Century Europe], Athens, Τυπωθήτω-Γιώργος Δαρδανός, 2005.

[Solōmos] Σολωμός, Δ., *Ύμνος εις την Ελευθερίαν, μελοποιηθείς υπό του ιππότου Νικολάου Χ. Μαντζάρου* [Hymn to Liberty set to music by the knight Nikolaos Ch. Manzaros], Λονδίνον, Clayotn & Co, R., Athens, Εκδόσεις του Φοίνικα, [1873] 2000.

[Stathēs] Στάθης, Γρ. Θ., "Τα 'επαναστατικά τραγούδια' του Ρήγα και το μέλος τους" [The 'revolutionary songs' of Rigas and their melos], *Αντί*, 652, 1998, pp. 52–55.

[Typaldos-Iakōvatos] Τυπάλδος-Ιακωβάτος, Γ., *Ιστορία της Ιόνιας Ακαδημίας* [History of the Ionian Academy], Athens, Ερμής, 1982.

[Tzerbinos] Τζερμπίνος, Στ. Ν., *Φιλαρμονικά Ζακύνθου (1816-1960)* [Philhramonics of Zakynthos (1816-1960)], Zakynthos, Φιλόμουση Κίνηση Ζακύνθου, 1996.

[Vrokinēs] Βροκίνης, Λ., *Έργα [Α΄] Βιογραφικά σχεδάρια, τεύχη Α΄ & Β΄* [Works I. Biographical sketches, volumes I & II], επιμ., Κώστα Δάφνη, Corfú, Κερκυραϊκά Χρονικά 16, 1972.

——, "Γεωργίου Προσαλένδου, ανέκδοτα χειρόγραφα αφορώντα την κατά το δόγμα της ορθοδόξου εκκλησίας βάπτισιν του άγγλου φιλέλληνος Κόμητος Γυίλφορδ νυν πρώτον εκδιδόμενα…" [Geōrgios Prosalendēs, unpublished manuscripts concerning the baptism of the English philhellene count Guilford to the Christian orthodox dogma, that appear for the first time…, in *Έργα β΄* [Works II], Corfú, Κερκυραϊκά Χρονικά 17, 1973, pp. 1–34.

Walton, B., *Rossini in Restoration Paris. The Sound of Modern Life*, Cambridge, Cambridge University Press, 2007.

[Xepapadakou] Ξεπαπαδάκου, Α., "Ο Μάρκος Βότζαρης του Παύλου Καρρέρ: μια 'εθνική' όπερα" [Markos Botzarēs by Pavlos Carrer: a 'national' opera], *Μουσικός Λόγος*, 5, 2003, pp. 27–63.

Zarlino, G., *The Art of Counterpoint. Part three of Le Institutioni harmoniche, 1558*, trans., Guy A. Marco & Claude V. Palisca, New Haven & London, Yale University Press, 1968.

Chapter 7

The Greek National Music School

Yannis Belonis

The founding of a National Music School is undoubtedly related to the nation's socio-political status quo. It is a practice that may rightfully come across as an attempt to conserve that nation's idiosyncratic difference and redefine its national identity through the updating of its goals. One particular instance of such relativity is the Greek National School; from the very beginning of its establishment, the National School in question came to serve the grandiose ideology of the so-called "Great Idea" and was consequently set in full accordance with the political orientation of Eleutherios Venizelos (Belōnēs [Μπελώνης] 2005: 16–17). The founding father of the Greek National School, Manōlēs Kalomoirēs[1] (1883–1962), aligned himself totally with that noble goal as much as with every other political move that Venizelos was to make.

An exuberant persona, full of enthusiasm and ambitions, Kalomoirēs succeeded in obtaining high funds for serving the school's goals and became highly established in the artistic environment during the first half of the 20th century. Through endless efforts and personal sacrifices he managed to build a monocracy onto the fruitful grounds of full support that his friend, Venizelos, had provided. Although this rule might have been partly reliant on the political base that Venizelos – at that time retiring from the political scene of Greece – had previously set, what eventually became acknowledged was that it kept growing stronger thanks to Kalomoirēs alone. His success lay upon his glowing and persistent personality together with the flexible policy that he followed, which allowed much room for the consent of almost all the authority centres.

Of course, this on-going activity of his was not to be welcomed by everyone. Quite the contrary, both his dominant appearance in the music affairs of Greece, which struck like a bolt out of the blue in 1908, along with the preferential treatment that he had been enjoying in Venizelos' days, proved sufficient enough to make him a primary target of attack from the anti-Venizelian circles. What further intensified this negative atmosphere around Kalomoirēs was his firm attitude towards the place of the musician within society. His belief, put down in words in his "Manifesto on the founding of the Greek National Music School" in 1908, was that, through his art a musician should interact with all manifestations of the society that bears it. Kalomoirēs' theory was soon to be set to practice through his intervention in the storm-tossed language issue.

From the very beginning of the dispute, the composer fell in with the users of the demotic language (the spoken language in mainland Greece). This fact railed the whole progressive party of the Athenian *intelligentsia* round him, as they came to regard *him* as their most important representative in the field of Greek music (Belōnēs [Μπελώνης] 2005: 16–17).

Manōlēs Kalomoirēs with his daughter, Krinō. Manōlēs
Kalomoirēs archives.

Thus once more, like many times in the past, music would be used as a vehicle of propaganda in the way that it enables the communication of political meanings to the public. After all, it so happens that, whatever the orientation a given political authority may have, it is bound to influence both the audience's perception and the cultural status of music. From that point onwards, those in power set out specific institutional competences towards the promotion of the works that belong to "indicated" composers. Particularly, when it comes to works that are innately connected with speech, like for instance the genres of opera,[2] oratorio or song, it goes without saying that the listeners are instructed through even clearer meanings (Frangou-Psychopaedē [Φράγκου-Ψυχοπαίδη] 2002).

After his final settlement in Athens in 1910 Kalomoirēs started teaching at the Athens Conservatoire (1911). During that period the institution fell under the management of Geōrgios Nazos, a man of a rather dubious music education. Nazos, however, held the same views with Kalomoirēs and sided up with him in the act against the Italy-orientated and thus "non-Greek" composers of Heptanese (Ionian Islands). The reverberation of this spar was the withdrawal of the Heptanesian Spyros Samaras' nomination for the managerial post of the Athens Conservatoire. This was very unfortunate since Samaras, also favoured by a big part of the press, happened to be the only Greek composer of an international reputation at the time. Kalomoirēs, having taken Samaras' origin too much into consideration, saw into his possible nomination a forthcoming threat to his interests. Thus, he turned against Samaras yet without previously becoming acquainted with his compositional work. Of course, later on and at a time when nothing was at stake, he came to retract this attitude of his by paying his respect to Samaras' work.

Another parameter that proved to be a drawback concerning Samaras' case was his favourable disposition towards the Royal Family. This fact set off the existing negative climate around his nomination, while – at the same time – proved the ruthless rivalry existing between the opposite ideological parties. Nevertheless, Samaras was bound to lose favour with the Royal Family under the pressure of governmental and business circles. The reason for this was their opposition to the composer's suggestions in his last opera, *Rhea,* on the constitution of a Greek-Western alliance against the Turks (Belōnēs [Μπελώνης] 2005: 16–17).

With the prospect of consolidating his position and his proclamations in the country's music affairs Kalomoirēs sought the establishment of various music institutions, for most of which he became in charge.[3] To his mind these would also enable him to set the ground for the founding of the Greek National Music School. Indeed, despite some opposition and dispute, the fact was that the ideal of creating a Greek National Music actually functioned as the unifying element during the period of the school's foundation. In 1911 Kalomoirēs was already working at the Athens Conservatoire as a music instructor for piano, harmony and counterpoint classes. From that year onwards he would commit himself totally to the circulation of both his views on the Greek National School and his compositional work, through a number of new publications, lectures, concerts and writing of educational books.

The first phase of Kalomoirēs' artistic and constitutional activity in Greece coincides with a period of social and political fermentations. These soon led to the optimistic view that the creation of a strong Greek state and culture, lying between Asia and Europe, would not take long to be realised. The Treaty of Sèvres in 1920 came to enlarge the above aspirations as it verified the annexing of East Thrace and the islands of Tenedos and Imvros to Greece, together with Greek rule upon the province of Smyrna. However, things did not go well for the Greek army, when it marched further east towards Ankara. As a result, close to 1.400.000 Greek nationals came to Greece as refugees. In doing so, they brought their civil and cultural customs along, thereby contributing to the creation of an idiosyncratic, mixed cultural and artistic consciousness (Frangou-Psychopaedē [Φράγκου-Ψυχοπαίδη] 1990: 114–117). Naturally, after the refugees settled in mainland Greece the character of the country transformed into a new reality. Social oppositions were aggravated and the working class, now revitalised with the new refugee force, would claim a primary role in the socio-political realignments. After the Asia Minor catastrophe[4] and the expulsion of the Dynasty and within an electrified social climate, the first Greek democracy is born.

The Asia Minor catastrophe in 1922 also came to signify the closure of the National School's first period of existence. Immediately after 1922, both the character and the overall grounds of the Greek National School were to change. Kalomoirēs, too, changed his compositional language towards introversion. This change coincided with the reverberation of two devastating events: the catastrophe of his birthplace, Smyrna, and the death of his beloved son, Jannakēs (1923). Now, the grandiose style and the epic works of the previous period give way to a more introspective and lyrical music language, since the whole ideology, and the goals upon which these characteristics and the creation of the National School had sprung, collapsed.

Despite this unfavourable climate, the music ideology that Kalomoirēs introduced had already been communicated to many other Greek composers of the time, while others were already by his side and would become the most important representatives of the Greek National Music School. Composers like Varvoglēs, Riadēs, and Petridēs offered new perspective to the creation of Greek music. Their ideological placement within the bounds of the same movement, however, did not result in similar styles. In fact, each of them was influenced by different sources of the European art music scene and succeeded in forming their own personal music dialect. Other parameters that had determined the stylistic differences among them were: the different places of origin and social environments they were coming from, together with the different aspects of music education they received. In spite of these differences, the principles that kept them all going were common. These were: the exploration of music material from the Greek tradition in their work; their consensus on the way they would like to see Greek music abroad; and the creation of those institutions and foundations that would promote its development.[5]

During that period, that is, after the founding of the National Music School in Greece, Kalomoirēs begins to compose works of a quite nationalist character, versifying them with the lyrics of a fellow ideological companion in the field of poetry, Cōstēs Palamas. Later on, Kalomoirēs will turn to other contemporary poets and literary figures, and will also lend a favourable ear to the new social demands that derived from the overall disappointment, the collapse of visions and the state of refugees of his times.

Palamas' work deeply influenced both his contemporary poets and his predecessors, especially through the last decade of 1910, when his superiority in the field of poetry in Greece was total.[6] Later on, however, the generation who first made their publishing début in late 1910 was not totally intimidated by Palamas' dominant presence; actually, it set off some high-class poets and literary figures, like Kazantzakēs and Sikelianos (both of whom would relate their work to that of Kalomoirēs). These creators may have borrowed elements form Palamas' poetry, but each of them certainly manipulated that material in a totally personal, new light.

From the late 1920s new innovative tendencies are already occurring in the European music scene, finding their primary expression in the works of Mitropoulos and Skalkottas. Nevertheless, the composers of the so-called National School – with Kalomoirēs as a kind of a 'patriarch' of Greek music – were the ones to have actually taken up all posts, in both sectors of Greek music education and music institutions. Meanwhile, younger composers spring up (Ponēridēs, Sklavos, Nezeritēs, Kōnstantinidēs, Xenos, Kydōniatēs, Evangelatos), who follow the National School's dominant track, despite the fact that similar movements across Europe were already considered long past.

Through the decade of 1940s and the beginning of the 1950s, the usual issues of the National School composers were mainly taken from the Occupation years and the National Resistance that followed, as a natural resonance of the conditions and needs of that society. Of course, many composers had modernised their music style by selectively enhancing it with innovative elements of the European music scene. Although many valuable music works were created during the time, it soon became obvious that the life-course of the National School was due to conclude, after about half a century of music production and contribution to the cultural life of Greece. Says Nikos Maliaras (Maliaras [Μαλιάρας] 2003):

> The reasons for which the National School gradually moved out of the creative music scene rely upon the fading out of those reasons for which it had been created. The National-liberal movement along with the 'Great Idea' had been forgotten for decades, if not degraded or devalued. The turn towards tradition is no longer a demand but the dominant reality translated into creative impulse for literature and culture, in general. Moreover, the new compositional techniques in Europe have changed to such an extent that [...] any persistence in conserving National Schools could only be perceived as a meaningless attachment to the past.

Manōlēs Kalomoirēs (1883–1962)

What becomes clear from the above is that Manōlēs Kalomoirēs was the figure who changed the course of history of Greek art music, by playing the most vital role in the formation of music institutions in Greece, during the first half of the 20th century. The dynamic personality and the perfect music training he provided enabled him to lead music life in Greece for a noticeably long period and set the grounds for the creation and development of the Greek National Music School. His ability to always hold a key post by being on good terms with people in power, enabled Kalomoirēs to promote both his work and beliefs, as well as be actively involved in the founding and management of almost all music foundations and institutions of the time. Besides, his great contributions to the music life of the country do not rely solely upon his compositional work but – perhaps to a greater extend – upon his inestimable gift to music education and music institutions.

Biographic note

Manōlēs Kalomoirēs was born in Smyrna, Asia Minor, on 14 December 1883. His parents, Iōannēs Kalomoirēs, a doctor from Karlovasi of Samos and Maria Hamoudopoulou, (member of a glorious family) from Smyrna, were bourgeoisie people of a quite satisfactory economic status. They raised their son in a relatively privileged environment, offering him high quality education and thereby set the prerequisites for a promising future. Most of young Kalomoirēs' family members and social circle happened to be educated and cultivated individuals, among whom he sought exemplars.

His first exposure to music learning was the lessons he took at Palladio Boarding School, in his hometown (1890); during the piano sessions with his instructor Digenēs Kapagrossas, Kalomoirēs demonstrated his music talent for the first time. In 1894 he and his family settled in Athens, where he continued his piano lessons under the instruction of Timotheos Xanthopoulos and concurrently followed classes at the National Lyceum (1894–1899). In 1899 he went to Constantinople, where he attended the Greek-French Hatzēchrēstos Lyceum (1899–1900). At the same time, he continued his piano lessons with Sofia Spanoudē, a figure who played a significant part in the formation and the development of the future composer's physiognomy. That was the period when Kalomoirēs was introduced to the Greek folk song and the popular linguistic idiom. Particularly, it was at one of Aramis' concerts in Constantinople where, apart from the standard foreign repertoire, Kalomoirēs got the chance to listen to a series of arrangements of Greek folk songs. This, together with the reading of Psycharēs' book, *My Journey,* brought Kalomoirēs in touch with the demotic language and left an indelible mark in his life. What, however, proved a real turning point in his life was his acquaintance with Kōstēs Palamas. The work of this enlightened man, to which Kalomoirēs was first introduced during that period, totally magnetised the young artist. Consequently, he too came to favour the use of the popular idiom, of which Palamas was such a warm supporter. The summer of 1901 (August) finds Kalomoirēs settled in Vienna with the prospect of following a new series of music classes at the Friends of Music Conservatoire. In Vienna, as part of his piano studies, he participated in numerous student concerts. In 1902 he made his first conscious attempt to compose – an activity which he continued throughout the whole duration of his study in Vienna (1901–1906). Apart from composition, Kalomoirēs also made sure to maintain his interest in the use of extreme demotic language, through the magazine entitled *Noumas.* Little by little, the "demotic idea" was evidently growing stronger in him. While, through his summer visits to Constantinople to see his family, he stayed in touch with Greek reality and cultivated the wish to aid the creation of a national consciousness. Nevertheless, what came to arouse his national aspirations more was a political figure: Eleutherios Venizelos.

In 1906, after completing his studies in Vienna, Kalomoirēs decided to settle in Harkov, so to become profoundly aware of the works of the Russian composers of that National School. Clearly, at the back of his mind also existed the prospect of undertaking similar action in Greece – a thought inspired by the performance of Rimsky-Korsakov's *Scheherazade* under the music direction of Gabrilovich, which made a huge impression on the Greek composer (Kalomoirēs [Καλομοίρης] 1988: 97). In Harkov, Kalomoirēs worked as a piano instructor at the Obolenski Music Lyceum (Kalomoirēs [Καλομοίρης] 1988: 123–124). During his stay there, he came to realise his affinity with the "popular idiom movement". As a result, he became a regular subscriber to *Noumas,* while he also began correspondence with many demoticists: Pallēs, Psycharēs, Tangopoulos, Ephtaliōtēs and, none the least, Palamas (to whom he showed great respect and admiration). Moreover, he started writing articles for

Noumas and openly expressed his views on language issues as much as on the need for the creation of a Greek National Music School.

At the beginning of 1908 he decided to give a concert in Athens; through this he meant to push forward the idea for a potential founding of a Greek National Music School along with presenting some of his works to his compatriots, as most of them had not previously heard of the young, ambitious composer.

The Greek National Music School manifesto

Throughout the whole duration of Kalomoirēs' stay abroad his patriotism and nationalist sentiments had become invigorated, while the seeds for his dream about a Greece born anew were already growing in him. This was due partly to his isolation in a foreign environment and partly to the high-spirited and ambitious visions and goals that he'd always had.

Kalomoirēs, standing always as an advocate of the demotic language, polarised the Athenian audience from the very first moment that he set foot in Athens, through his much-celebrated concert of 11 June 1908, as well as the publication of his manifesto. Many were the Athenians who endorsed his views, particularly those coming from the progressive environment; however a lot more went against him. Through the Greek National Music School founding-manifesto what became clear was Kalomoirēs' belief as to the necessity of enabling the musician to take part in socio-political and cultural developments, as a kind of a "seismographer" of his times. This belief of his was numerously incarnated through his subsequent attitude, as well as the numerous texts he would write about the National School and the Greek composers. His conscious ideological direction, in favour of the popular idiom from the very beginning and in favour of Venizelos and the "Great Idea" later on were nothing but practical confirmations of his beliefs. What was also clarified through the 1908 manifesto was Kalomoirēs' attempt to include Greek music in the bigger picture of National Music Schools worldwide, and therefore use it as a vehicle for visions of national ideals. His reference to language and the connection he drew between speech and music are characteristic qualities of the composers belonging to National Schools. He also made reference to the Greek folk song and the ways in which a composer should use its structural elements for the creation of National Music.

The whole progressive team of Greek intellectuals sided with Kalomoirēs, since his ideas on the language issue automatically located him as an expert on Greek music. He argued that Greek composers should set their creations side by side with those of all the other intellectual and artistic figures (poets, writers, painters) so that the Greek presence could finally reach a point of completeness. In that context, the creation of a national music language recognisable to the European set and – at the same time – distinguishable from that of other nations was necessary and unavoidable. At the same time, and through the same spectrum, he was excluding every composer who used foreign texts and who did not draw material from the sources of Greek tradition. Thus, right from the start Kalomoirēs was clearly marginalising the Heptanesian composers, whom he considered *Italians*.

Traditional folk song and Greek language proved to be fruitful grounds for the creation of a Greek National Music School and at the same time a battlefield for Greek composers of the early years of the 20th century. Realising the total absence of any national music in Greece (in contrast to the presence of Greek literature), Kalomoirēs felt obligated to respond to this need through the founding of a National School in the form of the existing National Schools around Europe. Kōstēs Palamas, whom naturally Kalomoirēs regarded as an intellectual ringleader, had taken an analogous action in the field of poetry. The course of Greek poetry and literature felt an immediate connection with the foundation of the Greek National Music School, especially with the works of its first generation composers. However, although Greek poetry and literature had already come quite a long way since Greek literary figures started following European developments, this was not the case for Greek music, which was in its infancy.

Until he finally settled in Athens, Kalomoirēs continued his teaching at Harkov and regularly wrote articles for *Noumas,* where he could analyse his views on both the language issue as much as the urge to create a Greek National Music School. Through his articles he could also respond to his critics and, at the same time, set the grounds for his great and permanent settlement to his country.

Compositional activity: influential factors for the formation of his musical language

Kalomoirēs moulded a music language of his own, based on small structural units of Greek folk tradition, so to give out the *Greek colour* he aspired for. This music language was set upon the modes, the rhythmic and melodic patterns of our folk tradition, while in several occasions it borrowed elements from legends, fairytales, traditions and customs (Maliaras [Μαλιάρας] 2001: 12–21). The existence of a poem within Kalomoirēs' works is of special significance, as lyrics lie in a rather idiosyncratic relationship with the music. Particularly in the case of Palamas' poems this relationship becomes even stronger; after all, the bond between the composer and Palamas went way beyond their artistic cooperation – both shared the same opinions concerning the art's reference to tradition and its involvement with the European movements.

Further crucial factors that influenced Kalomoirēs' music language are listed as follows:

a) His music studies in Vienna during the period 1901–1906

The period in question happened to be the most fruitful one for the composer concerning his music training since – apart from his studies at the Friends of Music Conservatoire of Vienna – he was also given the chance to familiarise with a culture of great music tradition, to associate and exchange views with musicians from all over Europe and, of course, attend ample music performances.[7]

At no other place could he have got to know Richard Wagner's works so profoundly, whom he often referred to as his exemplar for his operatic work. Nevertheless, the relationship between Kalomoirēs' operatic works with those of Wagner lies on an external level only, since both the interaction between drama and music (as much as the reference to popular legends and historical events of the past) were practices belonging to the overall ideological frame of romanticism. Besides, if we were to compare Kalomoirēs' compositional style to that of Wagner, we would find that the first used a lot more lyrical elements, while the latter composed on a thicker and more dynamic layer (Rōmanou [Ρωμανού] 2006: 131). In his songs, Kalomoirēs seems rather influenced by the style of German composers such as Hugo Wolf, Max Reger and Franz Schreker, "which liberated from the neurosis of symmetry, […] that leads towards the formation of a melodic technique, 'a kind of musical prose', like Reger likes to put it" (Frangou-Psychopaedē [Φράγκου-Ψυχοπαίδη] 1990: 126).

b) His stay at Harkovo (1906–1910)

It so happened that those four years of Kalomoirēs' stay in Harkovo, Russia, proved very determinative for the crystallisation of his ideology around the National Schools; it was here he became familiar with the forerunner and most authentic National School of all – the Russian. If one were to compare the socio-historical circumstances in Russia at the time that the Russian National School's formation took place (the middle of 19th century) to those that set off the founding of the Greek National School half a century later, one would discover ample similarities and analogies. In Harkovo Kalomoirēs got in touch with a very different music culture from his own, through listening to the works of The Five and through his occasional participation at various cultural events. It is therefore only natural to expect that he would adopt all the necessary elements that would aid the formation of a Greek National Music School, as this had always been his intention.

c) His relation to French culture

From a very young age, Kalomoirēs started learning French and as a student went to schools that were all French-speaking. Thus, in a way, he was exposed to French culture and music from his childhood. On top of that came the cosmopolitan environment of his birthplace, Smyrna, and of course his enrolment at the Greek-French Hatzēchrēstos Lyceum in Constantinople; these factors would later on function as a motive for his approach to French poetry, literature and music and their integration within his own works.

Throughout the 1920s and 1930s Kalomoirēs exploited those bonds with French culture by promoting both his work as well as those of the rest of the composers belonging to the

Greek National School; he made several trips to France, where he became acquainted with the works of many French composers. He also ensured that many of his students went to complete their music education in France, while he never neglected his friendships with musicians and music directors who had built a career in France. Also, he was very happy to see his daughter, Krinō Kalomoirē, settling in Paris. These facts all contributed to the invigoration of Kalomoirēs' bonds with French art.

This also had an impact on Kalomoirēs' music language, which changes from 1920 onwards; this change – also pin-pointed in his writings – depicts a clear move away from Wagner's world, in terms of compositional style, although the sentiments of admiration towards the grand composer were never to fade away (Kalomoirēs [Καλομοίρης] 1928). Thus, although Kalomoirēs preserved the principles of the National School's ideology, he moved onto the sphere of impressionism – where he would remain for the duration of the following decades of 1920 and 1930. This period would leave its mark on his later works, through the adoption of a rather subjective compositional style (after 1940) where he selectively integrates various stylistic elements.[8] Besides, apart from the programmatic character that Kalomoirēs' works obtain through the connection of words and music – a character evident in the compositional works all over Europe towards the end of the 19th century and the beginning of the 20th – "the so-called 'exoticism' of French music may be related to the subjectivism of the works of many Greek composers, who sought their sources of inspiration in our folk melodies […] in a similar manner to that of the elite European tendency towards the reconstruction of their folk culture" (Frangou-Psychopaedē [Φράγκου-Ψυχοπαίδη] 1988: 43–54).

During the 1930s Kalomoirēs' style turns to more modernist techniques and symbolist contents of the French art nouveau and impressionism (Frangou-Psychopaedē [Φράγκου-Ψυχοπαίδη] 1988: 54). What contributed to that tendency was the gradual appearance of new 'modernist' national composers, like Petros Petridēs who came to revitalise the Greek National Music Movement and also Nikos Skalkōtas who was to become the antipode of Kalomoirēs' music persona.

> Kalomoirēs does not turn a blind eye on the international developments that also influence Greek reality but he pinpoints them creatively and later on comments upon them, through his genuine critiques. Nevertheless, to him this represents a decline as far as the style of his symphonies is concerned, whose characteristics are already evident in the idiosyncratic style of chamber music. (Frangou-Psychopaedē [Φράγκου-Ψυχοπαίδη] 1988: 54)

To sum up, one could identify elements of a variety of influences in Kalomoirēs' works, such as those of romanticism, post-romanticism, impressionism, National Schools, not to mention elements of more modern tendencies of the time, as much as elements from the Greek folk and church music. Nevertheless, the way in which all the above are interwoven in Kalomoirēs' music language is deeply personal and thus unique (Frangou-Psychopaedē [Φράγκου-Ψυχοπαίδη] 1990: 95).

His work

In Kalomoirēs' operas, the situations, the characters or the Gods being presented are manipulated symbolically, through the construction of a web of leitmotivs and perpetual melodies in the orchestral parts. This practice clearly derived from the distinct Wagnerian manner and was based on the form of the Romantic epic-lyrical opera. Of course, in the works of the Greek composer this Wagnerian discipline is explored in a looser sense, as a Romantic background and an expressional technique. As C. Cui points out, in Wagner the leitmotivs constantly reoccur and the vocal part is often overlapped, something that is not evident in Kalomoirēs's works (Frangou-Psychopaedē [Φράγκου-Ψυχοπαίδη] 1990: 63–65). Besides, what drove Kalomoirēs away from the Wagnerian ideology towards the more modern movements of national romanticism was mainly his anxiety to be regarded as the most important representative of the Greek National Music School – a wish clearly reflected in his attitude during the last two decades of his life – and to see his work recognised, internationally.

Thus, his technique gradually deviates from the Wagnerian idiom like in his opera, *East* (1945), where Kalomoirēs abandons the leitmotiv to introduce the notion of "characteristic tunes", in a manner analogous to that of the Czech composer Smetana (Kalomoirēs [Καλομοίρης] 1953). This new technique was also evident in Kalomoirēs's next opera, *Fairy Waters*, but not in his last work *Constantine Palaeologos*, where an attempt to return to Wagnerism is observed that reminds the listener of the composer's first music drama, *Master Builder*.

Kalomoirēs often borrowed themes from the Greek folk or Byzantine music, which is, however, normally not used verbatim in his works. What he did, rather, was to exploit the modes and rhythm of the Greek music tradition in a way that would help him construct his own patterns. Nevertheless, when he did use identical themes of mainly folk and Byzantine music traditions, he did so in order to reach the listener's subconscious and to remind him of popular melodies that were landmarks for the Greek nation; it was like a psychological trick that often had a deep emotional impact on the listener. Examples of this broad practice may be found in *The Death of the Valiant Woman*. There he uses the main melody of the traditional song, *The Dance of Zalongo*, while in his *The Mother's Ring* he uses the chant *Virgin Mary Today*; also in his *Master Builder* Kalomoirēs uses the song *Forty Young Builders* and so on. Nevertheless, in some occasions, this practice symbolises a kind of personal recollection of the past; a flashback to the composer's childhood, at time when he, as a young boy, would listen to his nanny's numerous folk songs – a confession that he himself makes in his autobiography (Kalomoirēs [Καλομοίρης] 1988: 16–17). Such dreamy wanderings are very commonly evident in his works; for instance, in his *Symphonic Concerto for Piano and Orchestra* one can identify tributes of the song *Lynx the Gallant* and then again in the final part of his *Quintet with Song* the folk couplets of "the violin player who wove a song for his wife" may be heard.[9]

The text plays a primary role in the way Kalomoirēs shapes his works. As Giōrgos Leōtsakos puts it,

> […] poetic speech on the one hand functions as a motive to his inspiration and as a bridle on the other, and perhaps is the greatest determinative for the shaping of his vocal music. And by poetic speech I do not mean his operas […] but mainly his songs for one voice and orchestra, one voice and piano or one voice and other instruments.[10]

Surely, it does not take much for one to detect the need for some text to be present so to give shape to his composition. The fact that Kalomoirēs consciously makes use of the text for the above reason seems obvious, as it possibly helps him limit some of his weaknesses, like avoiding making prolonged references or unnecessary repetitions and leading him towards simpler, more sensitive and better processed pages, something clearly evident in his songs.[11]

Kalomoirēs may be characterised as a 'drama' composer, who seems to depend a lot on poetic speech in both his operas and his songs as much as in his instrumental or orchestral works, since any extra-musical reference (of poetic, historic or even autobiographic nature) may activate his stimuli for composing music. When one takes a glance at the catalogue of his works (Anōgeianakēs [Ανωγειανάκης] 1964; Tsalachourēs [Τσαλαχούρης] 2003), he may easily come to the above conclusion, since most of his works are dominated by the presence of text. Another obstacle that the composer had to overcome was to successfully combine two totally different worlds, in his compositions: European polyphony and Greek tradition. One of the characteristics that not only provided a certain amount of coherence between such heterogeneous materials, but also functioned as his moving force, is his unrestrained and often grandiloquent dramatic tone.

In Kalomoirēs' music the element that determines his harmonic language is the vocal melodic line. Vertical harmony, particularly in the works for grand *ensembles*, is often the consequence of the parallel development of two or more melodic lines, or even two or more different levels of composition. In this manner Kalomoirēs succeeds in creating a totally personal harmonic language upon which he incorporates various forms and styles that he borrows from different sources; these sources include modes of Greek traditional folk music, contrapuntal and other techniques of development in western tradition, and many other European practices of music composition.[12] His harmonic language, together with the texture of his music, present significant range from very simple harmonic structures that accompany a melodic line: from a parallel or chromatic use of harmony, counterpoint, polyphony or homophony, to whole parts that touch the boundaries of atonality (especially in the works of his last decade), bitonal 'hints' or even twelve-tone themes. Regarding Kalomoirēs' rich and often complex harmonic language, one may observe that the more it refers to extra-musical material, such as poems, narratives, programmatic layout or visual prompts, the more autonomous and independent it becomes.

Despite the above observation, it seems that Kalomoirēs remains faithful to the Romantic and post-Romantic writing onto which he selectively comes to incorporate more modern techniques, through the passage of time. Besides, as early as the 19th century there had been a lot of other composers who implanted the alternative element of chromatic harmony in their musical writing – in the sense of expanded tonality and modality, as a consequence of the spreading interest around the past, around folklore and Eastern music. During the early years of the 20th century, rhythm, counterpoint and timbre move into the foreground, while the role of harmony in a musical work becomes vague, blurry and difficult to detect. One would generally say that at the beginning of the 20th century harmony becomes generally undisciplined and less signifying.

What at times drives the composer towards epic, brave and dynamic outbreaks that may sometimes seem grandiloquent, is the same quality that, on other occasions, leads him towards wide, deeply lyrical or dramatic expressions: trusting the music instinct he possesses. Usually, the thickening of music writing and the increase in the number of dynamic culminations results in a richer orchestral impression that is supported by doublings of instruments and openings in full orchestra. The real matter of fact is, however, that his music writing thins out and music events are reduced either through the transformation of the initial diatonic manner to a chromatic one, or through the persistence of a given motif, rhythmic pattern or diatonic interval. A common characteristic of his orchestral works and his chamber music is the use of a cyclic form that contributes to the firm counter-balancing of the required stability of structure, while, at the same time, it gives out the impression of a vague dramatic programme. It is possible that Kalomoirēs, being aware of his tendency towards verbalism, used the cyclic form as a means to affirm what had previously been mentioned and to avoid expanding into a long-winded music dialogue (of which he was liable).[13]

Fearing a possible upsetting of structure that the constant insertion of new music ideas would bring to his works, Kalomoirēs tried to subdue such impulses to pre-existing forms of music writing. Of course, this was not always possible; in fact many are the occasions where one finds themes that are not exploited during the work's development or, when exploited, the work grows beyond limits. His tendency to expand his work to the point that he starts facing problems of either duration (as happens in his *Quintet with Song* (1912) and his "Trio for Piano, Violin and Cello" (1921) with a total duration of over forty minutes or again in his opera *Master Builder*) or structure, is easy to detect. This is particularly evident in his early works, when the young composer seems unable to tame his nerve in writing, and is often forced to call forth all his knowledge on counterpoint or instrumentation in order to handle his rich, expansive but also hectic product. Gradually however, he managed to stick to more shaped structures and created works of great elegance.

Kalomoirēs' great worry was that Greek composers had not yet reached the stage where they were able to assimilate the new international and anti-national techniques within their music writing without negatively interfering with the character of their national identity. His fear was justifiable, since the Greek National Music School had only begun to take its first steps, and thus did not have the sufficient music tradition or the music background that would otherwise permit the adjustment of new techniques to its national music language. This enriching practice could be, and was, adopted successfully by countries which already possessed a crystallised national music language. However, that was not feasible for Greek music, thus what Kalomoirēs sought to do was create an autonomous, identifiable national music style. In his late writings he offers an overview of this attempt, saying that the Greek national music style he pushed forward

> may not have been in tune with the latest international experimentations towards modernisation and may have ignored the twelve-tone system, concretism, or [the use of] electric equipment, however that proved to be its great advantage. (Kalomoirēs [Καλομοίρης] 1954: 557)

However in his article on Greek music in the periodical *Musikē Zōē* [Music Life], he notes that

> what will turn the dream of Greek music creation to reality is the outstanding of charismatic musicians who will combine the latest technical knowledge with an inherent understanding of the aesthetic and artistic texture of our traditional music. (Kalomoirēs [Καλομοίρης] 1931: 2)

An overview of Kalomoirēs as a composer shows a man inherently impulsive, hardworking, full of ambitions and passion for his work; a rather cyclothymic man constantly possessed by worries and insecurity, a plethoric persona that did not think twice when it was to express his beliefs, a man with countless goals around which he devoted his whole life and work, and a powerful character who proved that he was more than capable of leadership during a given battle. As years passed, the composer may have become more condescending and, on some occasions, may have sought to keep a lower profile and limit his former excessive reactions; but on the whole, the main features of his character, like enthusiasm and ambition, remained present and did not fade over the years.

If we wanted to give an overall estimation of his work, we would be able to say that Kalomoirēs managed to change the musical status quo of a whole country, completely on his own. His achievements stand out greatly, as not only did he produce a vast compositional work but he also changed the given system of music education; he set the mentality of all those people who were involved with the country's music affairs on a completely new track, thereby influencing Greece's entire music life.

Aemilios Riadēs (1880–1935)

Biographic note

Aemilios Riadēs[14] happens to be one of the most mysterious figures of Greek music, since Greek musicologists have explored a very small amount of his works. Given that a great part of his compositions remain unknown, unpublished and thus unperformed, many elements in Riadēs' music language are still undefined and so are many sides of his personal life, concerning his family affairs and his education.[15]

Aemilios Riadēs was born in Thessalonica in 1880 where he died in 1935. His real name was Khu and he was the eldest son of the Austro-Hungarian chemist-pharmacist Heinrich Khu and Anastasia Grēgoriou-Ninē, of Greek origin. Riadēs' family was most likely well off, a fact that allowed him to study at the Greek Gymnasium, the only Greek school of secondary education there was in Thessalonica during the Turkish occupation. At the same time he studied music (piano and harmony) with the most skilled musician in town, the composer Dēmētrios Lallas (Dēmētriou [Δημητρίου] 2002).

From a very young age Riadēs wrote poems, most of which were inspired by the severities of the Greeks under the Ottomans and the Macedonian Struggle. According to Diamantopoulou-Cornejo, the origin of the composer's pen name, "EleutheRiadēs", derived from the word "Eleutheria" (meaning freedom) and the Macedonian surname ending "iadēs", a name that Riadēs used for his first poetic publication. While G. Vaphopoulos claims that the name the future composer chose was "a symbolic manifestation of his lust for freedom [...], [and functioned as a] [...] shield for keeping his identity hidden from the Turkish persecution" (Diamantopoulou-Cornejo 2001/i: 106–107).[16]

After completing secondary education, his parents decided to send him to Piraeus, where his brother worked as a merchant, in the hope that he too would follow this profession since being a musician at the time was not considered a decent occupation. The possibility that the publication of Riadēs' early revolutionary-patriotic poems caused trouble to his family may have been an additional motive for them to send him to Piraeus. Those poems, however, were only the beginning of a series of actions that extended to his involvement with the developing National Movement; Riadēs set the basement of his house at the revolutionaries' disposal, where they held their meetings and hid their weapons for the forthcoming Macedonian Struggle (Dēmētriadou-Karayiannidou [Δημητριάδου-Καραγιαννίδου] 1990: 7). Consequently, it was only natural to expect that Riadēs would soon return to Thessalonica, which he did, after two months' stay in Piraeus (Karatzidēs [Καρατζίδης] 1937: 170).

Thessalonica: historical facts

Riadēs' hometown, Thessalonica, happened to be the second most important town of the Ottoman Empire with Constantinople being the capital, and undoubtedly provided the fruitful cultural background for the formation of the young composer's artistic persona. The long period of the city's Turkish occupation, characterised by numerous catastrophes, pogroms and trials did not intimidate the citizens' will to maintain their cultural tradition and regain their freedom.[17] Within the torment of demographic changes, national and linguistic reclassifications, expatriations and the founding of new colonies, the previously known art of the Byzantine Empire developed into what is now referred to as post-Byzantine art. During this period Thessalonica was growing stronger, both economically and culturally, among the Balkan cities. Perhaps this prosperity could be attributed to the coexistence of various cultures, religions, customs, values and morals of its residents (Greeks, Armenians, Turks, Jews and many more) that formed a multicultural mosaic, which also proved very beneficiary for Riadēs' personality (Kambourē-Vamvoukou [Καμπούρη-Βαμβούκου] 1997).

During the years of the second half of the 18th century the Russian support aided Greek mercantile activity to the organised Jewish and Frank commerce. The Greek merchants were soon to gain economic strength and play a leading part in both the liberating movement and in several other issues of social nature. Through the bribing of Turks this mercantile class provided the Greek civilians with far better living conditions. However, a greater contribution was their intervention in the establishment, at a time prior to the Greek Revolution of 1821, of the first Greek school in Thessalonica as well as a number of Greek Orthodox churches.

Within this climate of intellectual activation and national unity, Filiki Etaeria (the Greek revolutionary secret society that planned the revolution of 1821) found fruitful ground among the Greek civilians of Thessalonica. Thus, not long afterwards, the educational institutions multiplied along with several other unions, which enforced the formers' educational action. The graduates of these schools would become those teachers and priests who would later form the leaders of the Macedonian Struggle, within the greater territory of Macedonia.

Around that time Bulgarian guerrillas, known as *komitatzēdes*, were also about to take action, through a number of manifestations that at first took place in the outskirts of the Macedonian territory and later on reached the city (1903). A year later, in 1904, Greek officers of the regular army confronted the guerrillas, initiating the Greek opposition to them. At the centre of the Macedonian Struggle was the Greek consulate of Thessalonica and the Cathedral (1904–1908), while in 1908, the Neo-turkish uprising occurred in Thessalonica (Ristelhueber 2003: 125). Eventually, on 26 October 1912, Pasha Tahsin signed the protocol of Thessalonica's surrender to the Greeks (Castellan [Καστελλάν] 1991).

The cultural movement in Thessalonica at the end of the 19th and the beginning of the 20th century

There is very little information evident concerning the state of music life in Riadēs' hometown, during the years it was still under the Ottoman Occupation (the end of the 19th century). Certainly, there cannot have been any proper cultural action on behalf of the Greek population, since the priority was shaking off the Turkish yoke. If one takes a look at what was happening culturally in other Greek cities of the time, one will find that music entertainment consisted of wandering music groups, and also of occasional performances of foreign orchestras, most likely Italian.[18] Presumably, the same activity was also going on in Thessalonica. Moreover, there were sporadic music initiatives on behalf of the people of Thessalonica that found their expression at the founding of cultural unions, like the Music Lovers' Society (1889), the Amateur's Society (1892), Orpheus (1904) and many more. Those unions actually maintained wind bands, as well as mandolin ensembles and choirs, and really promoted the city's music life. While, after the town's liberation of 1908, Thessalonica's cultural activity would reach its peak.[19]

During the years of Turkish occupation another institution, this time an orphanage, was founded that was meant to play a significant role in the development of Thessalonica's music life; from its very first year of foundation (1903) the Papapheio Orphanage inserted music in its curriculum. Along with the theoretical and technical training it provided, the institution gave a lot of weight to the teaching of wind instrument playing. Soon, the orphanage had its own wind band, which fell under the command of the "Superior Parish Committee". President of the committee was the Eparch himself, who supervised all the institutions of the Greek community. Being the only orchestra in occupied Thessalonica, the wind band played in all the religious and cultural events organised across the city. While later, when the Greek liberating troops were marching into Thessalonica, it was the very same ensemble that welcomed the soldiers and accompanied the celebration events around the city.

In the following years the number of institutions being founded increased. In 1911 Sōtērēs Graekos, former student of Dēmētrios Lallas took the initiative to form the first private conservatoire in Thessalonica ("Graekos' Conservatoire"). The conservatoire maintained classes in violin and piano, as well as other instruments, which were initially taught by the Italian musicians Tiberio and Markezini. In 1914 another conservatoire was founded, the State Conservatoire of Thessalonica. As expected, the new institution, being antagonistic to the private conservatoire of Graekos, absorbed a good number of students (thereby harming the prestige and the popularity of the latter). The founding of a state conservatoire (according to statute 349/5.11.1914) was Eleutherios Venizelos' initiative, as he thought that there ought to be a public conservatoire in the liberated Thessalonica in order to train the youth of the area: the cultural development of the citizens was his vision. Alexandros Kazantzēs was appointed as the director of the institution, a man whom Venizelos had personally invited from Brussels for his assignment to that post.[20]

Venizelos' aspirations concerning the public conservatoire's role became realised, since – for the greatest part of the 20th century – the institution remained the prime vehicle of the city's music education and life. What is essential to pinpoint, however, is that beyond the conservatoire's obvious contribution it also signified the locus where the northern parts of Greece first came into contact with the European art music tradition and music education. Besides, the conservatoire became the meeting place for a few of the most distinct Greek musicians; people who returned to Thessalonica after completing their studies and work abroad, as well as people who were already staying in the city (like Vasileios Theophanous, Euripidēs Kotsanidēs) and foreigners (like the Belgian, Theo Kauffmann), all of whom worked at the conservatoire from the first years of its establishment.

A few years before the 1850s, a relative mobility in the field of literature is observed in Thessalonica. This becomes more noticeable in the early years of the 20th century, especially after 1930, when Greek poetry and literature strengthen and step into the cultural life of the city.[21]

The social and political tendencies of revitalisation, development, and florescence of poetry existing in Thessalonica at the time, differed a lot from equivalent tendencies across the rest of the country, including the city of Athens. Especially in the case of prose, the difference became more noticeable with the Macedonia genre been innovative and certainly in tune with the European movements. On the contrary, literature in the rest of Greece had maintained a far more traditional character (Kounenakē [Κουνενάκη] 1997; Vitti 1994: 388).

Nonetheless, knowing the above information still does not fill the huge gap in our knowledge about Greek literature before the 1850s. In fact the chronology "1850" signified a turning point in the intellectual life of the city, since it was the year that the first Greek printing house was inaugurated. Before that, there was no presence of domestic literate figures, with the translation of foreign books being the sole intellectual activity in the city of Thessalonica. The fact that, after the second half of the 19th century, the Turkish servility got less tight was also a factor that set off the mechanism of intellectual quest.

Riadēs' literate activity during his youth

As already mentioned, Riadēs first became known as a poet (under the pen name Eleutheriadēs), with his artistic nature being expressed from a young age. Yet, later, even when music absorbed his total attention, he never stopped writing poems but actually started setting a number of them to music and thus created his famous songs. A significant amount of his work is currently kept at the Music Library of Greece "Lilian Voudouri" which is situated in Megaron, Athens Concert Hall. As Stephania Merakou (the person in charge of his archive) informs us, it consists of over 600 handwritten pages (Merakou). Quoting Merakou, what is evident in those manuscripts, is: "the poet/composer's constant effort to achieve perfection and an ongoing processing of his [music] ideas, even after they had been printed and published" (Merakou).

Before going abroad to study music, Riadēs had the chance to see a few of his poems published at the press of Thessalonica. It is very likely that his first two poems were released at the magazine *Pharos tēs Thessalonikēs* [Lighthouse of Thessalonica] in 1904 (under the name Aemilios Khu), while several other publications followed at various magazines of both Thessalonica and Athens (where, for instance, the poetic collection *From the Collection of Patriotic Poems of Aem. Eleutheriadēs*, was published in 1905). Along with the manuscripts kept at Riadēs' archive, a small notebook is also present, where he used to gather newspaper clips of his own publications of the period 1904–1906. Those publications, however, have barely been looked upon up to the present day, since his researchers are preoccupied with his later works. During the Macedonian Struggle and despite his youth, Riadēs secretly published a number of anonymous patriotic poems, in the journal of Skokos, in the *Macedonian Journal* and in newspapers of the time (Dēmētriadou-Karayiannidou [Δημητριάδου-Καραγιαννίδου] 1990: 5).

It was around that time that Riadēs received his first music lessons on harmony and piano from Dēmētrios Lallas (1848–1911), perhaps the most important and best-trained music teacher of Thessalonica.[22] It is worth mentioning that a few of Riadēs's first poems are dedicated to him. Of those, we may mention *The Owl*, a poem written in Munich in 1909 during the composer's studies (that was published a lot later, on 30 December 1928 at the illustrated review *Epochē* [Season]) as well as the poem entitled *At the Parthenon*. Many of his poems were set to music by the composer himself, with a number of them being written in French possibly during his studies in France. Most of those poems were published in Paris, in the form of songs, by the firms M. Senart and Chepelier (Merakou).[23]

The years in Munich (1908–1910)

At the beginning of the 20th century the 'Movement of the Neo-Turks' obliged every Ottoman citizen to join the Turkish army. Being a citizen of Thessalonica, Riadēs was considered to be an Ottoman, so, under pressure to join the army, he decided to leave Thessalonica, in the summer of 1908.[24] His destination was Munich, where he intended to study music. With the recommendations of Dēmētrios Lallas (his former teacher), Riadēs joined the Royal Music Academy (Königliche Academie der Tonkunst). He studied music analysis, instrumentation, "theme and variations" and fugue under the tuition of the composer-pedagogue Anton Beer-Walbrunn (1864–1929). He also took piano lessons with Mayer Gschrey and choir lessons with Becht and Stich. Also, there are sources that mention Riadēs as a student of the great maestro Felix Mottl (1856–1911); however, according to Leōtsakos these sources are of doubtful reliability. What can be considered as a fact, though, is that Riadēs studied at the Academy of Munich from 16 September 1908 to 10 July 1910. During his stay in Munich he carried on with his writing of prose and poems, which were published in the press of Thessalonica. Still, there is very little information concerning his overall stay in Munich (Leōtsakos [Λεωτσάκος] 1988: 147–151).

The years in Paris (1910-1915)

After leaving Munich (1910), Riadēs went to Paris, where he stayed until 1915. Paris, at that time, had turned into a "metropolis" for arts. Every significant cultural event was taking place there, within an atmosphere of artistic unrest. The prestigious presence of the great French composers Ravel and Debussy along with that of the Russian Ballets, which gave a number of performances, enhanced the cosmopolitan character of this city's life. Due to all this activity Paris had become a pole of attraction for a significant number of important people of literature and arts. A lot of pioneer artists also came to Paris, with whom Riadēs (especially after 1914) had the chance to become acquainted and exchange opinions. That was the time when he decided to abbreviate his initial pen name "Eleutheriadēs" to "Riadēs"; his new pen name was later endorsed by the Greek Government as his official name, in the belief that it was more appropriate for an artist.

So the composer became known as 'Riadēs' in the art world of Paris; he also became integrated with the wider Parisian artistic circles and became associated with many important figures of both Greek and international cultural life. A few of his Greek new acquaintances were Skipēs, Malakasēs, Psycharēs, Calo[25] and Varvoglēs. Still, the information available on that particular period of Riadēs' life is fragmentary and often quite vague.

Another matter of dispute concerning his activity in Paris is whether he had actually been a student of all the famous figures that are presented as his professors in his biographies. Recovering the whole truth around this matter may be an impossible task, since much of the information we have on Riadēs simply cannot be confirmed.[26] Dimitra Diamantopoulou-Cornejo has undertaken assiduous research on the matter and comes to the conclusion that Riadēs never actually followed the lessons of Charpentier or Ravel, except for a few pieces of advice (Diamantopoulou-Cornejo 2001: I/109).

"Although there can be no doubt about Riadēs' great respect for Ravel's works – particularly his piano pieces – still there is no sufficient evidence of any personal contact between these two men" (Diamantopoulou-Cornejo 2001: I/109).

It is very likely that, on returning to Thessalonica in 1915, Riadēs overstated the meetings he might have had with the French composer, in an attempt to create a myth around his name and magnify the importance of his studies abroad. Leōtsakos offers an account of the composer's nature:

On his return (to Thessalonica) he gradually created a myth around his name that proved very misleading for the historians, in order to satisfy his 'ego' and keep the undesirables away. A Narcissist figure, a polyglot (he spoke English, French, German, Italian, the Hebrew dialect of Thessalonica, while he had a deep insight of the Japanese language and culture), with a yearning after the exotic, an inherent democrat, who had always been regarded as an odd figure, sometimes blithe yet totally harmless. (Leōtsakos [Λεωτσάκος] 1992a: 8)

Riadēs became known to the wide circle of musicians, through the presentation of his compositions at the city's concert halls as well as via the publication of his works by French music publishers (Dēmētriadou-Karajannidou [Δημητριάδου-Καραγιαννίδου] 1990: 8–9). It is possibly through these intellectual circles that Riadēs met Debussy (Diamandopoulou-Cornejo 2001: I/112). Nevertheless, despite all doubts concerning the composer's apprenticeship with Debussy and Ravel, Riadēs' music is undoubtedly influenced by French music of the beginning of the 20th century.

Return and permanent settlement in Thessalonica (1915–1935)

As previously stated, Thessalonica had been liberated on 26 October 1912. Nevertheless, Riadēs was temporarily arrested in Paris in 1914, a little after the break-out of World War I, due to the fact that he had neglected to renew his old passport and was still registered as an Ottoman citizen (Merlier 1952). The following year he returned to Thessalonica where he got a post as a piano teacher and then, around 1920, he became vice-principal of the State Conservatoire of Thessalonica (Leōtsakos [Λεωτσάκος] 1992a: 8).[27] At the same time, he was playing the grand cassa in the military band of which Manōlēs Kalomoirēs happened to be in charge. This band, based in Thessalonica, was playing daily in favour of the revolutionary government of Eleutherios Venizelos.

Polyglot as he was and passionate about anything exotic, Riadēs got involved with Eastern music and gave lectures on issues that were previously unknown to Greek composers, concerning "Chinese Music", "ancient Egyptian Music", "traditional Japanese Music" and so on. In fact, one of his writings about the History of Music has survived and it is believed that it functioned as the composer's guidebook for teaching during the years 1915–1935. This is an uncompleted piece of work, at a length of 197 pages, which the composer marked as the "first volume". According to Merakou, "the work seems complete, although there is no indication of a second volume in the composer's rough notes" (Merakou).

In it there is information concerning the music creation and the music practice of ancient civilisations (Egyptians, Sumerians, Persians, Japanese, Chinese, Hindus, Hebrews and Greeks). A study of that kind must be the first ever written by a Greek musician. On the other hand, Riadēs' passion about Far Eastern culture is evident in his writings about the music and poetry of those people. Towards the end of that work Riadēs makes reference to ancient Greek music (among others, to tragedy, dithyramb, music instruments, harmony, tetrachords and scales). He carries on with a historical review of the Byzantine period, with references to the chants and the tonal system and concludes with Greek folk song, which he juxtaposes with Byzantine chant (Merakou).

His compositional work

The largest part of Riadēs' archive is kept at the Music Library of Greece 'Lilian Voudouri' in Athens, while a smaller part is kept at the library of the State Conservatoire of Thessalonica. Nevertheless, it is only a small number of his works that have been researched, mainly due to the following two factors:

1. Until very recently there were no copies of the composer's manuscripts available at any institution or organisation for the musicologists and researchers to study.
2. Even when copies became available they are full of revisions and corrections on behalf of the composer (a fact that also applies to the published material, which is still corrected anew on the very edition) as well as unsolved pages (like for instance in his chamber music, where he wrote various parts without clarifying to which specific work they belonged) that disable any attempt to draw a solid conclusion.[28]

Perhaps it was the composer's perfectionism, or even his insecurity that is to blame for the sloppy writing of his compositions and poems; write-offs, corrections in different coloured ink, cross-outs of whole sections, unintelligible writing, ambiguous parts, unfinished works, works with titles of two different versions and work drafts, are a few of the characteristics of Riadēs' manuscripts. Thus, apart from some of his songs (that were published in Paris and in Athens) the rest of his work remained unknown in the main, up to the present day. Contrary to Kalomoirēs' neatly arranged material, Riadēs did not take any measures for preserving his work in the best possible way. The result was to leave a real "chaos" behind. "[…] whatever trouble the works of the many Russian composers may cause, […] is nothing in comparison to the problems that arise when one is confronted with Riadēs' works expecting to restore them", as Leōtsakos characteristically mentions (Leōtsakos [Λεωτσάκος] 1994: 344).

His songs

During his lifetime, and even up to the present day, Riadēs was known for his songs, which constitute the most complete part of his otherwise problematic material. For Riadēs, engaging his music with poetry provided a more ordered and defined frame in which he could develop his music thoughts. This practice, along with the fact that his songs were usually written for solo instrument (most often piano) and voice, led to the creation of more legible final versions that, even after their "revision" and rewriting, were still easy to read and perform.

Within the frame of modern Greek art music Riadēs' music language stands out as a very exceptional one. The vocal melodic line is usually characterised by folkloric colorations, in terms of both its modes and its rhythms, with the latter being borrowed from various Greek dances; it follows the content of the poem, usually in a sort of free recitation. On the other hand, the harmony is without doubt influenced by the writing style of French impressionists, especially Ravel, and is often driven away from any sense of "accompaniment", sinking in its own chromatic speculations and quests, independent from the content of the given text, but yet serving it. This idiosyncratic juxtaposition of a "Greek" melody with the accompaniment of an ethereal impressionist character that moves from lyricism to drama and from nostalgia to sarcasm, may generally be alluring, however it lacks solidity in its sounding (Foulias [Φούλιας] 2005: 129–130).

Marios Varvoglēs (1885-1967)

Biographical note

The composer Marios Varvoglēs[29] comes from an honoured family of Macedonian origin, whose members played a particularly important role in the Liberation Struggle – with some serving as soldiers, and others as politicians. Although born in Brussels during one of his father's many business trips, Varvoglēs always stated Athens as his birthplace. His father was a professor in the Army Cadets' School; his profession, like all military posts, was very

Amedeo Modigliani's portrait of Marios Varvoglēs (1920).

prestigious at the time and provided a life full of comforts for young Marios. The name Marios was his grandfather's pen name with which he used to publish articles at *Literary Hermes*, a Greek magazine edited in Vienna.

Marios' artistic nature emerged from a very young age, specifically in the field of painting. Thus, he attended the School of Fine Arts where he apprenticed with Nikēphoros Lytras and Giōrgos Roilos, while at the same time he took music lessons. This artistic flair of his, however, did not appeal to his parents, who were prejudiced against such occupations; fearing that their son would find himself on the "wrong track", they sent the seventeen-year-old Marios to Paris to study political sciences and thereby continue the family tradition. In Paris, Varvoglēs became acquainted with the artistic circles of Montmarte and, despite the disapproval of his family, he took a decisive turn towards the art of music (Vorazakē-Arzimanoglou [Βοραζάκη-Αρζιμάνογλου] 1982: 209–211).

Studying in Paris

Varvoglēs remained in Paris until 1920, without ever following the studies that his family had aspired. Instead, he enrolled in the Paris Conservatoire where he apprenticed (under the instruction of Xavier Leroux and Georges Caussade) for an indefinable duration of time. Looking at the chronologies of Varvoglēs' works and articles one may conclude that between the years 1910–1912 the composer was living in Vienna and Düsseldorf; it was in the latter city that a number of performances of his works took place in 1912. On his return to Paris the following year he registers to the Scola Cantorum as a student of Vincent d' Indy (Rōmanou [Ρωμανού] 1985: 16).

Before completing his studies Varvoglēs had already composed a few works, many of which he had the pleasure to direct or merely attend at the Parisian concert halls. Together with his articles in *Noumas*, which he began writing for in December 1909, these early compositions depict his commitment to writing music that was within the spirit of the Greek National Music School. Through his articles in *Noumas* he takes part in the discussion following Kalomoirēs' first concert in Athens, and becomes fully aligned with him. Through their writings the two men started paying compliments to one another, without previously having met or being aware of each other's works; what bonded them, however, was the sense of aiming towards the same direction. During his stay abroad Varvoglēs began to adopt a music language based upon the Greek traditional modes and rhythms, in the same manner that Kalomoirēs had done before him (a coincidence of particular interest, given the fact that the two composers had grown up and been educated at completely different environments) (Rōmanou [Ρωμανού] 1985: 16). Nevertheless, Varvoglēs' compositional technique differed in that it was influenced by French music, as a result of the composer's long stay and studies in Paris. Being that as it may, both Kalomoirēs and Varvoglēs decided to follow a more conservative line in their music writing; they thought this would be more resonant with their compositional quests and goals. The fact that they had both studied in the very two cities that were considered as the 'metropolises' of all the congruent, pioneer and subversive artistic movements and tendencies, did not seem to distract them from their own goals even for a moment.

In Paris, Varvoglēs got associated with a few of the most important figures of the art world, such as Modigliani, Saint-Saëns, Casella, Ravel, Varèse, and among others, the Greeks Riadēs, Skipēs and Jean Moréas. Jean Moréas (whose real name was Iōannēs Papadiamantopoulos, 1856–1910) had a great impact on Varvoglēs; as Rōmanou points out,

> that "central" figure of Quartier Latin who attracted intellectuals and artists with his spirited *dicta* and his elegant speech and whose poetry – at the time that Varvoglēs made his acquaintance – was purely classic, full of nostalgia for Greece, is regarded to have been determinative for the composer's development, by the commentators of Varvoglēs' work. (Rōmanou [Ρωμανού] 1985: 20)[30]

In fact, it was Jean Moréas who kept Varvoglēs away from the nonconformist extremities of the various "Schools" of his time (Rōmanou [Ρωμανού] 1985: 2).

Return and permanent settlement to Athens

In 1920 Varvoglēs returns to Athens where he settles permanently. Right from the start he entered the Athenian artistic circles and knitted up friendships with many other composers and performers as well as writers and painters. From that period onwards and until the end of his life, Varvoglēs failed to be assigned to high posts due to his left wing ideology, despite the fact that he always enjoyed the deep respect and gratitude of the art world.[31] Particularly in the field of music education his contribution is inestimable, if one considers that most of the composers of the following generation had been Varvoglēs' students.

Compositional work

Varvoglēs' compositional work may not be extensive but it is valuable and solid, embracing elements of both the Greek tradition and the manner of the French composers of the second half of the 19th and the beginning of the 20th century. Yet, these elements are built in his work in a very personal way that intends to come across as very simple, and gives out a scent of impulsive inspiration.[32] As far as the works he composed while in Paris (1902–1920) are concerned, they show a deep influence by the aesthetics of the neoclassical perspective of Moreas' poems (Kalogeropoulos [Καλογερόπουλος], 1998: "Varvoglēs, Marios").

Apart from Varvoglēs, the city of Paris hosted another two important representatives of the Greek National Music School, Riadēs and Petridēs. All three composers studied in Paris at the beginning of the 20th century being lucky enough to be staying at the greatest, perhaps, intellectual centre of their times. In the early years of the 20th century Paris was the ultimate centre of the arts, hosting a number of musicians, dancers, painters, sculptors and engravers, from all over Europe and the US. As early as 1900, when the World Exhibition was taking place at the Grande Pallais with a great part of the exhibition being devoted to the arts, Paris had intrigued artists from all around Europe. Since then, and for the following twenty years, the city became a home for the various artistic movements and tendencies that emerged during the early years of the 20th century.

The emergence of modality in the works of French composers of the time – as the antipode to the vast chromaticism of the German School – that sprang up through their interaction with foreign cultures including the Greeks, and the so-called exoticism of French music, were practices that found common ground with the Greek composers' efforts to promote folk and traditional elements in their works; as a result, the Greek composers' work found a warm audience in French music halls, and that was the prime reason why their compositions were performed in the Parisian concert halls and published by French music editors. Of course, Greek composers were also influenced by French culture and music to a great extent; especially in the case of Varvoglēs, the influence of the French mélodie is particularly evident. What is also evident in their works, is impressionism, which by that time was in decline, and not, as one might have expected, the adoption of other, more up to date and innovative tendencies and movements of the times.

Varvoglēs' music writing often gets introspective and melancholic, creating a nostalgic mood; a number of motifs and phrases that originate from the Greek folk tradition are used in reoccurrence, while the overall structure is marvellously balanced and very articulated. The rich, sweet and gentle melodic lines of his works – especially the ones composed after 1930– are enhanced with harmonic chromaticism, extended use of contrasts and shifting of chords and intervals of unidentifiable relations to one another, an overall practice which, at times, touches upon the boundaries of atonality.

Lastly, it should be mentioned that Varvoglēs happened to be one of the first Greek composers who composed music for theatrical plays, and there were several occasions on which he collaborated with the National Theatre.[33]

Petros Petridēs

Biographical note

Petros Petridēs[34] was born in Nigdé, Kappadokia, in 1892 and died in Kifissia (Attica) in 1977. A man of vast knowledge on various fields of science and art, who is rightfully placed among the most cultivated and educated Greek composers of the first half of the 20th century; his assignment to numerous posts and offices abroad together with his long, creative and active presence certifies the extent to which he was valued. His music style is entirely original, characterised by many modern influences that are brought together with elements of the Greek tradition (like ancient modes, Greek rhythmic patterns, Byzantine echoi etc.).

Petridēs' childhood was not spent in his birthplace but in Constantinople (1899–1911), where he went to the Zōgrafeio Gymnasium and the American Robert College. From a very young age he was introduced to the art of music since his family was very fond of art, with both his older brothers being amateur musicians. Later on he took piano lessons in a more systematic way under the instruction of Hegey, until he went to Paris in October 1911, with the intention to study law in Sorbonne and political sciences at the Liberal School of Political Sciences.

The following year (1912) Petridēs returned to Greece in order to take part in the Balkan Wars as a volunteer of the Greek Army, and then, in 1913 he went back to Paris having – in the meantime – acquired Greek Citizenship. It was then that Petridēs decided to devote himself entirely to music, thereby quitting his other studies. Despite the few years of his apprenticeship with Albert Wolff (1914) and Albert Roussel (1919), for the biggest part Petridēs was self-taught. During the years 1915–1920 he worked as a correspondent in Paris for the foreign press, such as London's *Musical Times,* and Boston's *Christian Science Monitor,* while at the same time collaborated with numerous other Greek, French, English and American newspapers and magazines, in the domain of music as well as cultural issues, in general.[35] He had also been the head of the Greek Embassy's information office in London (1918–1919) giving, at the same time, lectures on the topic of Greek folklore and music at King's College, University of London. During the years 1919–1921 he was a lecturer of Modern Greek philology at Sorbonne (at the newly established department of the Neohellenist Hubert Pernot). However, after 1922 he would split his time between Paris and Athens. Occasionally he worked as a music critic, collaborating for longer periods of time with the Greek newspapers *Eleuthero Vēma* [Free Tribune] (1922–1925), *Prōïa* [Morning] (1934–1936), *Hē Kathēmerinē* [The Daily] (1939–1941), *To Vēma* [The Tribune] (1955–1957) etc. He worked for many European festivals and international music symposia and competitions. In 1958 he was elected as a corresponding member of the French Academy of Fine Arts (his predecessor was the great Jean Sibelius). In 1959 he was elected as a regular member of the Academy of Athens (Kalogeropoulos [Καλογερόπουλος] 1998: "Petridēs Petros").

Compositional work

Petridēs regarded himself as a self-taught composer, although he did receive a series of lessons from eminent musicians. His overall view of the systematic apprenticeship of music at a conservatoire or privately – which proved determinative for his further course – was that the only benefit this may have is to facilitate the ordering of his music material and to be taught a methodical way to go through that material. From that moment onwards what takes over is each composer's talent and imagination in the way he will manipulate his material so to create subtle and inspired works. Petridēs's own style was a very idiomatic one, characterised by counterpoint, polytonality and polymodality, which offer a sense of homogeneity to the totality of his work.

The most important part of his compositional writing is located between the years 1921–1977, as his early works (mostly songs) did not foretell his future compositional course. The symphonic idiom that Petridēs developed during the early years of his major music creation met its best expression in the *Greek Suite* (1929). This work reveals the technical perfection of a mature composer, who wisely reserves the potentials of a big orchestra avoiding any idle, grandiose manifestations. If we were to compare his music idiosyncrasy with that of the rest of the composers of the National School we would find that it bears the characteristics of a more rational and intellectual style of music writing: a kind of writing that is characterised by the economy of the music material, the solid and distinct structuring of each work as well as the homogeneity of music language, yet without depriving the overall work of musicality or sensitivity. In Petridēs' music, the impressionistic style of the French composers meets the spirit of Baroque and Greek music traditions. The composer's creativity is betaken by a great sense of morphological unity which is never disturbed despite the variety of images in his orchestral and instrumental works. The multi-coloured character of his orchestrations, the mannerism of counterpoint and the contrasting themes and motifs do not affect the solid and grandiose architectural structure of his work.

From 1932 Petridēs moves towards a "rationalist codification of modal scales" while in the years that followed he also experimented with Byzantine chant: a fact that is evident in both the work *Byzantine Sacrifice* and the oratorio *Saint Paul*. Naturally, the use of elements from the Greek Byzantine and traditional music could not but be channelled through the various techniques and structures of European polyphony. Besides, no other composer belonging to the Greek National School had studied the Byzantine echoi to that extent and with such thoroughness as Petridēs had. That is a fact that enabled him to use these echoi extensively in his works, especially the works that belong to religious genres, wherein the dominance of the *isokratema* (the pedal tone, characteristically evident during the narrator's recitation in *Saint Paul*) and the Byzantine echoi is unexceptionable. It was through this practice that Petridēs successfully managed to bring together the heterogeneous elements of western polyphony with those of the Greek music tradition. In fact, at times, he harmonises the selfsame Byzantine chants according to the western compositional techniques, thereby driving the work towards a forceful climax and creating immense tension.

Among other composers of the National School mentioned earlier, Petridēs is the only one to have composed oratorios. He showed great commitment to that genre, and created works of great value. Through his religious works in particular, one may see reflections of the composer's personality; an artist who, through his devoutness and dynamism, manages to communicate to his audience the grandiose idea that lies within his works. This communication is not achieved through the deployment of pompous music manifestations but rather through the deep understanding of the impact that given music events are bound to have upon the listener (Dounias [Δούνιας] 1951).

Although musicologists have failed to look closely into Petridēs work up to the present day, it seems that, in his day, his works were actually being performed abroad – a pleasure that very few Greek composers seemed to have enjoyed. According to the most important music critic of the times, Minōs Dounias, who also happened to be best informed in the cultural issues outside the Greek borders,

> Currently, no one has an insight of the Greek production, not even the composers themselves were given the chance to listen to a performance of their own works, except Petridēs who is known and whose works are performed in the big centres. (Dounias [Δούνιας] 1937)

Petridēs' compositional activity expands around most music forms. As far as his orchestral and instrumental work is concerned – and most particularly his symphonies – he seems to be developing his music in enviable clarity, often driven by the main theme, which in most cases he frames with a second theme, without the usual long-winded, void tone-colour quests and dashing climaxes to which his colleagues often resorted. Nor was he ever interested in submitting to the spirit of the times that demanded an extended use of folklore material in music: he was not after the audience's approval. What drove him instead was correspondence with a deep, inherent, rather strict, philosophised, intellectual and often-intrinsic world, which usually makes his works inapproachable (Dounias [Δούνιας] 1945). This, however, never seems to undermine the Greek character that derives from his works, and aids the existence of traditional and Byzantine modes as much as the tone of his music, which always sounds familiar in its totality, despite any deviations – such as the use of bitonality or other 'hints' of modern techniques – from those manners that theoretically lie closer to the Greek tradition.

Notes

1. Also written: Manolis Kalomoiris or Kalomiris.
2. One of the most distinguishing characteristics of a National Music School – besides the use of a nation's folk tradition is the use of language, one of the most crucial bonds of unification within a nation. Therefore, music nationalism finds its expressional means first and foremost in opera, which offers the composer the possibility to combine music with words on a two-level basis; firstly, by enabling him to refer to tradition on a foreground level and at the same time making use of vocal or orchestral forms that are based on the interaction between music and speech, this time without the element of scenic action. Besides that, opera, especially in the National Schools of the 19th century, functioned as the starting point of their creation. It is also very common to find extra-musical motives with references to historical and socio-political events, in the works of composers of National Schools. However, it did not take long for National Schools to break out of the narrow operatic boundaries in order to compose works that would derive from the whole repertoire of art music.

3. He was the General Inspector of Military Musicians [(1918–1920) and (1922–1937)], principal of the Hellenic Conservatoire (1919–1926), principal and founder of the National Conservatoire (1926–1948, but remained an honorary chairman until his death), permanent music reviewer for *Ethnos*, a Greek newspaper (1926–1958), founder of the Melodramatic Society (1933–1935), president of the Greek Composers' Union (1936–1945), general principle (1944–1945) and president (1950–1952) of the managerial Council of the National Lyric Theatre, member of the Athens's Academy since 1945, vice-president of the Management Supreme Council of Music, president of the Greek Composers, Writers and Editors' Association (1947). Moreover, he received the National Prize of Literature and Arts as well as many more Greek and foreign distinctions.

4. Thus is called in Greece the extinction of all Greek communities of Asia Minor.

5. See also, Oikonomidou [Οικονομίδου] 2005.

6. The poets born a decade after Palamas were gradually isolated from the main stream of 20th century poetic matters that tended to follow the general rules of symbolism. That generation of poets instantly connotes the failure of the realisation of the "Great Idea", despite the fact that most of them had formed their themes and technique long before the year 1922. The new course that poetry of that generation seems to take suggests a sentiment of indifference towards the "Great Idea", a fact that is evident in Palamas' works of 1910 onwards, even before the military defeat and the upset of the Greek's expansive plans.

7. During those years in Vienna the dominant genre that proved to be the most popular happened to be opera. Most of the operatic repertoire was based on the Wagnerian operas, while of equal popularity were the operas of Mozart, Richard Strauss, Verdi and Meyerbeer. The next most popular genres were symphonies and concertos. Being exposed to the works of the composers of the Viennese School (Haydn, Mozart, Beethoven) and those of the following Romantic era like Schubert, Wagner, Brahms, Bruckner but also Reger, Mahler and Richard Strauss, Kalomoirēs got the chance to feel the pulse of German culture (Bolstein 2001).

8. The fact that the majority of foreign poetry used in Kalomoirēs' compositional work is taken from the works of French poets is not incidental. The musicologist Giõrgos Vlastos draws out attention to this matter: "[…] *The First Balade* (1905) for piano is inspired by Victor Hugo's poem *En Mer, les Hardis Écumeuns,* belonging to *Les Orientales.* While in the third part of Kalomoirēs' *Symphony of the Ignorant and Good People* (1925–1931) he borrows the poetry of Jean Richepin translated by Zacharias Papantōniou and, finally, the opera *Fairy Waters* (1950) is based on Veta Pezopoulou's paraphrase of William Butler Yeats' homonymous poem. It is worth mentioning that this Irish writer, whose dreamy world and overwhelming authenticity may easily connote the French symbolist poets of the end of the 19th century, was to become – along with a number of other English-speaking poets – one of the most dominant, influential figures of the French impressionism. Besides, the fact that Kalomoirēs first listened to Yeats' poem while in Paris, in 1926, is not circumstantial. Another thing that needs to be highlighted is that Kalomoirēs' inspiration for the creation of the ballet *The Death of the Valiant Woman* (1943) derived from the true story of Simone Seailles, the heroine that fought against the Germans during World War II" (Vlastos [Βλαστός] 2002).

9. More information about Kalomoirēs' elaboration on demotic melodic themes in: Maliaras 2001: 10–31.

10. Typed unpublished text, which is treasured in the archives of Manōlēs Kalomoirēs's Society – with the writer's kind assignment (Leōtsakos [Λεωτσάκος] no date: 7).

11. Leōtsakos notes: "one immediately realizes the extent to which poetry bridles Kalomoirēs' tendency to expand in his instrumental works. It is as if, when left without the aid of poetic

speech, he wants to expand in order to say – through pitch and timbre – what he subconsciously feels that only poetry may express" (Leōtsakos [Λεωτσάκος] no date).

12. See also Little 1978: 87–121.

13. See, "Sonata for Violin and Piano", "Trio for Piano, Violin and Cello", *Quartet quasi Fantasia, Quintet with Song, Symphony of Bravery*, etc.

14. Also written: Emilios Riadis.

15. For a biographic note of Riadēs see, "Ριάδης Αιμίλιος" ["Riadēs Aemilios"] in: Kalogeropoulos [Καλογερόπουλος] 1998.

16. See also Leōtsakos [Λεωτσάκος] 1992a: 7–15. The author clames that the name "Eleutheriadēs" is his mother's family name, which was then abbreviated to "Riadēs".

17. Before falling in the hands of Turks in 1430, Thessalonica had been at its greatest peak culturally. This long cultural tradition, enhanced by the regenerating spirit of the Palaeologian dynasty, celebrating human passion through art, glowed beyond the town's borders. In fact, Thessalonica transmitted the universal Byzantine art across the whole region of the Balkans. The monuments of unique splendour that lie within the town depict its status as the leading cultural centre of the times.

18. By the beginning of the 20th century a few musicians had already established their names, like Tiberio, who was the organ player of the Catholic Church, Markezini, who was the Church's violinist and the pianist Errikos Orpi. See Kalogeropoulos [Καλογερόπουλος] 1998: "Θεσσαλονίκης, περιληπτική μουσική παρουσίαση" ["Thessalonica's Brief Music Presentation"].

19. The *Apollon Society* had already formed a wind orchestra that gave performances and sold tickets possibly as its contribution to the Macedonian Struggle. (See Leōtsakos [Λεωτσάκος] 1992: 227–228). Moreover, Motsenigos mentions that, during the Turkish occupation, the wind orchestra of the Israeli organisation "Maccabi", by Greek civilians, as well as the Israeli wind orchestra "Alliance", were founded in Thessalonica (Motsenigos [Μοτσενίγος] 1958: 284).

20. One of the first choirs to be founded was in the Michaēl Hatzēmichalēs' Mandolinata (1915, the Mandolinata of Thessalonica), joined by Greek and Jewish workers who used to sing the labour songs of the time. The Mandolinata was a complete conservatoire that maintained theory, mandolin, violin, piano and choir classes with Michaēl Hatzēmichalēs on the lead. The conservatoire's choir often took part in concerts within the city of Thessalonica as well as the Macedonian outskirts. Together with the orchestra of the White Tower, which functioned as the seed-bed for the later founding of the public orchestra (1919), these two ensembles paid great contribution to the city's music life.

21. Literature, around the 1930s, was the dominant genre for the literate figures, who were mainly connected to the magazine *Macedonikes Hēmeres* [Macedonian Days]. However, after the war they sought to expand their work in new directions, leaving their former preoccupation with the peculiarity of their own city behind. Thus they redefined their literate identity through the adoption of specific ideological aesthetic and political tendencies of the time. This new orientation left its mark on the development of Greek Literature, through their authentic, often subversive and provoking interference.

22. Dēmētrios Lallas' presence played a significant role in the music life of the city. He had studied music at various European cities. The most important one proved to be Bayreuth, where Lallas studied as Wagner's apprentice. He settled permanently in Thessalonica in 1881, where he taught singing at the Supreme Girls' School, while giving private piano lessons to the children of wealthy families and conducting the orchestras and choirs of cultural associations (Music Lovers, Orpheus, and Apollo) concurrently.

23. Quoting Merakou, in Riadēs' archive in the Music Library of Greece "Lilian Voudouri", "there is also a rough sketch of an opera, entitled *Tutahoroa, Sentier des âmes pour la nuit eternelle*, en

quatre actes, Paroles et musique, d' Aemilian Reiadis". As Merakou notes, "it takes place at the edge of Australia, near the island Tararao of Polynesia, at a time when the (feathered) Toupapahou still wandered among the living".

24. The Neo-Turks was a National Liberal Movement inspired by the French Revolution that attempted to overturn the outworn state system held responsible for Turkey's decadence. It should have been a revival of Turkish patriotism, under new disguise; it was quite chauvinist but also passed for a movement of great liberty, supposedly promoting a kind of scepticism that was actually congruent to the severe dogma and practice of Islam. Despite their persecution by the authorities, the Neo-Turks had such a great appeal, mainly to the big rural centres, like Constantinople and Thessalonica, that they even attracted students and young officers. The movement expanded day by day in high secrecy. Eventually, when the revolution broke out in July 1908, under the Neo-Turks' methodical planning, it completely took the Turkish authorities by surprise (Ristelhueber 2003: 272–275; Castellan [Καστελλάν] 1991: 504–513).

25. Speranza Calo was the pseudonym of the Greek singer Elpis Calogeropoulou.

26. In his biographies Riadès is said to have attended the classes of Maurice Ravel, Gustave Charpentier and Claude Debussy. However, it seems that this information is invalid and came from the articles of his friend, Kōnstantinos Karatzidès at the Macedonian Press (Karatzidès [Καρατζίδης] 1937: 169–176).

27. In the same text Leōtsakos mentions that so far the document which proves Riadès' appointment to that post has not been found.

28. The most recently updated catalogue of Riadès' works is in: Diamantopoulou-Cornejo 2001: II/753–777.

29. Also written Mario Varvogli or Varvoglis.

30. The writer also provides a text by Sophia Spanoudē in Prōïa [Morning] of 19 June 1931, where she cites: "Marios Varvoglēs had a special aesthetic view in his music. His Greek Inspiration is characterised by a frugality of expression, a music lyricism that is gentle and melancholic [...]. This Atticism of style that is evident in the works of this young Greek composer remained unaffected all those years in Paris, when Varvoglēs moved around the most revolting artistic circles [...]. Within this blurry atmosphere of influences of every kind, Varvoglēs always kept the clarity and lucidness of Greek nature's lines. In that sense, the way Jean Moréas – the maitre of the artistic circles to which Varvoglēs also belonged – influenced the composer proved more than beneficiary [...] The Greek poet [...] communicated, through his own work, 'wise simplicity' and the grand art, which constitutes one of the fundamental dogmas of his School".

31. Characteristically, in 1945, he got arrested and was kept imprisoned at an English camp as a result of being friends with Varnalēs and Augerēs... A lot later, a time when circumstances allowed it he was nominated for the Cross of Palm as a tribute to his significant contribution to the Greek culture and especially to the field of music (1965). Before that he had been nominated with the National Distinction of Arts and Letters (1923) and in 1937 with the music award "Takēs Kandyloros Award" of the Arts' Academy.

32. Some of his works exist in two or three versions, for various sets of instruments. It is possible that, given the lack of potential for the arrangement of a larger set of instruments, he was often forced to transcribe his works for smaller sets, in order to hear them performed.

33. See a catalogue of his works in: Kentrōtēs [Κεντρωτής] 1998.

34. Also written: Petridis.

35. In 1916 he publishes in the Hesperia newspaper a number of articles where he analyses his views on Greek music. For a re-publication of those articles, see Fidetzēs [Φιδετζής] 1989: 119–146, 152–163.

References

[Anōgeianakēs] Ανωγειανάκης, Φ., *Κατάλογος Έργων Μανώλη Καλομοίρη, 1883–1962* [Catalogue of the Works of Manōlēs Kalomoirēs, 1883–1962], Athens, Ίκαρος, 1964.

[Belōnēs] Μπελώνης, Γ., *Η Μουσική Δωματίου του Μανώλη Καλομοίρη* [Manōlēs Kalomoirēs chamber music], unpublished Ph.D. dissertation submitted to the Music Department of the National University of Athens, 2003.

——, "Ισορροπώντας ανάμεσα σε Αριστερά και Δεξιά" [Balancing between the Left and the Right], in newspaper *Η Καθημερινή*, 6 July 2005.

Bolstein, L. 2001. "Vienna, §5 (iii)" in *The New Grove Dictionary of Music and Musicians* 26, London, Macmillan Publishers, 2001, pp. 566–572.

[Castellan] Καστελλάν, Ζ., *Η Ιστορία των Βαλκανίων* [The history of the Balkans], trans., Βασιλική Αλιφέρη, Athens, Γκοβόστη, 1991.

[Dēmētriadou-Karayiannidou] Δημητριάδου-Καραγιαννίδου, Μ., *Αιμίλιος Ριάδης-Η ζωή και το έργο του* [Aimilios Riadēs- his Life and Work], Unpublished thesis submitted to the Music Department of the Aristotle University of Thessalonica, 1990.

[Dēmētriou] Δημητρίου, Ν., *Καταγραφή του μουσικού αρχείου του Αιμίλιου Ριάδη στο Κρατικό Ωδείο Θεσσαλονίκης* [Recording of Aimilios Riadēs's Music Archive at the State Conservatoire of Thessalonica], unpublished thesis submitted to the Music Department of the Aristotle University of Thessalonica, 2002.

Diamantopoulou-Cornejo, D., *Les mélodies pour une voix et piano d'Emile Riadēs: Aspects esthétiques entre les musique française et grecque au début du XXe siècle*, Université François Rabelais, Tours, ANRT, 2001.

[Dounias] Δούνιας, Μ., "Από τις συναυλίες" [From the Concerts], in newspaper *Νεοελληνικά Γράμματα* [Neohellenic Letters], 11 December 1937.

——, "Η Συμφωνική. Έργο Π. Πετρίδη", [The Symphonic Orchestra. Work by P. Petridēs], in newspaper *Η Καθημερινή*, 15 December 1945.

——, "Πέτρου Πετρίδη: Ορατόριον *Άγιος Παύλος*" [Petros Petridēs: *Saint Paul* Oratorio], in newspaper *Η Καθημερινή*, 6 July 1951.

[Fidetzēs] Φιδετζής, Β., "Πετρίδης: Κείμενα για την Ελληνική μουσική στην εφημ. *Εσπερία*. Τα πρώτα (;) κείμενα", [Petros Petridēs: Texts on Greek Music in the *Hesperia* newspaper. The first (?) texts] *Μουσικολογία*, 7–8, 1989, pp. 119–168.

[Foulias] Φούλιας, Ι., "'Αντίς για Όνειρο'. Απόπειρα αποκατάστασης και κατανόησης ψηφίδων της Έντεχνης Νεοελληνικής Μουσικής" [Instead of a Dream. An attempt to restore and apprehend the mosaic of Greek Art Music], *Πολυφωνία*, 7, 2005, pp. 93–146.

[Frangou-Psychopaedē] Φράγκου-Ψυχοπαίδη, Ο., "Πολιτισμικές Σχέσεις Γαλλίας και Ελλάδας στη Σύγχρονη Ελληνική Ιστορία της Μουσικής" [Cultural Relations between France and Greece in Recent History of Greek Music], *Μουσικολογία*, 5–6, 1988, pp. 43–54.

——, *Η Εθνική Σχολή Μουσικής-Προβλήματα Ιδεολογίας* [The National School of Music-Ideology Problems], Athens, Ίδρυμα Μεσογειακών Μελετών, 1990.

——, "Μουσική και Πολιτική στην Ελλάδα" [Music and Politics in Greece], in newspaper *Η Καθημερινή*, 13 January 2002.

[Kalogeropoulos] Καλογερόπουλος, Τ., *Το Λεξικό της Ελληνικής Μουσικής: Από τον Ορφέα έως Σήμερα* [Dictionary of Greek Music: From Orpheus till today], Athens, Γιαλλελής, 1998.

[Kalomoirēs] Καλομοίρης, Μ., *Το Δακτυλίδι της Μάνας* (πρόλογος) [The Mother's Ring (introduction)], Athens, Γαϊτάνος, 1928.

——, "Το Λαϊκό Μοτίβο στη Μουσική Δημιουργία ΙΙ" [The Folk Motif in Music Creation II], *Μουσική Ζωή*, 2: 1, 1931, p. 2.

——, "Η Νέα Τεχνοτροπία στην Διεθνή Συνθετική και η Ελληνική Μουσική Δημιουργία" [The New Technique in the International Compositional Practice and The Greek Music Creation], *Πρακτικά Ακαδημίας Αθηνών* [Proceedings of the Academy of Athens], 29, 1953, pp. 549–559.

——, "Γύρω από την *Ανατολή*" [About *East*], in *Ανατολή* [East], Athens, Έκδοση των φίλων της Ελληνικής Μουσικής, 1954, pp. V–VII.

——, *Η Ζωή μου και η Τέχνη μου* [My Life and Art], Athens, Νεφέλη, 1988.

[Karatzidēs] Καρατζίδης, Μ. Κ., "Ο Εκλιπών Καλλιτέχνης Αιμίλιος Ριάδης, In Memoriam" [The Extinct Artist Aemilios Riadēs, In Memoriam], in *Μακεδονικό Ημερολόγιο* [Macedonian Diary], Thessalonica, 1937, pp. 169–176.

[Kambourē-Vamvoukou] Καμπούρη-Βαμβούκου, Μ., "Μεταβυζαντινή Αρχιτεκτονική" [Post-Byzantine Architecture], in *7 Ημέρες: Θεσσαλονίκη* [7 Days: Thessalonica], 22, Athens, *Η Καθημερινή*, 1997, pp. 10–13.

[Kentrōtēs] Κεντρωτής, Κ., *Θεματικός Κατάλογος Έργων Μάριου Βάρβογλη* [Thematic Catalogue of the Works of Marios Varvoglēs], unpublished thesis submitted to the Music Department of the Aristotle University of Thessalonica, 1998.

[Kounenakē] Κουνενάκη, Π., "Λογοτέχνες της Θεσσαλονίκης" [Literature Figures of Thessalonica], in *7 Ημέρες: Θεσσαλονίκη* [7 Days: Thessalonica], 22, Athens, *Η Καθημερινή*, 1997, pp. 96–97.

[Leōtsakos] Λεωτσάκος, Γ., "Το ύφος του Καλομοίρη" [Kalomoirēs' Style], unpublished text kept in Kalomoirēs' Archives, n.d.

——, "Αιμίλιος Ριάδης (1880–1935): Πορτρέτο για Εγκυκλοπαίδεια" [Aemilios Riadēs (1880–1935): Portrait for an Encyclopaedia], *Παρατηρητής*, 6–7, 1988, pp. 147–151.

——, "Δημήτριος Λάλλας. Ο Μακεδόνας μαθητής και οικείος του Ρίχαρντ Βάγκνερ (1844–1911)" [Dēmētrios Lallas. The Macedonian student and friend of Richard Wagner (1844–1911)], in *Ο Βάγκνερ και η Ελλάδα* [Wagner and Greece], Athens, Μέγαρο Μουσικής Αθηνών/ Μορφωτικό Ίδρυμα Εθνικής Τραπέζης, 1992, pp. 208–245.

——, "Αιμίλιος Ριάδης (1880–1935)" [Aemilios Riadēs (1880–1935)], notes in the Cd *Αιμίλιου Ριάδη Έργα I* [Aemilios Riadēs Works I], Athens, Lyra, 1992a.

——, "Αιμίλιος Ριάδης, το μισοτελειωμένο όραμα: προβλήματα διάδοσής του" [Aemilios Riadēs, the unfinished vision: problems of its spreading], in *Επιστημονική Επετηρίδα του Κέντρου Ιστορίας Θεσσαλονίκης του Δήμου Θεσσαλονίκης* [Scientific Yearbook of Thessalonica's History Centre of the Municipality of Thessalonica] IV, Thessalonica, Κέντρο Ιστορίας Θεσσαλονίκης, 1994.

Little, S. Bl., *The Symphonies of Manolis Kalomiris*, unpublished thesis, Southwest Baptist University, 1978.

[Maliaras] Μαλιάρας, Ν., *Το Ελληνικό Δημοτικό Τραγούδι στη Μουσική του Μανώλη Καλομοίρη* [The Greek Demotic Song in the Music of Manōlēs Kalomoirēs], Athens, Παπαγρηγορίου Νάκας, 2001.

——, "Ελληνική Εθνική Σχολή" [Greek National School], in newspaper *Η Καθημερινή*, 23 March, 2003.

[Merakou] Μεράκου, Στ., "Αρχείο Αιμίλιου Ριάδη" [Aemilios Riadēs Archive], Text in the official site of the Music Library of Greece "Lilian Voudouri": www.mmb.org.gr/notebook/col/Riadēs/ Riadēs_gr.htm

Merlier, O., "Prologue" (non paginated and untitled) in *Emile Riadis, Liturgie de Saint Jean Chrysostome et autres compositions religieuses pour choeur*, Athènes, Collection de l'Institut Français d'Athènes 5, 1952.

[Motsenigos] Μοτσενίγος, Σπ. Γ., *Νεοελληνική Μουσική* [Modern Greek Music], Athens, 1958.

[Oikonomidou] Οικονομίδου, Μ., "Η Πολύπλευρη Κληρονομιά" [The Multilateral Legacy], in newspaper *Η Καθημερινή,* 15 May 2005.

Ristelhueber, R., *Ιστορία των Βαλκανικών Λαών* [History of the Balkan People], trans., Αναστασία Μεθανίτη & Αθαν.Δ. Στεφανής, Athens, Παπαδήμα, 2003.

[Rōmanou] Ρωμανού, Κ., "Μάριος Βάρβογλης (1885–1967)" [Marios Varvoglēs (1885–1967)], *Μουσικολογία,* 2, 1985, pp.13–47.

——-, *Έντεχνη Ελληνική Μουσική στους Νεότερους Χρόνους* [Greek Art Music in Modern Times], Athens, Κουλτούρα, 2006.

[Symeōnidou] Συμεωνίδου, Α., *Λεξικό Ελλήνων Συνθετών Βιογραφικό – Εργογραφικό.* [Dictionary of Greek Composers], Athens, Φίλιππος Νάκας, 1995.

[Themelēs] Θέμελης, Δ., "Η μουσική ζωή στη νεώτερη και σύγχρονη Θεσσαλονίκη" [Music life in recent and contemporary Thessalonica], in Τοις αγαθοίς βασιλεύουσα Θεσσαλονίκη Ιστορία και Πολιτισμός [Thessalonica, the queen of the good. History and civilisation], Thessalonica, Παρατηρητής, 1997, pp. 138–159.

[Tomanas] Τομανάς, Κ., Η καλλιτεχνική κίνηση στην Θεσσαλονίκη [Artistic life in Thessalonica], Thessalonica, Νησίδες, 1996.

[Tsalachourēs] Τσαλαχούρης, Φ., *Νέος Κατάλογος έργων. Μανώλης Καλομοίρης 1883–1962* [New Catalogue of Works. Manōlēs Kalomoirēs 1883–1962], Athens, Σύλλογος "Μανώλης Καλομοίρης", 2003.

Vitti, M., Ιστορία της Νεοελληνικής Λογοτεχνίας [History of Modern Greek Literature], Athens, Οδυσσέας, 1994.

[Vlastos, G.] Βλαστός, Γ., "Μια σκιαγράφηση των σχέσεων του Μανώλη Καλομοίρη με την Γαλλία και τη γαλλική μουσική" [A sketch of Manōlēs Kalomoirēs' relations with France and French music], unpublished paper delivered at the conference *Manōlēs Kalomoirēs 40 years later,* hosted at Megaron-Athens Music Hall, in Athens, 5–7 April, 2002.

[Vorazakē-Arzimanoglou] Βοραζάκη–Αρζιμανόγλου, Έ., "Μάριος Βάρβογλης" [Marios Varvoglēs], *Επετηρίς Ιδρύματος Νεοελληνικών Σπουδών* [Calendar of the Foundation of Modern Greek Studies] II, Athens, 1982, pp. 209–222.

Chapter 8

Nikos Skalkottas

Katy Romanou

"Anyone who was my student became aware of the seriousness and morality of the mission of the artist; this awareness will, under any circumstances of life, bring him honor if he is able to remain true to it!" Arnold Schoenberg

Nikos Skalkottas (1904–1949) is recognised today as one of the most talented and original among Schoenberg's Berlin students and as the most important Greek composer of the first half of the 20th century.

Nikos Skalkottas belongs to the generation "buried" by the Third Reich. Although his is not exactly a case of what has been called the *lost generation*, he was a victim of the destruction of the artistic and spiritual environment he grew up in and of the forced proscription of the music he was accustomed to and which would have dominated the music scene in Europe and influenced, naturally, minor centres of western music like Athens.

His posthumous reputation, connected to the introduction of avant-garde music to Greece during Cold War cultural antagonism, begun at the end of the 1950s and was initially strongly influenced by politically motivated aesthetics.

Political circumstances as well as the stylistic pluralism of his compositions and the disorder of his documents contribute to many contrasting but persuasive presentations of his life, his character and his ideas, as well as of the reception of his work during his life in Germany and in Greece. Although the substantial quality of his music has been rapidly gaining appreciation in recent years,[1] his personality, many biographical facts and the causes behind them are much less likely to be understood. The scarcity of documents is a main reason.

Skalkottas' texts are relatively few. They consist of (1) various writings and (2) letters to friends.

(1) Among the "various writings", a small percentage was published in the monthly periodical *Musikē Zōē* [Musical Life] (Athens 1930–1931) in 1931; these are one article entitled 'Music Criticism' and five texts he sent to the periodical as a Berlin correspondent.[2]

A much larger body of texts was unpublished during his life (except for one, undated) and is kept in the Skalkottas Archive in autographed manuscripts. These are: twenty-two manuscripts (three to ten pages long) on technical or aesthetic subjects concerning music; a 166 page study entitled "The technique of orchestration"; nine analyses or forewords to his own works; and thirty-two analyses of folk songs he transcribed collaborating with the Melpo Merlier Archive.[3]

(2) His letters to friends are not kept in the composer's archives; most circulate as photocopies. The greatest bulk consists of his correspondence to Nellē Askētopoulou (31 letters)[4] and to Manōlēs Benakēs (55 letters). The former was a violinist who studied in the Athens Conservatory and then in Brussels. In Athens she was married to a wealthy man (Evelpidēs) and organised chamber concerts at her home. The latter was the son of a very wealthy Greek family who financed Skalkottas studies when his official scholarship ended. The existence of the corpus of Skalkottas correspondence with Benakēs was publicised for the first time in 12 November 1999 by John Thornley at a Nikos Skalkottas Symposium, organised by the Department of Music of the University of Athens.[5]

His life

Nikos Skalkottas was born in Chalkis, a small provincial town on the island of Euboea. His talent was recognised early by his musical father and uncle (members of the town's Philharmonic Society) and the family moved to the capital (in 1906 or 1910), where the child was able to study the violin at the Athens Conservatory.[6] He matriculated into Tony Schulze's second-level[7] violin class in 1914. In 1917 he entered the final stage of violin performance and participated in the student orchestra that was directed by Armand Marsick.[8] Skalkottas graduated in 1920, at the age of sixteen, receiving the highest prize of the institution as well as a scholarship to continue violin studies in Berlin.[9] He studied at the Berliner Musikhochschule with Willy Hess from October 1921 to June 1924.[10] Although a brilliant violinist, he terminated his studies before graduation, having been already involved and much attracted to composition. According to some sources (including a letter he had sent to Willy Hess on 13 June 1923)[11], he suffered from tendonitis of his left hand. It is possible, though, that this could have been an excuse he gave to his teacher. However, in a short biography published and signed by Octave Merlier, who almost certainly was informed by the composer, it is said that Willy Hess "engaged him to compose" ("l'engage à composer").[12] Most probably, Skalkottas did not plan to abandon the violin in order to become a composer (which indeed he never did). In two letters to Nellē Askētopoulou he expresses both an antipathy to specialisation and the wish to become both an orchestra violinist and a composer.[13] He wished to be broadly educated in cultural subjects and worked with vivacity to that end. Regarding music, he listened to many performances in the city and played on the piano whatever attracted his interest together with Yannēs Cōnstantinidēs, a Greek friend living near him in Lankwitz, a Berlin suburb where a number of Greeks lived. According to Cōnstantinidēs, Skalkottas was at the time playing the piano more often than the violin and had acquired an exceptional technique on that instrument. They played together symphonic works by Mahler, R. Strauss, Debussy, Ravel, Russia's Five and others.[14] Skalkottas studied the prerequisites for a composition course with Paul Juon, Robert Kahn[15] and Kurt Weill, and, in 1925–1927, he became a student of Philipp Jarnach.[16] Then, in November 1927, he was accepted by Arnold Schoenberg to his master class,[17] where he was an official student

Nikos Skalkottas in Berlin (1927).

up to June 1930. Although his fees were paid by the Academy, his expenses increased in 1927 when he became the father of twins (with his fellow violin student, the Latvian Matla Temko).[18] When his scholarship ended, Skalkottas managed, with the help of one of his Greek friends in Berlin, the pianist Spyros Farandatos, to get a regular (though, decreasing) monthly aid from Manōlēs Benakēs.[19] This aid lasted from 1928 to 1931; it enabled Skalkottas to move from Lankwitz to central Berlin and stop playing music at clubs and cinemas, as Benakēs had urged him to do.

In the Academy, Skalkottas was considered, by both Schoenberg and his fellow students, to be a promising composer.[20] We know of the following concerts for the master class students where his works were performed:[21]

On 19 June 1929 Skalkottas' two first Sonatinas for violin and piano and the 1st String Quartet were performed, together with works by Norbert von Hannenheim, Peter Schacht, Joseph Zmigrod and Alfred Keller.

On 20 May 1930, in the hall of the Singakademie, a concert of the master class students was performed by the Berlin Symphony Orchestra. The programme consisted of a *Serenade* by Winfried Zillig, a symphony by Norbert von Hannenheim and Skalkottas' *Concerto for Wind Instruments*. Skalkottas directed the two latter works.[22]

On 2 June 1931, a master class concert presented works by Erich Schmid, Natalie Prawossudowitsch, Norbert von Hannenheim, Peter Schacht and Skalkottas' *Octet* for four woodwinds and four strings, under the direction of Erich Schmid.

Moreover, in a concert sponsored by the Greek embassy on 6 April 1930, Skalkottas' Concerto no. 1 for violin and piano was performed together with his *Little Suite* for violin and orchestra under the direction of K. Mengelberg. The pianist was Polyxenē Mathéy-Roussopoulou and the violinist Anatol Knorre.[23]

On 21 January 1931, in a concert transmitted through the radio, Theodor W. Adorno presented his analysis of, among other pieces, Schoenberg's Lieder op. 6, Zilligs *Serenade* and Skalkottas' *Little Suite* for violin and orchestra.

The Athenian periodical *Musikē Zōē*, that promoted both contemporary music in general and Skalkottas in particular during the greater part of its short circulation (October 1930–October 1931) and whose pages were the first ever to host an edition of a Skalkottas' work,[24] informs on the performance of Skalkottas' first two quartets in Berlin on 21 May 1931.[25]

Skalkottas was also entrusted by Schoenberg with the rehearsals of three of his works: *Erwartung* (conducted by Zemlinsky on 7 June 1930 in Berlin's Krolloper), *Gurrelieder* (conducted by Schrecker in Berlin's Singakademie on 15 June 1931), *Von Heute auf Morgen* (presented in the Frankfurt Opera House on 1 February 1930, and, in another interpretation, transmitted by the Berlin Radio on 27 February).[26]

On 15 December 1931, in Schoenberg's absence,[27] Skalkottas accompanied on the piano the Greek singers Cōstas Mylōnas and Margarita Perra (engaged at Berlin's State Opera since 1927) in his own arrangements of four Greek folk songs. This was a Berlin Radio production presented by Curt Sachs and entitled "Greek Hour".

One of these arrangements, the folk song *Elafina*,[28] was published in Athens by Grēgorēs Cōnstantinidēs around 1939[29] and is the second of the three Skalkottas' works published during his lifetime. It is dedicated by Skalkottas to Margarita Perra.[30]

In August 1930, Skalkottas came to Athens. He went back to Berlin at the beginning of 1931 and stayed there – in contact with Schoenberg's master class – up until March 1933, when he returned to Athens, never to leave Greece again.[31]

The circumstances of both his 1930–1931 and his final trip to Athens are not yet absolutely clear. Most probably, the first trip was done at the anticipation of the termination of Benakēs' support; it is assumed that Skalkottas' aim was either to find another scholarship or to examine the possibilities of working in Athens.

During the first trip he presented himself as conductor and composer. On 23 November 1930 he conducted the Athens Conservatory Orchestra in a Sunday morning Popular Concert, featuring his own *Concerto for Wind Instruments* together with Schubert's Ninth Symphony,[32] Liszt's Second Piano Concerto, in A major (with Polyxene Mathéy-Roussopoulou at the piano) and Wagner's prelude to the *Mastersingers of Nuremberg*. On 27 November, an all-Skalkottas chamber music concert was given in the conservatory by its professors, Spyros Farandatos (piano), Frederikos Voloninēs and Vassilēs Skantzourakēs (violins), Nellē Askētopoulou (viola) and Achilleus Papadēmētriou (cello). They performed his *Easy Music for String Quartet*, his String Quartets nos 1 and 2, and his Sonatinas for violin and piano nos 1 and 2.

He got some indignant reviews for his compositions, to which he answered, on his return to Berlin, with a long, ironic article published with the news he sent to *Musikē Zōē*, for which he was acting as a Berlin correspondent.[33]

The periodical *Musikē Zōē* responded cordially to Skalkottas' trip to Athens in 1930–1931. Its director, the Ph.D. musicologist Cōnstantinos Oeconomou, a Guido Adler student,[34] expresses his admiration for contemporary modern trends and for Skalkottas at any opportunity. Starting from Issue 3 up to double Issue 9–10, every single issue mentions Skalkottas and contemporary trends in Europe.

The second movement of Skalkottas' Sonatina no. 1 for violin and piano (1929) is published in Volume 4 (31 January 1931, pp. 83–86) while his correspondence from Berlin, concerned mainly with contemporary composers, is published in every issue between Issue 5 and double Issue 9–10. In Issue 5, Stella Peppa publishes the first part of an article entitled "The Main Directions of Contemporary Music" where she speaks about expressionism, futurism, constructivism, neoclassicism, atonality, Busoni, Milhaud, Stravinsky and Schoenberg. She singles out the later as "the Titan reformer" and comments with pride on his Greek student, Skalkottas.

Skalkottas' article "Music Criticism" is published in Issue 6 (31 March 1931, pp. 124–126) together with his correspondence (pp. 138–139) and the second part of Peppa's article, which is about the influence of jazz on modern composers such as Stravinsky, K. Weill, Milhaud, Hindemith et al.

Without any notice or explanation, in Issue 13 (the first in the periodical's second year but also the final one of the periodical) C. Oeconomou is replaced by Stavros Prokopiou.[35]

Skalkottas' second trip to Athens is even less clear than the first. He was repatriated by the Greek Embassy, being in debt and unable to find work during this period of economic crisis. All his belongings and his works were left to his landlady, while his passport was confiscated by the Greek Foreign Ministry because Skalkottas had not served his military service.[36] Skalkottas also left behind his six-year-old daughter, who was in care in Berlin. The child's mother went to Sweden at the same time as Skalkottas.[37]

Roberto Gerhard told the pianist and conductor G. Chatzēnikos that Skalkottas was deeply depressed during the years 1931 to 1933 in Berlin.[38] This depression continued during the two first years in Athens. Possibly, among the causes of his depression were his relations with Matla Temko and Manōlēs Benakēs.[39]

Skalkottas' acclimatisation to Athens was painful; it would be correct to say that it never actually occurred.

He secluded himself in his parents' house during the first months of his arrival. In January 1934 he joined the Orchestra of the Athens Conservatory and later on the two other orchestras existing in Athens at the time (which shared, apart from Skalkottas, most of their members).

He did all sorts of jobs, such as copying music, arranging, harmonising; he also performed as a piano accompanist, even to violinists.[40]

From 15 June 1934 to 31 January 1935, Skalkottas worked for the project of the Melpo Merlier archive, i.e. the transcription of a large number of recorded folk music.[41] After that, Skalkottas completed his most popular *36 Greek Dances* for orchestra that he had begun in Berlin.

Skalkottas composed in Athens some commissions for friends who wished to help him. Polyxenē Mathéy-Roussopoulou and the choreographer Koula Pratsika, with whom she was collaborating in 1933, "tried" in the words of the former "to help him adapt to Greek reality".[42] On 9 June 1940, Mathéy's school performed in the Flower Festival for the National Youth Organisation of Ioannes Metaxas. The music (experts from Orff, J.J. Rousseau, Mozart, F. Mompou and Greek folk songs)[43] was rehearsed by Skalkottas at the piano. He was the conductor of a small ensemble at the performance. Five years later, Mathéy commissioned Skalkottas for an original dance suite, *The Land and the Sea of Greece*. This was orchestrated by Skalkottas in 1948 and separated; the "land" pieces forming the *Little Dance Suite – Four Dances for Ballet*, and the "sea" pieces incorporated in the ballet *The Sea* in 1949. He also wrote the ballets *The Elves* (1939) and *The Beauty with the Rose*[44] (1946) for performances by Koula Pratsika.

All this professional activity brought Skalkottas in contact with other artists in Athens and kept him occupied during daytime hours, but it was less important during his last years in Athens. During those years, Skalkottas composed the largest and most significant part of his oeuvre. When the day ended, he was on his own, penetrating into a wealth of music ideas, composing.

The absolute frustration Skalkottas felt at his return to Athens is a fact. However, to speak of a conspiracy of Athenian figures that blocked his recognition as a composer[45] is to ignore the facts about the composer, and about Athens and Berlin during these times.

Nikos Skalkottas, having left his small provincial city at the age of six, and his provincial country at seventeen, lived the most creative and the larger period of his life (1921–1933) in Berlin, in Arnold Schoenberg's circle, in the most progressive musical circle of a world-class music capital. With no strong inner resistance, his ideas, his knowledge, his taste, were formed in those years. The environment in which he lived during those years was, to his perception, the normal environment for a person to live in. Indeed, he writes in November 1935:

For me it would have been much better if I'd remained in Germany and carried on working with Schoenberg.[46] Here, in my humble opinion the time I spend working is wasted….I just can't get any further…In parting from the Schoenberg-pupils, from my friends, by coming back here, I have lost nearly everything that you could call the existence of a "normal" human being; it's very strange, abroad I found love and a normal life more natural, more a matter of course, than here – and almost with everyone, without exception! Here I'm afraid everything has been stolen from me, I've been properly robbed

– if not dirtied from head to foot, perhaps both. One doesn't see it so easily, so it's probably much filthier in reality than I can describe it to you.[47]

This letter, written in German, is important because it shows the ignorance that prevailed in Greece on the situation in Germany, even before the censorship enforced by the dictatorship of Iōannēs Metaxas in 1936. It is also important as one of the most sincere among Skalkottas' letters. The letters he wrote to his Greek friends produce the impression of a restraint, of holding back his profound feelings and his sincere thoughts. Reading some letters to Nellē Askētopoulou, one is not always certain whether he is humorous, ironic or sincere. To Manōlēs Benakēs he writes in a manner that could mean either that Benakēs has changed Skalkottas' views or that Skalkottas is pretending to have changed his views in order to satisfy Benakēs.[48] His correspondence with those two friends is written at an age when he was still convivial and battling for his recognition in society, while in 1935 he was reclusive, fighting his battles inwardly. Also, Skalkottas' handling of the Greek language is problematic.[49] He applies many foreign words (a lot of French[50] as well as German), uses certain Greek words in their etymological meaning and not in the meaning they have acquired by their use,[51] and, at times, makes up his own words, translating from foreign languages.

Crucial changes and moves in Skalkottas' life were most untimely. His early years in Athens occurred during a period of optimism for the future of the country. Besides, a great percentage of the circle of the Athens Conservatory he was in contact with consisted of foreigners and Greeks who often travelled abroad. Before leaving for Berlin, Skalkottas had only faintly realised the quality of Athenian society. Even this had much altered during his stay in Berlin, as Greece had suffered the catastrophic consequences of the failed 1922 campaign to Asia Minor; this halted all progress and was disastrous for the economy but also for the morality of the people.[52]

While Skalkottas was in Berlin, the city was also at its peak of cultural vitality. What followed after he left the city was cultural isolation and stylistic regression in music. Serial music (and all music connected to Jewish musicians) was completely effaced from concert halls, music schools and most memories. Karl Holer, Werner Egk, Wolfgang Fortner, Paul Graener, Ernst Pepping, Wilhelm Maler, Gerhard Frommel, Max Trapp, Hans Pfitzner, were among the composers representing the New German School, with Karl Orff and Paul Hindemith considered the most progressive. The regression of musical style promoted by the Third Reich's cultural policies was complete when, in 1935, Germany ended its isolation (projecting a liberal image for the coming Olympic games of 1936) and begun exchange cultural programmes with other western countries.

The propagation of tonal and modal music was well accepted not only on political but also on aesthetic grounds over much of Europe. When, in 1935–1939, the Permanent Council for International Cooperation amongst Composers (founded by Richard Strauss in 1934) organised exchange cultural programmes, German music was cleared from all its "demolishers", among whom Schoenberg, Kurt Weill and other Skalkottas acquaintances were eloquent examples. During one of those exchange programmes, on 5 December 1938,

Philoctētēs Œconomidēs directed Berlin's Philharmonic Orchestra in the Singakademie in an all-Greek music concert organised by the Prussian Academy of the Arts, the Ministry of Propaganda and Popular Education, and the Ambassador of Greece, Mr. A. Rangavēs. The works performed were: four songs by Aemilios Riadēs; the second movement of Kalomiris' two-movement *Symphonic Concerto for Piano and Orchestra*; four *Greek Dances* for orchestra by Nikos Skalkottas; Antiochos Evangelatos' *Introduction to a drama;* and Petros Petridēs' *Greek Suite.*

This was the last performance of Skalkottas' music organised by the Prussian Academy of Arts in Berlin during his life; a performance which did not do a Schoenberg student much honour. I am not aware of any comments by Skalkottas on that occasion.[53] Other participating composers saw those exchange projects as the recognition of Greek music as a branch of European music.

An all-German music concert was performed, in exchange, in Athens on 28 February 1939. The conductor was Erich Orthmannn, and the works performed were by Hans Pfitzner, Paul Graener, Max Trapp, and Baron von Reznicek.

Henry Missir, serving as music correspondent from Athens to *La Revue Musicale*, wonders "why such a splendid school as the German School considers it an obligation to illustrate its musical creation of today with symphonic pages of composers whose style is most often rococo and imitative, as if the evolution of actual procedures in composition is ignored".[54] A remark that may be added to the numerous signs showing the ignorance of Greek musicians to the situation in the Third Reich.

The Music

It is estimated that Skalkottas' lost works are at least 28 and at most 70 (Papaïōannou [Παπαϊωάννου] 1997/ii: 213). His works preserved in any form (including orchestral works in piano reduction, or partially orchestrated) are close to 100 (Papaïōannou [Παπαϊωάννου] 1997/ii: 204-212). They include large suite-like works consisting of a great number of movements (*36 Greek Dances* for orchestra; *32 Piano Pieces*); monumental works in one or more movements (*Ulysses'Return* overture; two Orchestral Suites in six movements each); works in classic forms (a Classic Symphony in A for wind orchestra, harp and double bass, a Symphonietta, many concertos,[55] four string quartets, two piano trios, one violin sonata and one for violin and piano, sonatinas etc.); various shorter works in one or more movements (such as his two dance-movement quartets for piano and wind, sets of theme and variations, short suites, piano studies etc.); stage music (especially dance music); songs.

Today, every serious researcher recognises as an achievement of Schoenberg the strong personalities of his (talented) students, none of whom imitated him or each other. Furthermore, since the 1990s American theorists and musicologists have shown tonal implications in Schoenberg's own twelve-tone works, of both the American and the European periods (Milstein 1992: 4–5). Therefore, to project as Skalkottas' singular achievement the independent treatment of the method and the tonal reminiscences it produces[56] is convincing no more; nor is this realisation downgrading Skalkottas' work.

Schoenberg himself was very much aware of the potential repercussions of the method's propagation and was reluctant to publish a manual on it. For him and his best students, the method was a help to fortify "music logic" in an atonal idiom, and it was this "music logic" that he was trying to theorise before publicising anything on the method. He wrote:

> For nearly twenty years I have been collecting material, ideas and sketches for an all-inclusive textbook of composition. When I shall finish it, I do not know. In any case: I have published nothing about "composition with 12-tones related to one another" and do not wish to do so until the principal part of my theory was ready: the "Study of Musical Logic". For I believe that meaningful advantage can be derived from this composition when it is based on knowledge and realization that comes from musical logic. And that is also the reason why I do not teach my students: "12-tone composition", but "composition", in the sense of musical logic; the rest will then come, sooner or later by itself.[57]

Schoenberg, an insightful reader of history, had foreseen the hyperbole of the method's adoption by composers as well as the fading of its consequence. Speaking, the year of Skalkottas' death, of his evolution (Schoenberg 1975: 87–88) he wrote:

> Usually when changes of style occur in the arts, a tendency can be observed to overemphasise the difference between the new and the old. Advice to followers is given in the form of exaggerated rules [...]. Fifty years later, the finest ears of the best musicians have difficulty in hearing those characteristics that the eyes of the average musicologist see so easily.

We might assume that time has given the method the importance Schoenberg's circle understood it to have. In 1931 Skalkottas explained the method to his Greek readers:[58]

> With his twelve-note system its inventor does not certainly mean, as many erroneously believe, the continuous "scholastic" repetition of the twelve notes in principal and secondary [polyphonic] parts of the work, but [he means] a law similar to that of the heptatonic system: the laws, the limits and the collection of the entire modern material into a solid modern system. Main points of this system are: a) the avoidance (as much as possible) of octaves, b) transparency of writing, c) the limitless horizon of exploitation of [polyphonic] parts and harmony.

This broad appreciation of the method conforms with Schoenberg's search for a theory of musical logic, as well as with all information about Schoenberg's lessons which consisted of analyses of great works (Gradenwitz 1998).

Not less important, in Skalkottas' case, was Schoenberg's transmission to his students of a missionary role. In a letter sent to the Prussian Academy of Arts from the United States in 1933 (Ennulat 1991: 7), Schoenberg summarised his teaching in Berlin:

[…] when I gave in to the temptation of the academy's flattering offer, it was because they appealed to my ambition as a teacher, and held up to me my duty to disseminate my knowledge, and because I knew what I was able to do for the students. This indeed I have done and more. Anyone who was my student became aware of the seriousness and morality of the mission of the artist; this awareness will, under any circumstances of life, bring him honor if he is able to remain true to it!

It was this awareness that armed Skalkottas with creative impulse, despite the oppressing and humiliating circumstances of the last Athenian period of his life.

Skalkottas was a serious, or if you like, a moral composer, whatever the subject and the inspiration of his works, which were indeed richly diversified.

A very characteristic aspect of his work is his genuine humour and a sunny joy influenced by light music and the music of Kurt Weill (whose collaboration with Bertolt Brecht took place in the years Skalkottas studied with him and with Schoenberg). His tangos, fox trots etc. are bursting with vitality and are embroidered with witty details, which add light and colour to the dancing pace and the singing line.

As was a trend among his generation's composers in Berlin (Kurt Weill, Ernst Krenek), Skalkottas is an eclectic composer. He wrote in a rich variety of styles that are independent of the technique or the method applied. As put from the analyst's point of view: in Skalkottas' music one is faced with "the frequent lack of aesthetic differentiation between the atonal and the twelve-tone works" (Zervos 2008: 66).

Skalkottas' eclecticism is observed not only in the sense of works differing to each other. It is also present as an uncommon coexistence of styles, influences and quotations within one work, that sound normal when listening to the music but look strange if described in words. For instance in the ballet *The Maiden and Death*, based on a folk legend, a manly folk dance (containing a quotation of his *Tsamikos*, the first of his published *Quatre Danses Grecques*), a type of Weill brassy fanfare, and a valse-lente (geographically displaced by a jazzy drums accompaniment) all follow each other smoothly and convincingly.

On the first level, one is impressed by the rich concepts of time in his music. In his monumental symphonic works, as in the *Return of Odysseus* overture,[59] time unfolds in broad, slowly formatted contours. In fact, his linear counterpoint is enclosed in a counterpoint of music shapes, some of which have rich interior life. In his collective works, the movements of his suites, and among his short, autonomous pieces, time is often developed as though under a miniaturist's magnified glass.

Multi-level polyphony, requiring transparency to be comprehended, becomes extremely demanding in solo music. His music for the violin and, especially, his music for the piano pose immense technical problems (Laaris [Λαάρης] 1999).

Skalkottas' *32 Piano Pieces* although written in one summer (1940),[60] do represent, like Beethoven's 32 piano sonatas, the composer's development as a composer; the work seems to contain all his compositional propositions. In fact the years 1935–1940 were very productive and certainly at the end of that period Skalkottas had in his mind the problems and issues he was confronted with during its course (Demertzēs [Δεμερτζής] 1991).

Both the diversity and the art are admirable. One is charmed by a Schumannesque child's logic, tenderness and pianistic polyphony (no. 1, "Klavierstück", no.16, "Nachtstück"), purely neo-Baroque atmposphere (no. 22, "Gavotte"), Bartókian music games (no. 2, "Kinder-Tanz", no. 8, "Vierstimmiger kleiner Kanon"), modern dance joy and sentimentality in his many dances. One is stunned by the pitiless virtuosity (Kontossi 2007: 93) either theatrically exhibited (no. 4, "Katastrophe auf dem Urwald") or concealed (no. 8)

The piece no. 15, entitled *Passacaglia* (a piece published individually and often performed thus), is an example of his non-serial treatment of the twelve-tone method. On (but not always over) an ostinato melody with strong baroque characteristics (two tied semitones and a chromatically descending segment) which is a twelve-tone row, unfold twenty compact variations (two 9/8 meters each) on styles dispersed in western music history from Bach to the 20th century. They are extremely diverse to each other, but compose a tightly constructed work not only by means of the ostinato melody, but also through use of the same sets of pitches over the same ostinato segments and the reappearance of the theme as the beginning of variation xvi, which is the peak of a contrapuntal build-up. After variation xvi, the pianistic shapes become all the more chordal, concluding, in the final variation, in the exposition of those sets, as blocks, over the corresponding ostinato segments; like an explanation of the technical foundation of the entire work. The last block of the work contains in the right hand all the notes of the set on a c of the left hand; this is repeated for the first time after the end of the ostinato melody (which ends on a C sharp).

Skalkottas has not left any hints on programmes even of works whose titles suggest their programmatic nature. However, his piano piece no 24, entitled "Italian Serenade" might well be a very descriptive programmatic piece. The pianist and musicologist Christophe Sirodeau observes that the piece's "slight whiff of vulgarity" might be related to "the anti-Italian situation in 1940 with the imminent invasion of Greece by Mussolini" (Sirodeau 2000: 13–14). Indeed, Skalkottas' piece seems to describe clearly the torpedoing of the Greek ship 'Ellē' by the Italian submarine 'Delfino', during the panhellenic festivities for the Virgin on the island of Tēnos.[61] The simple melody, the peaceful harmony and rhythm, repeated in variations over and over, are completely shuttered and overturned, after the massive ascending thirds (mm. 45-46: the Italian torpedo ?) smash the joyous atmosphere.

Skalkottas' relation to Greek folk music needs a special discussion. In an unpublished and undated text (estimated by Cōstēs Demertzēs to be written in 1935–1936), entitled "Folk Song", Skalkottas is explicitly expressing his idea that folk song if treated by a *great* composer will be perfected and become compelling to modern listeners. This sounds like an echo of Béla Bartók's "On the significance of folk music" (Suchoff 1976: 345-347) written in 1931 and published in German translation in 1932:[62]

folk music will become a source of inspiration for a country's music only if the transplantation of its motives is the work of a great talent. In the hands of incompetent composers neither folk music nor any other musical material will ever attain significance. If a composer has no talent it will be of no use to him to base his music on folk music or an other music. The result will in every case be nothing.

In the articles sent from Berlin to *Musikē Zōē*, Skalkottas expresses his admiration for Béla Bartók. In one instance he writes about a performance of the two *Rhapsodies* for violin and orchestra: "Those two rhapsodies by Béla Bartók are folkloristic works, full with rhythm and superbly orchestrated. After Schoenberg, Bartók is without any doubt the most interesting and serious musician of our times" (Skalkōtas [Σκαλκώτας] 1931c: 163). In another article, comparing Kodály to Bartók he admires Bartók's use of folk songs "with new harmonies, contemporary forms and pure artistic freshness" (Skalkōtas [Σκαλκώτας] 1931a: 112). It is obvious from Skalkottas' writings that he was fairly well acquainted with the music of Bartók. In fact, Cōnstantinidēs, Skalkottas' friend mentioned above, recalls a Bartók week in Berlin, in 1923, with the composer performing at the piano in some of his chamber music concerts.[63] He also remembers having heard Bartók playing his 1st piano concerto, which may have been the first world performance of the work, given in Frankfurt on 1 July 1927 (Gillies 1993: 558).

It might not be a coincidence that Skalkottas' first piano concerto, written in 1931, is undeniably alluding to Greek folk melodic and rhythmic characteristics and applies some Bartókian developmental techniques (such as the extension of a chromatic theme into diatonic and vice-versa), even though it is a twelve-tone work. Bartókian characteristics, including a "night music" section, are also observed in his Violin Sonata, another work preserved from the Berlin years.

Skalkottas was a free spirit and his musical perception was penetrating. Even under the spell of Schoenberg's personality, he was observing his music's "aggressiveness and problematic sonority"; (Skalkōtas [Σκαλκώτας] 1931b: 113) he was enjoying Stravinsky's "humorous pleasure and his ironic playing with both classic and modern composers" (Skalkōtas [Σκαλκώτας] 1931b: 113) and he was admiring Bartók's treatment of folk music and the inspiration he got from it. His music shows evidence of all three influences, as well as the influence of Kurt Weill and other contemporary composers. Equally evident is his deep knowledge of western traditional literature, the study of which constituted, as mentioned, Schoenberg's composition lessons.

It is now certain that Skalkottas did not share his teacher's opinion on "*synthetic* national music, bred like horses or plants" (Schoenberg 1975: 168, original emphasis),[64] and that the possibility of following Bartók's direction occupied his thoughts during the Berlin years.

The similarity of much of his music to Bartók's[65] is not exemplified only in the numerous cases where folk or folkish themes, rhythms and modes are used, but also in a character of purity, truth and sentimental immediacy through restraint and concision, or at times, the character of a strongly anti-Romantic earthly strength; a character that might be associated with the understanding of the elemental nature of Eastern European folk music.

Posthumous fame

Skalkottas' music begun to be studied and appreciated in Athens in the 1950s, when avant-garde music was introduced and strongly supported as part of Cold War cultural antagonism and propaganda.[66] The recovery of his music was initiated by Yannēs Papaïōannou, an amateur musicologist (an engineer by profession) with undisputable talent and knowledge, who was a leading figure in organising the avant-garde music movement in Athens. This is well reflected in the way he interpreted Skalkottas' work, life and personality in his writings.

Papaïōannou lead the foundation of a Society of Skalkottas' Friends in 1961,[67] organised a workshop of contemporary music – with Günter Becker – at the Goethe Institute of Athens in 1962 and played a leading role in the Greek section of the International Society for Contemporary Music in 1964 and the Hellenic Association for Contemporary Music (HACM) in 1965 (the latter two shared a large percentage of their members and directorships). In 1966 Papaïōannou initiated the Greek Festivals of Contemporary Music, which were financially supported by both the Greek Tourism Organisation and foreign institutions (Goethe Institute, Italian Institute, the Cultural Office of the American Embassy, The Ford Foundation). Papaïōannou succeeded in creating a circle of good musicians and a lively audience for avant-garde music, and in establishing good relations with foreign related agents and artists. Among other Greek music works performed in the festivals, several works by Skalkottas had their world premieres.

Papaïōannou begun the publication of Skalkottas' work in 1968 with Universal Editions (twenty-five works). In 1969 he published a catalogue of the composer's works which includes information on the autographs kept in Skalkottas' archives. That same year he organised the English Bach Festival (presided over by the Greek harpsichordist Lila Lalandi); a festival dedicated to Skalkottas in order to commemorate the twenty year anniversary of his death. Nineteen works were performed and for their execution the Society undertook to publish them hastily in editions named *Provisional Editions* (by copyists; the project was financed by The Ford Foundation). Those provisional editions, however, continued to be produced (funded by another Ford Foundation grant) after the Bach Festival as they were judged to be efficient. In 1980, Gunther Schuller got interested in publishing Skalkottas' work and did so with Margun Music Inc., which was incorporated into G. Schirmer of New York in 1999.

In his texts, as well as in a catalogue of Skalkottas' works, Papaïōannou divided his compositions into atonal (including twelve-tone), that he calls *main* works, and tonal (or modal). He promoted the theory that Skalkottas was obliged by the depressing, conservative atmosphere in Athens to abandon his progressive music language and turn to tonality and the use of Greek folk songs in his music. Indeed, as Nikos Christodoulou writes: "Papaïōannou (who disapproved of tonal music as a legitimate language for a then modern composer) called emphatically, in his many articles and book, as 'two great voids' those periods where Skalkottas was mostly composing tonal works" (Christodoulou 2008: 134).

A conspiracy theory, initiated by Papaïōannou, has been widely circulated to explain Skalkottas falling into obscurity as a composer during his life in Athens. This theory, supported or repeated by John Thornley (Thornley 2008: 344–354) and many others, names as main conspirators Manolis Kalomiris and Philoctētēs Œconomidēs, followed by Petros Petridēs, Spyros Farandatos, Giōrgos Ponēridēs, Dimitri Mitropoulos and others.[68]

For the liberties he took, Papaïōannou has received criticism from recent Skalkottas researchers. However, as Cōstes Demertzēs – whose Ph.D. dissertation is the first large-scale published study on Skalkottas – has said, without Papaïōannou's valuable contribution it is very possible that Skalkottas would be a *"nomen nudum"* (Demertzēs [Δεμερτζής 1998: xx).

Demertzēs thus reminds us that if Papaïōannou made the mistake of interpreting Skalkottas through the prism of avant-garde enthusiasm, we should not repeat this mistake by judging Papaïōannou through the prism of postmodern "maturity".

The pianist and conductor Giōrgos Chatzēnikos was also very important in the dissemination of Skalkottas' music. In October 1953, he was the soloist at the premiere of Skalkottas' Piano Concerto no. 2 given in Hamburg by the orchestra of the Northwest German Radio, under the direction of Hermann Scherchen.[69] Although his recordings of Skalkottas' work are few, his interpretations communicate fully the musical logic of the pieces. He is also credited with having found, in a Berlin secondhand bookshop in December 1954, three of Skalkottas' lost works; his *Octet*, two String Quartets, and the Piano Concerto no.1.

The first collective recording of Skalkottas' works was a four LP album by EMI/HMV issued in 1980. It contains chamber music performed by nearly all the Greek musicians who performed in the avant-garde music concerts of the 1960s and 1970s in Athens. They are: the pianists Diana Vranoussē, Nellē Semitecolo and Yannēs Papaïōannou himself; the violinists Tatsēs Apostolidēs (leader of the Hellenic Quartet whose other members were Ersē Kangelarē, Yiannēs Vatikiōtēs and Sōtērēs Tachiatēs), Nina Patrikidou and Dēmētrēs Vraskos; the violist Yiannēs Vatikiōtēs; the cellists Sōtērēs Tachiatēs and Chrēstos Sfetsas and a small string orchestra directed by Tatsēs Apostolidēs.

In the last decade of the 20th century, a second renaissance of Skalkottas' work begun. This has brought forth a startling number of unexpectedly good interpretations of his works. Most among the splendid performers of the recordings that circulate are young Greek musicians, some of which have gained recognition in Greece through their Skalkottas interpretations. It should be reiterated here that Skalkottas' writing for all instruments is very demanding; in order to communicate the musical thoughts of the composer, the instrumentalist has to overcome extreme technical problems. This Skalkottas renaissance has therefore led to a very interesting phenomenon: a community of anti-star, young, Greek musicians following a career both in Greece and abroad and being recognised for their supreme musicianship, outside the craze of mass media. It should be added that Skalkottas' works quite often require serious editing, which is, in many cases, undertaken by the interpreters themselves.

The cellist and conductor Byrōn Fidetzēs, a crusader for the promotion of Greek music and the present director of the Athens State Orchestra, has conducted the premiere of the entire *36 Greek Dances* with the State Philharmonic Orchestra of the Urals (recorded by Lyra, 1991).[70]

From February 1998 to July 2008, the Swedish company BIS has circulated seventeen CDs (including some boxes of two) of Skalkottas works. Among the Greek artists participating in this project, the conductor Nikos Christodoulou has the lead; the conductors Byrōn Fidetzēs and Vassilēs Christopoulos each appear on one CD. The orchestras participating are the Iceland Symphony orchestra, the Thessaloniki State Symphony Orchestra, the BBC Symphony Orchestra, the Caput Ensemble and the Malmö Symphony Orchestra.

The violinist Giōrgos Demertzēs has performed, either as the leader of the New Hellenic Quartet or as a soloist, all of Skalkottas' relevant works. Other string players include the violinist Simos Papanas, the violist Chara Seira, the cellist Maria Kitsopoulou and the double bass player Vassilēs Papavassiliou, who is the soloist at the superb concerto for double bass.

Among pianists, Nikolaos Samaltanos and Maria Asteriadou perform on several CDs, while Lorenda Ramou plays Skalkottas' arrangements of his ballet music. Samaltanos has recorded the *32 Piano Pieces*, a work that was premiered in 1979 in Athens by Geoffrey Douglas Madge. Madge participates in the BIS project by performing Skalkottas' 1st and 2nd piano concertos, and his *Concerto no 3 for Piano and Ten Wind Instruments*. The interpretations of the mezzo soprano Angelica Cathariou and the percussionist Dēmētrēs Desyllas are also remarkable.

Among the Greek interpretations that are not recorded in the BIS project, one should mention a Decca/Universal CD containing the world premiere recording of Skalkottas' neoclassic, sparkling C major *Concertino* for piano and orchestra (together with his *Concerto no 3 for Piano and Ten Wind Instruments*) performed by the Montpellier National Orchestra under the direction of Friedemann Layer, with Danaē Karra as soloist.

Vassō Koutsobina, compiling a Skalkottas discography in 1999, lists 77 records (Koutsobina 1999). In 2008 Thōmas Tamvakos lists 144 records containing Skalkottas' music (Tamvakos 2008), the second greatest number of records for a "serious" Greek composer after Iannis Xenakis.

Notes

1. Despite the facts that a large part of his work is extremely demanding for instrumentalists, still remains unpublished and is difficult to access.
2. Skalkōtas [Σκαλκώτας] 1931: 111–113, 124–126, 138–139, 163–164, 179, 213.
3. In Demertzēs [Δεμερτζής] 1998 the "Technique of orchestration" is thoroughly analysed. The subjects of the short texts are given in Demertzēs [Δεμερτζής] 1998: 8. For his folk song transcriptions, see Dragoumēs [Δραγούμης] 1978–1979.
4. See their list in Demertzis 2008: 294–295.
5. The letters were written by Skalkottas to Manōlēs Benakēs from November 1928 to January 1933. Today, these letters are missing. However, Thornley had read them and obviously had obtained copies of them (it is not clear if he copied all of them) which he cited in the paper read at the conference, later published in revised form (see Thornley 2002).

6. The only music school in Greece, at the time, that had introduced the programmes, the methods and the repertory of German music academies and the Parisian Conservatoire. From 1872, when it was founded, to 1891, music was taught practically. Then, under the direction of Geōrgios Nazos, who had studied in Munich, the institution was radically reorganised, its new staff consisting primarily of German, French and Belgian professors. This determined the transition from Italian to German influence in Greek music life.

7. Studies in Greek conservatories are organised in three multi-years levels.

8. Marsick, who had come to Athens at the end of 1908, taught in the conservatory up to 1920, when Saint-Säens visited the city. Dimitri Mitropoulos was Marsick's favourite student and his right hand in the orchestra. Marisck's wish and effort to get assimilated into Greek music life is remarkable: he had composed several works on Greek subjects, using folk modes and rhythms, and he participated in the first well-organised expedition of the Athens Conservatory for the collection of folk songs in Peloponnēsos. On 25 February 1922 he moved to Bilbao.

9. Dimitri Mitropoulos had received a piano diploma one year earlier, also with the highest distinction, and prizes, as well as a scholarship to continue his studies in Brussels. He stayed for a short time in that city and left for Berlin as well.

10. He was on the list of Hochschule students up to the end of the summer semester (Jaklitsch 2003: 170). He performed in student concerts of 31.5.1922, 3.2.1923, 26.1.1924, 13.2.1924, 7.3.1924, 4.6.1924. (Mantzourani 1999: 35). Nina Jaklitsch also gives the works performed by Skalkottas in those concerts (Jaklitsch 2003: 174–175).

11. Cited in Jaklitsch 2003: 177–178. See also, Thornley 2002: 178.

12. Skalkottas 1948: [1].

13. Cited in Demertzis 2008: 306.

14. Cōnstantinidēs' autographed manuscript notes entitled "Skalkottas". They were shown to me by the musicologist Giōrgos Sakallieros.

15. In Octave Merlier's biography of Skalkottas (Skalkottas 1948: [1]), the names of those two are mixed up and Skalkottas' teacher is called Paul Kahn; this has created some problems for later biographers. (See Papaïōannou [Παπαϊωάννου] 1997/i: 67).

16. From 1921 to 1924, Kurt Weill was in Ferucio Busoni's composition master class at Berlin's Academy of the Arts and from 1923 to 1929 he gave private lessons in composition. Kurt Weill studied counterpoint with Philipp Jarnach, at the advice of Ferucio Busoni.

17. Arnold Schoenberg succeeded Busoni in August 1925. (See Alsmeier 2001: 78). In the Arnold Schoenberg Archive, the following note is kept "Herrn Nikolaus Skalkottas habe ich nach vorheriger Prüfung in die mir unterstellte Meisterschule aufgenommen, und bitte um seine Zulassung zur Immatrikulation. Berlin, den 8ten November 1927, Arnold Schönberg" (http: // www.schoenberg.at/).

18. Temko gave birth to Artemis and Apollo (or Giōrgo). The boy died very early. The couple had divorced by the summer of 1928 (Thornley 2002: 186) and their daughter was given to a foster-mother in Berlin.

19. On his relations with N. Skalkottas, see Thornley 2002. On the information of Farandatos' intervention, see Thornley 2008: 356.

20. See Gradenwitz 1998: 169–183.

21. Alsmeier 2001: 79–80.

22. Hannenheim and Skalkottas wrote a letter, dated 23 May 1930 and signed by both, thanking Schoenberg for offering them the opportunity, through this concert, to perform their works. The letter is reproduced in Gradenwitz 1998: 173.

23. Thornley 2002: 191. The programme of this concert is reproduced in Ramou 2008: 420. Polyxenē Mathéy-Roussopoulou (1902–1999) was married to the German painter Georg Mathéy. She studied with Karl Orff from 1935 to 1937 and in 1938 she founded a school in Athens where she introduced Orff's methods to Greece.

24. The second movement of his Sonatina no. 1 for violin and piano (1929), in volume 4 (31 January 1931, pp. 83–86).

25. This information is given with the occasion of a remark on the "musicality and sweet voice" of Skalkottas' sister who sang at a students concert in Athens. The unsigned text concludes: "We believe that Miss Skalkotta will continue her studies in Berlin, by her brother, the known Greek composer. By the way, we note that Mr Skalkottas, who is living in Berlin, has already composed an Octet for four strings and four wood winds which will be performed in the German capital on 2 June. Two of his quartets, nos 1 and 2, were also performed in Berlin on 21 May. *Musikē Zōē* expresses to Mr Skalkottas and his parents the most cordial congratulations." *Musikē Zōē*, 8, 31 May 1931, p. 192.

26. Thornley 2002: 189. (The details in parentheses are from Thornley's paper read at the Skalkottas Symposium of the University of Athens on 12 November 1999, not included in its published revised form.)

27. Schoenberg's teaching contract required him to be at the post six months per year. After an asthma attack, he moved to Barcelona (as advised by his physician) from October 1931 to May 1932 (see Ennulat 1991: 152).

28. According to Papaïōannou, this is not a folk song but a composition by Lambelet (Papaïōannou [Παπαϊωάννου] 1997/i: 34). He does not specify who among the three Lambelet brothers is the composer.

29. Bichsel 2008: 486.

30. Thornley says that she was one of the persons to whom Skalkottas asked for economic support, when Manōlēs Benakēs ceased his own; the other being Papastratos and Kyriazēs (Thornley 2008: 356). The same author says that Margarita Perra's brother, Tēlemachos Perras, was the doctor who operated on Skalkottas the day he died, on 19 September 1949 (Thornley 2002: 205).

31. In May 1933 Schoenberg left for the USA (through Paris). He had resigned from the Academy on 20 March (Holtmeier 2008: 269).

32. Called Seventh Symphony in the Greek press (a number given often to the *Unfinished Symphony* in those years, and very seldom to the Ninth).

33. The article is published entirely in Greek and with an English translation, in Skalkottas 2008: 323–329.

34. One of those Greeks who, like Skalkottas himself, take the lead so prematurely that they become ineffective and marginalised. Oeconomou gives a fine description of Adler's definition of musicology and an introduction to this new science (Oeconomou [Οικονόμου] 1930: 29–31). Nothing is known about this musicologist, besides the very little information he gives on himself in his writings in the periodical (e.g. that he had studied in Vienna and that Guido Adler was his teacher, p. 30) and in his editing notes in various texts that give an idea of his anti-Romantic taste.

35. In Thornley 2002: 195, we read the following quotation from a Skalkottas' letter to Benakēs, written about March 1932: "In connection with last year's rows, I feel like going down to Athens to beat up Oeconomou. Who gave him the idea of annihilating me with his acts of malevolence and his nasty remarks?". Given the fact that Oeconomou supported Skalkottas, this is strange; Skalkottas either refers to some event that we do not know about, or this is an ironic remark.

36. Skalkottas was exempted from military service again through the intervention of Spyros Farandatos (Thornley 2008: 356). See also note 19 above.
37. Thornley 2008: 334.
38. Chatzēnikos [Χατζηνίκος] 2006: 46.
39. Chatzēnikos [Χατζηνίκος] 2006: 47.
40. See Lalaounē [Λαλαούνη] 1945, where Skalkottas is mentioned to have accompanied the violinist Alecos Chatzēdēmētriou, who performed his own compositions.
41. See Dragoumēs [Δραγούμης] 1978–1979.
42. Ramou 2008: 422.
43. Such choreographic "pasticcios" were much used by modern dance pioneers in Athens, who were exceptionally musical.
44. These are arrangements of music by Bartók, Stravinsky, and others, most possibly proposed by Pratsika herself. See Rikakis 2008: 402.
45. See 'Posthumous fame' below.
46. Skalkottas was probably unaware that Schoenberg had been forced out of Germany by the Nazis in May 1933.
47. Letter to Matla Temko in Sweden quoted in translation (from the original German) by Thornley 2002: 214–215.
48. Thornley observes this in various occasions. See for example Thornley 2002: 201.
49. One of the holes in Skalkottas' biography has to do with his schooling. It is most possible that he did not complete the twelve years of Greek schooling.
50. In the Athens Conservatory of Music, the French language was prevailing. There exist recital programmes of Schubert's Lieder, where their titles are in French.
51. This might be the reason why Papaïōannou finds the treatment of language by Skalkottas outstanding (Papaïōannou [Παπαϊωάννου] 1997/i: 63).
52. Besides the thousands of people who were forcefully expelled from their homes during the retreat of the Greek army, the Exchange of Populations Treaty brought within the boarders of a poor and worn-out country of 5.500.000 inhabitants close to another 1.400.000 Greek nationals, all refugees. See Pentzopoulos 2002: 98–99. See also Yannis Belonis' chapter "The Greek National Music School" in this book.
53. I am not aware, either, of any comments by him on the three performances of Manolis Kalomiris' opera *The Mother's Ring* in Berlin's Volksoper, between 2 and 10 February 1940. For further information on these performances, as well as the situation in Greek music life during the Ioannes Metaxas dictatorship and the Axis occupation, see Romanou 2009.
54. Missir 1939.
55. They are two piano concertos, one concerto for piano and wind orchestra (ten instruments), a concertino for piano, a concertino for two pianos, one violin concerto, one concerto for two violins, one concerto for violin and viola, one concerto for double bass, a concertino for oboe and one concertino for trumpet (Papaïōannou [Παπαϊωάννου] 1997/ii: 206–207).
56. A comprehensive description of Skalkottas' application of the method is given in Mantzourani 2008.
57. Goehr: 1977: 4 (cited in Milstein 1992: 1).
58. Reviewing a piano recital by Else Krauss who performed Schoenberg's piano *Suite*, opus 25, which he names as the first twelve-note work (Skalkōtas [Σκαλκώτας] 1931: 138).
59. An analysis of this twelve-tone work, applying non-serially many rows thematically connected to each other, see Giannopoulos [Γιαννόπουλος] 2003.

60. Cōstēs Demertzēs gives a foreword to this work written by the composer and much information on it (Demertzēs [Δεμερτζής] 1991: 32–53, 94–143).

61. On 15 August 1940. This act initiated the Italians' menacing stand towards Greece. They invaded Greece on 28 October 1940 and at this date Greece got involved in World War II. Very few among the 32 pieces are dated by the composer. The "Italian Serenade" is not. However certain of the dated pieces are written after 15 August 1940.

62. *Mitteilungen der Österreichischen Musiklehrerschaft* (Vienna), no.3 (May-June), 1932, pp. 8–10.

63. He also mentioned performances of his quartets by the Waldbauer Quartet. (Sakallieros [Σακαλλιέρος] 2005: 19).

64. Schoenberg's "Folk-music and Art-music", written c.1926. The passage on horses and plants runs as follows: "How, then, does one produce 'synthetic' national music, how does one breed it? As one breeds horses, or plants – by intermingling or grafting native and foreign products..."

65. The consideration of the Fibonacci series, observed in his *32 Piano pieces* (Sirodeau 2000: 10) might be added to Bartók's influence.

66. After World War II, Greece, as the only Balkan country belonging to the West, "turned into the largest beneficiary per capita of American largesse in the world" (Mazower 2000: 133).

67. From 1949 to 1961, an informal Skalkottas committee was formed by Minōs Dounias, Nellē Euelpidou (Askētopoulou) and Yannēs Papaïōannou. In 1961, they founded the Society of Skalkottas' Friends. They collected all of the documents Skalkottas had left in the two houses he had lived in in Athens (his sister's and his own, where he moved after his marriage in 1946). (Papaïōannou [Παπαϊωάννου] 1997 : 30–31).

68. See the chapter "The great collusion" (Papaïōannou [Παπαϊωάννου] 1997/i: 96-104). In the text he uses the word "conspiracy".

69. (Chatzēnikos [Χατζηνίκος] 2006: 17– 18). Because of the bad situation of the score, two movements were only played. This mutilated performance circulated in 1993 in an Arcadia CD.

70. Some of the most popular dances have been recorded in interpretations by Dimitri Mitropoulos and the New York Philharmonic Orchestra. The earliest was recorded in Athens in 1955 but only circulated on CD in 1991 to commemorate the thirty years since Mitropoulos' death.

References

Alsmeier, J., *Komponieren mit Tönen. Nikos Skalkottas und Schönbergs "Komposition mit zwölf Tönen"*, Saarbrücken, PFAU, 2001.

Bichsel, M., "The Nikos Skalkottas Archive manuscripts" in Haris Vrondos (ed.), *Nikos Skalkottas A Greek European**, Athens, Benaki Museum, 2008, pp. 482–513.

[Chatzēnikos] Χατζηνίκος, Γ., *Νίκος Σκαλκώτας. Μια ανανέωση στην προσέγγιση της μουσικής σκέψης και ερμηνείας* [Nikos Skalkottas. A renewal of the approach to musical thought and interpretation], Athens, Nefelē 2006.

Christodoulou, N., "Nikos Skalkottas. A centenary of his birth", in Haris Vrondos (ed.), *Nikos Skalkottas A Greek European*, Athens, Benaki Museum, 2008, pp. 128–175.

[Demertzēs] Δεμερτζής, Κ., *Ο Νίκος Σκαλκώτας ως συνθέτης μουσικής για πιάνο σόλο* [Nikos Skalkottas as a composer of piano solo music], Chalkis, Public Central Library, 1991.

---

* This is a bilingual publication, all texts appearing in English and Greek in opposite pages.

——, *Η Σκαλκωτική Ενορχήστρωση* [The Skalkottian Orchestration], Athens, Papazēsēs 1998.

Demertzis, K., "Musical ideas in Skalkottas' youthful correspondence" in Haris Vrondos (ed.), *Nikos Skalkottas A Greek European*, Athens, Benaki Museum, 2008, pp. 292–319.

[Dragoumēs] Δραγούμης, Μ., "Πέντε Σιφνέϊκες μελωδίες από τη συλλογή Μέλπως Μερλιέ σε καταγραφή Νίκου Σκαλκώτα" [Five melodies from Sifnos from the collection of Melpo Merlier, in Nikos Skalkottas' transcriptions], *Αρχείο Ευβοϊκών Μελετών* [Euboic Studies Archive], 22, 1978–1979, pp. 32– [64].

Ennulat, E., *Arnold Schoenberg Correspondece. A collection of translated and annotated letters exchanged with Guido Adler, Pablo Casals, Emanuel Feuermann and Olin Downes,* N.J., & London, The Scarecrow Press Inc., 1991.

[Giannopoulos] Γιαννόπουλος, Η., "*Η επιστροφή του Οδυσσέα* του Νίκου Σκαλκώτα: αναλυτικές προσεγγίσεις στο πρόβλημα του συνδυασμού ενός δωδεκάφθογγου ιδιώματος με μια συμβατική μορφή" [*Ulysses' return* by Nikos Skalkottas: analytical approaches to the problem of combining a twelve-tone idiom with a conventional form], *Μουσικολογία* [Musicology], 18: 3 (2003), pp. 150–163.

Gillies, M. (ed.), *The Bartók Companion,* London, Faber and Faber, 1993.

Goehr, A., 'Schoenberg's *Gedanke* Manuscript', *Journal of the Arnold Schoenberg Institute,* 2: 1 (1977), pp. 4–25.

Gradenwitz, P., *Arnold Schönberg und seine Meisterschüler. Berlin 1925–1933,* Wien, Paul Zsolnay Verlag, 1998.

Holtmeier, L., "Arnold Schönberg at the Prussian Art Academy" in Haris Vrondos (ed.), *Nikos Skalkottas A Greek European,* Athens, Benaki Museum, 2008, pp. 256–289.

Jaklitsch, N.-M., *Manolis Kalomiris (1883–1962), Nikos Skalkottas (1904–1949). Griechische Kunstmusik zwischen Nationalschule und Moderne* (Studien zur Musikwissenschaft, 51, unter Leitung von Theophil Antonicek und Elisabeth Theresia Fritz–Hilscher), Tutzing, Hans Schneider, 2003.

Kontossi, S., "La Musique Grecque pour Piano Seul. Quelques propositions de repertoire" in Danièle Pistone (ed.), *Pianistes du XXe siecle*, Observatoire Musical Français, Serie "Conférence et Séminaires", no 33, Université de Paris-Sorbonne, 2007, pp. 89–101.

[Koutsobina] Κουτσομπίνα, Β., *Δισκογραφία Νίκου Σκαλκώτα (1954–1999)* [Nikos Skalkottas' discography (1954–1999)], 1999, http://www.mmb.org.gr/

[Laaris] Λαάρης, Ν., "Τεχνικές Δυσκολίες στα έργα για σόλο Πιάνο του Σκαλκώτα" [Technical difficulties in Skalkottas' piano solo works], unpublished paper read in *Nikos Skalkottas Symposium* organised by the Music faculty of the University of Athens, 12 November, 1999.

[Lalaounē] Λαλαούνη, Α., "Τελευταία ρεσιτάλ" [Latest recitals], in newspaper *Βραδυνή*, 4 June, 1945.

Mantzourani, E., *Nikos Skalkottas. A Biographical Study and an investigation of his twelve-tone compositional processes.* Unpublished P.h.D. dissertation, King's College, London 1999.

—— "An introduction to Skalkottas' twelve-note compositional processes" in Haris Vrondos (ed.), *Nikos Skalkottas A Greek European*, Athens, Benaki Museum, 2008, pp. 88–125.

Mazower, M., *The Balkans. From the end of Byzantium to the present day,* London, Phoenix Press, 2000.

Milstein, S., *Arnold Schoenberg. Notes Sets Forms*, (Music in the 20th century), Cambridge, Cambridge University Press, 1992.

Missir, H., "Grèce", *La Revue Musicale*, xx/193, August–November, 1939, pp. 122–123.

[Oeconomou] Οικονόμου, Κ. Δ., "Η μουσική ως επιστήμη" [Music as a Science], in *Μουσική Ζωή* [Musical Life], Vol. 2, November, 1930, pp. 29–31.

[Papaïōannou] Παπαϊωάννου, Γ. Γ., *Νίκος Σκαλκώτας* [Nikos Skalkottas] i-ii, Athens, Papagrēgoriou-Nakas, 1997.

Pentzopoulos, D., *The Balkan Exchange of Minorities and its Impact on Greece*, London, Hurst & Company, 2002.

Ramou, L., "The presentations of the suite *The Land and Sea of Greece*. An unpublished letter by Polyxene Mathéy about her meetings and collaboration with Nikos Skakottas", in Haris Vrondos (ed.), *Nikos Skalkottas A Greek European,* Athens, Benaki Museum, 2008, pp. 418–439.

Rikakis, A., "Nikos Skalkottas, This prolific and 'unknown' composer of dance, dance drama and ballet", in Haris Vrondos (ed.), *Nikos Skalkottas A Greek European,* Athens, Benaki Museum, 2008, pp. 400–415.

Romanou, K., "Exchanging *Rings* under dictatorships", in R.Illiano and M. Sala (eds), *Music and Dictatorship in Europe and Latin America*, Turnhout, Brepols Publishers, 2009, pp. 1–38.

[Sakallieros] Σακαλλιέρος, Γ., *Γιάννης Κωνσταντινίδης (1903-1984). Η ζωή και το έργο του* [Yiannis Cōnstantinidēs (1903–1984). His life and work], unpublished Ph.D. dissertation, University of Athens, 2005, p. 19.

Schoenberg, A., *Style and Idea,* in Leonard Stein (ed.), New York, St Martins Press, 1975.

Sirodeau, Ch., "II. The 32 Pieces for piano", CD BIS 1133/1134 (Notes accompanying the CD), 2000, pp. 7–14.

[Skalkōtas] Σκαλκώτας, Ν., "Μουσική Κίνησις του Βερολίνου" [Musical activity of Berlin], *Μουσική Ζωή* [Musical Life], 5, 28 February, 1931a, p. 112.

——, "Πρώτη συναυλία της I.G.N.M. " [First concert of the ISCM], *Μουσική Ζωή* [Musical Life], 5, 28 February, 1931b, p. 113.

——, "Μουσική Κίνησις του Βερολίνου" [Musical activity of Berlin], *Μουσική Ζωή* [Musical Life], 7, 30 April, 1931c, p. 163.

Skalkottas, N., *Quatre Dances Grecques. Partition d'Orchestre,* edited by O. Merlier (Série Musicale no 3), Athens, Collection de l'Institut Français d'Athènes, 1948.

——, "Music Citicism", in H.Vrondos (ed.), *Nikos Skalkottas A Greek European*, Athens, Benaki Museum, 2008, pp. 322–329.

Suchoff, B., ed., *Béla Bartók Essays*, London, Faber & Faber, 1976.

[Tamvakos] Ταμβάκος, Θ., *Πλήρης κατάλογος ηχογραφημάτων των μουσουργώντων οποίων έργα παρουσιάζονται στις Ελληνικές μουσικές Γιορτές (Τέταρτος Κύκλος)* [Complete catalogue of recordings of the composers whose works are presented in the Greek Music Festival (fourth cycle)], Athens, Megaron Musikes, 2008, pp. 103–150.

——, *Δισκογραφία Νίκου Σκαλκώτα* [Discography of Nikos Skalkottas], 2008, http: //www.mmb.org.gr/

Thornley, J., "'I beg you to tear up my letters…' Nikos Skalkottas's last years in Berlin (1928–1933)", in *Byzantine and Modern Greek Studies*, 26, 2002, pp. 178–217.

——, "An encounter with 'Greek artistic reality' – Nikos Skalkottas' return to Athens in 1933", in H. Vrondos (ed.), *Nikos Skalkottas A Greek European*, Athens, Benaki Museum, 2008, pp. 334–367.

Zervos, Y., "Musical idioms and aesthetic directions in Nikos Skalkottas' work", in H. Vrondos (ed.), *Nikos Skalkottas A Greek European*, Athens, Benaki Museum, 2008, pp. 50–85.

Chapter 9

Chrēstou, Adamēs, Koukos: Greek Avant-garde Music During the Second Half of the 20th Century

Nick Poulakis

In this article I propose a comparative approach to the neo-Hellenic art music of the post-war period and I examine its resonance on the Balkan and European art music scene. This is critically presented through the paradigmatic cases of three contemporary Greek composers (Jannēs Chrēstou,[1] Michalēs Adamēs[2] and Periclēs Koukos),[3] who adopted diverse music, stylistic and philosophical viewpoints.

The ideological confrontations between the two opposing sides of the Cold War polarity (the western and the eastern) represented a nodal point in the turn of cultural politics in almost all European countries after the end of the Second World War. This reformation involved both the artistic-creative and the educational-informative dimension of cultural politics. Within the circumstances of political propaganda international forces founded institutes in various countries that became systematically active in the field of fine arts and sciences. These organisations supported the interests of their donors and, among other activities, they provided scholarships for art studies abroad; they also set up several festivals, exhibitions, concerts and seminars and they actively participated in the cultural life of local communities.[4]

More particularly, during the first post-war years the base was laid for new, pioneering quests and experimentations in western art music. The extensive use of atonality in combination with the unavoidable transition to total serialism, the use of aleatory techniques, the birth of electronic and electro-acoustic music, along with the spread of music theatre and multimedia works produced innovative music morphemes within a web of music universalism. The abolition of tonality and the cessation of the Romantic and national schools movements resulted in the gradual overthrow of the hegemony of West-European music and the development of particular music dialects.[5]

During the same period the socio-political, economic and cultural situation in Greece was characterised by great fluidity, at least until the change of polity (from military junta to parliamentary democracy) in the middle of the 1970s. Political fermentations and cultural transformations allowed traditional Greek society to accept novel ideological norms and material preferences. The significant rise in the urban population along with the subsequent modifications in the structure of production, the change of consumer practices and thus of personal expectations, the boosting and thickening of political activities concerning formal institutions (state, public administration) and mass politics (parties, collective individuals, society of citizens) radically reformed the older Greek cultural values.[6]

In the case of contemporary Greek music from 1950s onwards, cultural renovation stimulated a vivid mobility both within Greece as well as abroad. Greek composers participated, apprenticed and created within the frame of international art movements; they were keen on current developments and shaped modern tendencies through the fusion of indigenous (local or national) tradition with elements of western music culture.[7] The composers' adjustability to the demands of progressive music creation was related to the fact that the innovations adopted by western pioneers included features that were very coherent to those of the Greek music tradition, such as the use of micro-intervals and modes, free or controlled improvisation, as well as various special techniques of vocal and instrumental performance (Rōmanou [Ρωμανού] 2000: 167–168).

The constitution of the National Orchestra of Thessalonica, the creation of the Third Programme of the Hellenic Radio Foundation, the enactment of the Athens Festival, and the establishment of the Odeon of Herodes Atticus as the central venue for concerts represented crucial developments that were related to the reinforcement of art music life in Greece.[8] The charismatic composer Manos Chatzidakis established the Experimental Orchestra and developed a multiform activity in cultural affairs, emphasising music production and the promotion of the works of young composers. In 1962, a new institution was born in Athens, the "Manos Chatzidakis Composition Competition" of the Doxiadēs Technological Organisation. During this competition composers of contemporary avant-garde music were presented to the Greek public. Among them, one could discern the fascinating persona of Jannēs Chrēstou, who, until then, was living and working mainly abroad.

Born in Cairo in 1926 and coming from a wealthy family, Chrēstou was brought up in the cosmopolitan bourgeois environment of Alexandria in Egypt and stayed in close contact with the local elite. The composer's family and social environment, along with the fact that he spent his childhood and adolescence in a country with a long tradition in philosophy, had a dramatic effect upon his work.[9] Initially, he attended the English College of Alexandria, while at the same time he took his first music lessons from Alexander Plotnikoff and Gina Bachauer. In 1945 he travelled to England to study philosophy and logic with Ludwig Wittgenstein and Bertrand Russell at the University of Cambridge.[10] At the same time he was taught advanced music theory by Hans Ferdinand Redlich, former student of Alban Berg, while he frequently visited Italy to follow Vito Frazzi's classes of composition and Francesco Lavagnino's classes of orchestration and film music. Chrēstou considered himself as self-taught in the sense that he carried out most of his projects beyond his teachers' tutorship.

His brother's – Euangelos Chrēstou – attendance at the Zurich Institute and his encounter with Carl Jung's analytical psychology and alchemy drove the composer deeper into philosophical speculation and introspectiveness.[11] Euangelos was to him a personal mentor and spiritual guide; consequently, his death in a car accident in 1956 was a fact that haunted the composer during the rest of his life. This had a dramatic impact on both his temperament as much as on the field of his artistic activity. After this heavy loss, Jannē Chrēstou edited his brother's manuscripts and published them in one volume titled *The Logos of the Soul*. In the meantime, the composer returned to Egypt and married Thēresia (Sia) Chōremē, a young painter and friend of his since childhood.

Jannēs Chrēstou at the ancient theatre of Epidauros.

In 1960 he was forced to abandon Egypt due to political and financial changes, particularly in the field of industry. Chrēstou settled permanently in Greece, dividing his time between Athens and Chios. Despite his efforts to remain professionally independent and stay out of music events and shows, the public showed great appreciation of his work as well as of his charming personality. During the last decade of his life, his popularity spread rapidly. He was then working on the idea of creating a cultural complex, wherein it would be possible to host an international festival of contemporary music. Yet, the very night of his birthday, 8 January 1970, Chrēstou was killed in a car accident, just like his brother.[12]

Chrēstou's creation, according to the researcher Jannēs G. Papaiōannou, falls into six subsequent stages: a) First Period (1948–1953), b) Second Period (1953–1958), c) Third Period (1959–1963) d) Fourth Period (1964–1966), e) Fifth Period (1966–1968) and f) Sixth Period (1968–1970) (Papaioannou 1970). Another division of his work into three lengthier periods is also possible: a) First Phase (1948–1958), b) Second Phase (1959–1964) and c) Third Phase (1965–1970), in the manner that Giōrgos Leōtsakos has suggested (Leotsakos 2009b). Both these suggestions accord with the psycho-philosophical route of Chrēstou's artistic mutation, persisting on the composer's greatest works and innovative theses.

Chrēstou's first composition, if one excludes the early juvenile works, is *Phoenix Music* for orchestra (1948–1949). This work is based on the so-called "Phoenix Principle" (birth – growth – climax – death – rebirth), which is a dynamic procedure of transforming a fundamental initial motif into the central core of the whole creation, referring undoubtedly to Egyptian beliefs. The inclination towards the use of small intervals (small second and diminished third), the alternate use of music progressions and sonic collisions, the exclusion of any music development, together with the liberal structure of form – in this case, the symphonic poem – are elements that define the composer's style and characterise this work. Furthermore, the process of variations evident in *Phoenix Music* should be treated on an allegorical level; as Anna-Martine Lucciano explains, it "may no longer be regarded as a technique, but as a phenomenon. Thus, it no longer relates to the sound object itself but to the way in which this object is perceived" (Lucciano 2000: 4). Within the environment of free atonality, the short chromatic motif is constantly being transformed as a symbol of perpetual recreation of the mythical fowl and the renaissance of life.

The First Symphony (1949–1950) shares a lot in common with *Phoenix Music,* yet it communicates a more profound tragedy, a gradual complexity and a linear orchestral writing (Guarino 1955). In The First Symphony climax is not achieved through the increase of tension or thickness but rather through the mutation of the sentimental charge into looseness, as Chares Vrondos likes to put it (Vrondos [Βρόντος] 1983: 75). To serve this purpose, Chrēstou uses Thomas Stearns Eliot's poem, *Eyes that Last I Saw in Tears*: a poem which is also included in his later collection, *Six T. S. Eliot Songs* (1955). This middle part introduces the piece with the human element through its vocal presence, and functions as a compositional bridge on the one hand and as an antithetic projection between the first and the last part on the other.[13] Along with the above works, reference should be made to the *Latin Liturgy* (1951); this is a music interpretation of the sacred texts in their ceremonial sequence with influences of Stravinsky, which was later incorporated into the finale of his Second Symphony (1957–1958).

Chrēstou's *Patterns and Permutations* (1960) proved a landmark, as it reflects the composer's aesthetic turn and the establishment of a new route in his personal music system. Chrēstou names this special type of material organising "meta-serialism". This term may be rendered as "beyond serialism", since, although the twelve-tone series might be used as a starting point, the structure of the sonic phenomena is also based on further parameters that do not relate to serialism. In *Patterns and Permutations* the composer introduces a set of new terms while he also uses pre-existing ones in a different context: for instance the "permutations", the "patterns" (simple and complex), the "isochrones", the "mega-statement", the "anti-patterns", the "continuum" and so on. What is necessary to clarify at this point is that this method is not put forward as a normative form that needs to be coursed systematically; instead it functions as an outline of re-contemplation around the compositional morphemes and their dynamic traits, which serves the composer's music aspirations. The conception of the above idea offers Chrēstou the chance to work in a manner that is quick and technically flawless and which, at the same time, reveals the mysticism and spiritual-orientation of his inner world. The first performance of the work in 1963, by the Athens State Orchestra, took place in a rather triggered atmosphere under the threat of conflict between the supporters and the opponents of contemporary music. The oratorio *Tongues of Fire* (1964) summarises the characteristics of this "new system" putting particular emphasis on the asymmetric multi-rhythmic articulation of the voices being used.

Music for theatre in Chrēstou's work rightfully comprises a distinct section. His collaboration with Karolos Koun at the National Theatre of Greece was of significant importance in scoring for ancient Greek tragedy and comedy. *Prometheus Bound* (1963), *The Persians* (1965), *The Frogs* (1966) and *Oedipus Rex* (1969) belong to the last decade of the composer's life and affirm Chrēstou's beliefs on the performative texture of the ancient drama: through a climax of his psychological state the spectator is driven to the liminal state of catharsis. Chrēstou's theatre music relies upon the psychodynamic energy of ancient rites, the combination of particular rituals, as well as the sacramental experience of magic petitions. The use of concrete and electro-acoustic music, together with a reformation of the original theatrical texts, transfers the spectator directly to the thrill and the release of tension evident in the scenic action.

Experienced theatricality is inherent in Chrēstou's creation, even in works not designated as original music background in scene shows. This characteristic is particularly felt in the music of the composer's last productive decade and has resonance with his growing interest in life, and life after death – possibly as a result of his brother's early death. The works *Mysterion* (1965–1966), *Praxis for 12* (1966) and *Enantiodromia* (1965–1966) represent the different direction that his compositional expression takes as an osmotic procedure of merging music with other performing arts (with these being mainly acting and dance). Moreover, they function as an art manifesto of negation towards the inherited aesthetics by focusing on the liberating, participative and communicative nature of music (Lucciano 2000: 92).

On this basis one may come to conceive two of the central notions in Jannē Chrēstou's music: "Praxis" and "Metapraxis". Thus, according to the composer, "Praxis" represents a music action belonging to a particular rationale, whereas "Metapraxis" symbolises an action that opposes this logic or surpasses it. The one suggests, yet, concurrently undermines the other, threatening the very meaning of the medium itself. The turn in Chrēstou's approach manifests itself through the transition from the model of "Phoenix Principle" to the "Lunar Prototype" and the acceptance of the possibility of "Eclipse" being the dynamics of fortuity, of the unexpected. The three different forms of notating his music conception (synthetic, proportionate and measured), which the composer formulates and explicates, include plentiful audiovisual and spatiotemporal elements, concerning the constituents of the sonic events. In many of Chrēstou's works a combination of notational systems is evident, so that both extra-musical and para-musical factors are ascribed in the most complete possible way.

The rather eccentric work *The Strychnine Lady* (1967) departs philosophically from Carl Jung's book *Psychology and Alchemy* and was influenced by a dream that the composer had. The *Epicycle* (1968), on the other hand, sets the music background for the screening of a film within the scope of the Greek Week of Contemporary Music. These pieces unfold and establish former compositional techniques, like happenings, immeasurable controlled improvisation and mixed media that extend to the point of chaotic self-decomposition. *Anaparastaseis* [Re-enactments], a cycle of 30–40 works, refers to the event of ephemeral creation of performances. Of these numerous compositions, only *Anaparastasis I, Astronkatoidanykteronomigyrin*

(1968)[14] and *Anaparastasis III, The Pianist* (1968) were performed during Chrēstou's life time.[15] The rest exist in the form of unfinished, synoptic sketches. They are extraordinary musical psycho-dramatic forms, where the relationship between the performers and the audience gain particular healing gravity, whereas music is restrained to a prudent expression. The composer's lattermost conception happens to be the operatic adaptation of the Aeschylus' trilogy *Oresteia*. In this work, which remained incomplete, Chrēstou deals with mythical archetypes, paralleling them with the feeling of panic that man bears in his failing to solve the matter of existence.

Through a comparative approach to Jannē Chrēstou and Iannis Xenakis' works, Giōrgos Zervos mentions characteristically that "even in his most 'anti-musical' moments, with these being the moments of 'metapraxis' of the instrumental works and the 'anaparastaseis', Chrēstou remains deeply musical. [...] On Chrēstou's romantic, expressionistic, introvert and metaphysical mood, Xenakis juxtaposes an anti-romantic mood and a philosophical rationalism". And he continues: "Chrēstou's *Anaparastaseis* differ from Xenakis' *Polytopes* in the sense that they comprise more of a genre of primordial rituals, during which what is released is the most profound and violent subconscious powers of man, rather than an effort to revive a certain mode of life and expression of the ancient Greek society or a new Gesamtkunstwerk (total work of art) referring to a future or utopian society" (Zervos [Ζερβός] 1999: 145– 146).

For a deeper understanding of Chrēstou's work, it is really important to pinpoint that the composer also bears the substance of a metaphysical thinker, expressing, in a large degree, the speculations of the 1950s and the 1960s. His music, seen as direct emanation of his inner restlessness, is presented as personal intention, a consistent revelation and a gradual embodiment of his philosophical theories.[16] The antitheses, the confrontations and the ambiguities constitute basic characteristics of his music. The world of the primitive and the magical co-exists with that of contemporary massiveness and collective hysteria. Spiritual ecstasy, proto-performance and mystical rituals are combined with modern commonalities. The logical is correlated with the paralogical, the illogical and the alogical, while ritual is associated with representation. Also, everyday life meets with its excess and ordinariness is combined with exceptionality. The East is conceived through the West, whilst the past and the future are conceived as the "other" expressions of the present, and vice-versa.

The issues concerning the relation between eastern and western music tradition, and their assimilation into new music sets, are the central artistic and ontological keystones of Michalēs Adamēs' work. Adamēs was born in Piraeus and since the age of eleven he became systematically involved in both Byzantine and Western European classical theory and practice at the Athens and Piraeus Conservatories. Initially, he acquired the certificates for Byzantine music and chanting, while later he advanced to counterpoint, fugue and composition as a student of Jannēs A. Papaiōannou at the Hellenic Conservatory. During the period of 1949 to 1954 Adamēs attended the Department of Theology, at the University of Athens, while being actively involved in choir conducting. The years 1961 to 1965 proved of great significance for the young composer, since he went to Brandeis University of Boston for postgraduate studies in composition, Byzantine music palaeography and electronic music.

During his stay in the United States, Adamēs expanded his horizons to the technical potentialities and the speculations of contemporary music, while at the same time delved deeper into the core of Byzantine music. These two modes of expression coexisted as much in the studies he attended as in the shaping of his personal compositional style. Some of his chamber music compositions, like *Anakyklisis* (1964) and *Prooptiki* (1965), were performed in America for the first time, gaining considerable distinction. In the genre of electroacoustic music he composed works with the use of videotape, such as *Piece I* (1964) and *Piece II* (1964), as well as works with mixed media, like *Proschemata* (1964). Along with the particular works considered as milestones, this period marked the beginning of the composer's mature compositional phase.

In 1965 Michalēs Adamēs returned to Greece and created the first private electronic music studio, since at that time there was no alternative set-up place for music production via technology. In his studio he composed works through mostly electronic and electroacoustic sources.[17] This is not to say, however, that he did not create music for the conventional instruments of the western orchestra; in fact, he composed various vocal and choral pieces, chamber music and theatre music. In 1968 he was appointed as the director of the Music Department of Pierce College, making several appearances with its choir in various artistic performances around Athens.

Beyond Michalēs Adamēs' compositions, what is of equal importance is his presence as a musicologist, particularly in the field of Byzantine music. Among his studies, the most important was his paradigmatic reference to one of the earliest samples of Orthodox polyphonic music that dates back to the 15th century. Adamēs' manifold activity also extended to administration competences. In 1966 he was elected secretary of the Greek Society for Contemporary Music, while from 1975 to 1985 he was appointed to the position of the president. Adamēs was the president of the Special Committee of the Ministry of Culture responsible for the development of choirs and a member of the Administrative Committee of the Ionian University, which formulated the curriculum and the organisation of the newly established Music Department. Adamēs is also a member of the Greek Composers' Union.[18]

During a period of about forty years Adamēs succeeded in constructing a pioneering style, within which he transmuted not only the technical and aesthetic features of the Byzantine tradition but also its further symbolisms. Despite the fact that the basic principles and morphological characteristics of Byzantine music cannot conform to the melodic and harmonic hermeneutic models of western performance, Adamēs' music achieves vast sensation and is internationally appreciated by contemporary music audiences. This is mainly due to its linear form, its polyrhythmic, polymelodic and polymodal combinations, and furthermore, due to the Byzantine chanters' techniques being incorporated in many of his works (for instance, the idiomorphic sound structure, the micro-intervals, the *isokratema* or drone bass, the specific melismatic ornamentation, and so on).

A distinct quality found in many of Adamēs' pieces is the amalgamation of the West-European and the Byzantine notation; this practice beautifully serves the composer's utmost purposes, such as the attempt to bring together the western with the eastern music sphere. This encounter is also evident in the orchestration, through the interweaving – that is, the recomposing or the juxtaposition – of heterogeneous timbres. An example of this could be the use of Byzantine chorus and various traditional Greek idiophones together with conventional instruments of western music and also with electronic sources. The above stressed points, concerning the notation and the orchestration in the composer's work in connection with his stylistic and aesthetic attachment to the neo-Byzantine song, on the one hand, and to atonality, serialism and electronic media, on the other, led to the establishment of Michalēs Adamēs as a very special, yet solitary figure in Greek art music from the 1960s onwards.

In order to maintain – to an extent – the ideals of the senior Greek National School of Music, and incorporate them within the contemporary notions of nationality, many composers attempted to feature particular elements of Greek music tradition (Byzantine, demotic and folk) through its mixture with West-European music. At the time of Michalēs Adamēs' intense creativity, his attitude towards Greek tradition is considered as "courageous in Greece, where many Orthodox intellectuals still reject western music as incompatible with their ideas of national identity" (Conomos and Leotsakos 2009).[19] The formation of a rather idiosyncratic liturgical and musical ethos based – for the most part – upon the Byzantine cultural legacy is evident in works such as *The Sixth Seal of the Apocalypse* (1967), *Genesis* (1968), *Kratema* (1971) and *Tetelestae I* (1971).

The vocal and choral works of Michalēs Adamēs cover a big part of his creation, from the *Hail Mass* (1950) and the *Byzantine Passion* (1967) to *In Bethlehem* (1988), the *Lament of Virgin Mary* (1994) and the *Os Thessavron* (1994). His work for ancient drama performances is of great importance. During the period 1960–1974 Adamēs composed mainly for tragedies, most of which contained electronic music and were supported by live electronics. Moreover, between the years 1971–1973, he composed electronic incidental music for some theatrical plays. *The Seagull* (1977), a piece for flute, double-bass, percussion and videotape, tells the story of a bird that denied the main purpose of its existence – i.e. flying for food seeking – and turned to more profound values of life such as freedom, creation and love.[20]

The 1980s represent a liminal period for Adamēs' work. During this phase the composer devoted himself primarily to instrumental music, while in general his style went through a gradual modification.[21] By expanding his research to the Byzantine and traditional modes and the rhythms of the demotic song, Adamēs applied a kind of polymelodic counterpoint. This method was used, for example, in his pieces *Alliostrofa* (1986), *Eptaha* (1989), *Enestota* (1991), *Esothen* (1991) and *Hellenion* (1996). According to this technique, "independent lines combine to produce striking harmonic conflicts", in a quasi-kaleidoscopic effect with various alternating and overlaying tone-colours (Conomos and Leotsakos 2009). The linearity in Adamēs' instrumental composition and, consequently, the formation of dense melodic complexes and imaginable horizontal sound progressions – clearly depicted even

as to be interpreted as a whole and, at other times, it is opposed to music as an independent hermeneutic view. As for the last act of the drama, this is not simply given but is provoked as the spectator's subjective solution (Kōstios [Κώστιος] 1991).

Human voice through song acquires particular gravity in Koukos' works, as it becomes the most essential vehicle of communicating the composer's inmost intentions across his audience. The neo-Romantic nostalgia – a hovering sensation of parallel distance and proximity, an ambivalent relationship between the present and the recent past – constitutes the core of the formation of the song cycle *Diary for Passers-by at the End of the Century* (1993–1994).[27] The melodic-harmonic and the orchestration references to popular music of the 20th century (blues, jazz, rock, pop, etc.) are expressions of an individual but also a transnational music identity, which the creator wishes to highlight. Periclēs Koukos finely succeeds in combining various elements that seem contradictory. Through a kind of discourse that reforms music norms yet devoid of falling out with them, the composer uses former codes so to create a totally personal and, eventually, extremely characteristic language of interaction.

The search for contact between the composer and his social environment is one of the most crucial issues with which art music creation is engaged. In an attempt to respond to this need, contemporary avant-garde music at times wholly demolishes "the traditional" while at others attempts to transform older musical morphemes into new ones, thereby virtually giving birth to a "meta-musical" logic: a critical, aesthetic and political discourse that is far away from "pure" music; a discourse coming from music and being concurrently about and beyond music. In the work of each of the three composers the concept of "meta-music" is present, however, this takes on a different meaning in each case. Thus, in the case of Jannēs Chrēstou it emerges as a denial of the conventional means of performance, in Michalēs Adamēs' as a reformation of the lived tradition, while in Periclēs Koukos' it appears as an application of the established practices within different contexts of interpretation. The new generation of composers in Greece, following up closely with the procedures and the orientations of contemporary music, heads next to an internationalised and – at the same time – multicultural scene of art music and preserves its own perspective through the current polyphonic reality.

Notes

1. Also written: Jannis or Janis Christou.
2. Also written: Michalis Adamis.
3. Also written: Periklis Koukos.
4. Various foreign cultural organisations were created in Athens (for instance, the Italian Institute of Culture, the Goethe Institute and the Hellenic American Union), which, along with the pre-existing French Institute, engulfed the Greek art pioneers of the times (Rōmanou [Ρωμανού] 2000: 167–168; Dontas [Δοντάς] 2001).

5. For an overall estimation and an account of the tendencies and the figures of contemporary Neohellenic music, see Slonimsky 1965; Zervos [Ζερβός] 1999.
6. For further information concerning the socio-political and cultural setting of post-war life in Greece, see Lambiri-Dimaki 1983; Charalambis, Maratou-Alipranti and Hadjiyanni 2004; Mouzelis 1996.
7. Together with avant-garde music, popular song flourished in post-war Greece. Popular music fusions started from a similar attempt to bind together "western" and "eastern" elements but in a different style from that of the avant-garde. Various personalities in Greek musical and cultural life got involved in this process, in one way or another. The central point of reference turned out to be the Mikēs Theodōrakēs-Manos Chatzidakis dipole. As well as these two composers, whose work and attitude deeply influenced their epoch as well as the next generation of musicians, some other music creators (e.g. Stavros Xarchakos, Jannēs Markopoulos, Manos Loizos, Dēmos Moutsēs, Chrēstos Leontēs and Dionysēs Savvopoulos) followed a similar path, each one with a distinctive personal aesthetic, and ideological and socio-political view. More particularly, a new music genre, the so-called "art popular song", was created. Art popular song was characterised by a) an inner ambiguity, as is shown through the combination of the terms "art" and "popular" in its name, b) the composer's formal music education, c) the use of poetic lyrics, and d) a massive acceptance by the audience. For further information according to Greek popular and art popular music in the post-war era, see Holst-Warhaft 1997; Notaras [Νοταράς] 2001: 131–132; Mylōnas [Μυλωνάς] 1985.
8. The Greek National Tourism Organisation was mutated to the main vehicle of culture and development. Its fundamental concern was the construction of an – otherwise fictitious – image of cultural prosperity. Culture was clearly related to the mimic adoption of western social etiquette and modes of behaviour. See Rōmanou [Ρωμανού] 2003; Dontas [Δοντάς] 2001; Leotsakos 2009a.
9. Being a businessman, Chrēstou's father tried to direct his son towards economic studies, while his mother, a well-known poet and a warm supporter of spiritualism, influenced Chrēstou towards mysticism and meditation. Moreover, his relationship with the Egyptian *intelligentsia* and aristocracy of the time, and the overall religious orientation of the culture where he grew up, proved to be determinative factors concerning his future choices.
10. Chrēstou kept well in touch with England and France. The English language and education, in particular, had a great influence on him. Besides, English was the language the composer used to note down his personal, philosophical and music speculations as well as a detailed indication of his dreams.
11. Beyond his preoccupation with music composition, Jannēs Chrēstou devoted considerable time to the study of philosophy, anthropology, psychology, history, theology, science of religion, magic and alchemy.
12. For more information on Jannēs Chrēstou's biography and works, see Symeōnidou [Συμεωνίδου] 1995: 439–443; Lucciano 2000: xv-xviii, 169–178; Leotsakos 2009b; Kalogeropoulos [Καλογερόπουλος] 1998: 598–601.
13. For an analytical approach to Chrēstou's *Phoenix Music* as well as The First Symphony, see Sliōmēs [Σλιώμης] 2000.
14. "Astronkatoidanykteronomigyrin" refers to a strophe from Agamemnon by Aeschylus which means "I have become familiar with the assembly of all the stars of night".
15. For a more detailed analysis of the *Anaparastaseis,* see Zapheiropoulou [Ζαφειροπούλου] 2004.

16. Jannēs Chrēstou's "dream diaries" are of exceptional musicological interest, given the fact that they combine a significant number of historical and psychological parameters that refer to certain works of the composer.

17. For a review of Michalēs Adamēs' electroacoustic work, see Loufopoulos [Λουφόπουλος] 1999.

18. For further information concerning Michalēs Adamēs' biography and works see Symeōnidou [Συμεωνίδου] 1995: 16–20; Conomos and Leotsakos 2009; Kalogeropoulos [Καλογερόπουλος] 1998: 59–62.

19. Furthermore, in an attempt to interpret the overall tendency towards the use of folk and traditional music elements on behalf of young Greek composers, Giōrgos Zervos mentions characteristically: "Although the way and the degree of using the Byzantine chant is different in each occasion, the very fact that they all attempted to incorporate elements of the demotic or the Byzantine music tradition – a phenomenon that continued even after the National School era and keeps carrying on, yet limitedly, up to the present day (in a sense that approaches postmodernism) – indicates nothing but another attempt to enhance the questioned state of contemporary western music creation with a 'foreign' grand music culture that, in our case, is the Byzantine one" (Zervos [Ζερβός] 1999: 151–152).

20. This work is based on Richard Bach's novel *Jonathan Livingston Seagull* (1970).

21. The period in question is described as particularly difficult for Greek electronic music avant-garde. "The primary cause was the insufficient equipment and studio facilities as the demands were gradually growing higher, yet without having the analogous financial security. Faced up against this dead-end, many composers gradually abandoned electronic music during the late years of the decade and either turned to instrumental music (like Michalēs Adamēs in 1977) or abandoned composition on the whole. Other composers (like Ch. Xanthoudakēs, D. Terzakēs, Th. Antōniou) went abroad either to study or to find occupation in fully equipped studios in foreign countries" (Loufopoulos [Λουφόπουλος] 1999: 11).

22. For an insight into the composer's opinion concerning his own work, a kind of an autobiographical article, see Adamis 1995.

23. For further theoretical and methodological pinpoints concerning "new musicology", see Subotnik 1991; McClary 1991; Kramer 1995. See also Rōmanou [Ρωμανού] 1998.

24. For further information on Periklēs Koukos' biography and works, see Symeōnidou [Συμεωνίδου] 1995: 195–197; Kalogeropoulos [Καλογερόπουλος] 1998: 280–281.

25. The term "postmodern" refers, on the one hand, to a music style defined according to given characteristics and, on the other, to the status of contemporary cultural, social, economic and political reality. As a musical style, "postmodern" includes elements of the art that lies across, after and beyond "modern" and, more particularly, eclecticism, self-reference, ironic attitude, collage, multi-diversity and the diffusion of genres. As a situation, postmodern music represents an expression of the corresponding period that is distinct for its globalising sense in the sectors of finance and culture, the dominance of the mass media and the development of information technologies. For various approaches on the phenomenon, see Jameson 1991; Lyotard 1985; Turner 1990. Concerning the issue of "the modern" and "the postmodern" in music, see Albright 2004; Lochhead and Auner 2002. For the Greek perspective on this matter, see Lapidakēs [Λαπιδάκης] 2000; Zervos [Ζερβός] 1987.

26. For a thorough and deep analysis of the work, see Kōstios [Κώστιος] 1991.

27. Concerning the concept of "nostalgia", in the way that this is depicted in contemporary postmodern scientific and artistic tendencies, see Hutcheon 2000; Jameson 1989.

References

Adamis, M., "Within and beyond Symbolism: An Insight and a Perspective of Musical Creation", *Contemporary Music Review*, 2: 12, 1995, pp. 9–21.

Albright, D., *Modernism and Music: An Anthology of Sources*, Chicago, University of Chicago Press, 2004.

Charalambis, D., Maratou-Alipranti, L., and Hadjiyanni, A. (eds), *Recent Social Trends in Greece: 1960–2000*, Montreal, McGill-Queen's University Press, 2004.

Conomos, D., and Leotsakos, G. "Adamis, Mihalis" in *Grove Music Online* http: //www.oxfordmusic online.com/subscriber/article/grove/music/00165. Accessed 17 May 2009.

[Dontas] Δοντάς, Ν., "Νέο Ξεκίνημα" ["New Beginning"] in *7 Ημέρες: Η Ελλάδα τον Εικοστό Αιώνα: 1950-1970* [7 Days: Greece during the 20th Century: 1950–1970], Athens, Καθημερινή [Kathēmerinē], 2001, p. 56.

Guarino, P., "Compositeurs d' Égypte: Jani Christou", *Rhythme*, 5, 1995, pp. 3–6.

Holst-Warhaft, G., "Song, Self-Identity and the Neohellenic", *Journal of Modern Greek Studies*, 2: 15, 1997, pp. 232–238.

Hutcheon, L., "Irony, Nostalgia and the Post-modern", in R. Vervliet and A. Estor (eds), *Methods for the Study of Literature as Cultural Memory*, Atlanta, Rodopi, 2000, pp. 189–207.

Jameson, F., "Nostalgia for the Present", *The South Atlantic Quarterly*, 2: 88, 1989, pp. 522–537.

——, *Postmodernism, or the Cultural Logic of Late Capitalism*, Durham, Duke University Press, 1991.

[Kalogeropoulos] Καλογερόπουλος, T., *Το Λεξικό της Ελληνικής Μουσικής: Από τον Ορφέα έως Σήμερα* [Dictionary of Greek Music: From Orpheus till Today], Athens, Γιαλλελής [Jallelēs], 1998.

[Kōstios] Κώστιος, A., "Για τον Συνθέτη και το Έργο" [About the Composer and the Work], introductory text in the score Π. Κούκος [P. Koukos], *Ο Κονρουά και οι Κόπιες του* [Conrois and his Copies], Athens, Φίλιππος Νάκας [Phillipos Nakas], 1991, pp. 6–8.

Kramer, L., *Classical Music and Post-modern Knowledge*, Berkeley, University of California Press, 1995.

Lambiri-Dimaki, J., *Social Stratification in Greece 1962–1982: Eleven Essays*, Athens, Sakkoulas, 1983.

[Lapidakēs] Λαπιδάκης, M., "Σκέψεις ενός Συνθέτη στην Ελλάδα στο Τέλος της Χιλιετίας" [Thoughts of a Composer in Greece at the End of the Century], *Μουσικά* [Mousika], 5, 2000, pp. 59–73.

Leotsakos, G., "Greece, §III, 5: Art Music since 1945" in *Grove Music Online* http: //www. oxfordmusiconline.com/subscriber/article/grove/music/11694pg3, 2009a. Accessed 17 May.

——, "Christou, Jani" in *Grove Music Online* http: //www.oxfordmusiconline.com/subscriber/article/ grove/music/05716, 2009b. Accessed 17 May.

——, "Koukos, Periklis" in *Grove Music Online* http: //www.oxfordmusiconline.com/subscriber/ article/grove/music/O902510, 2009c. Accessed 17 May.

Lochhead, J., and Auner, J. (eds), *Post-modern Music, Post-modern Thought*, New York and London, Routledge, 2002.

[Loufopoulos] Λουφόπουλος, A., *Αρχειοθέτηση – Περιγραφική Ανάλυση των Ηλεκτροακουστικών Έργων του Συνθέτη Μιχάλη Αδάμη* [Archival and Descriptive Analysis of the Electroacoustic Works of the Composer Michalēs Adamēs], unpublished B.A. thesis, Corfu, Department of Music Studies, Ionian University, 1999.

Lucciano, A. M., *Jani Christou: The Works and Temperament of a Greek Composer*, trans., C. Dale, New York and London, Routledge, 2000.

Lyotard, J. F., *The Postmodern Condition: A Report on Knowledge*, trans., G. Bennington and B. Massumi, Minneapolis, University of Minnesota Press, 1985.

McClary, S., *Feminine Endings: Music, Gender and Sexuality*, Minneapolis, University of Minnesota Press, 1991.

Mouzelis, N., "The Concept of Modernization: It's Relevance for Greece", *Journal of Modern Greek Studies* 2: 14, 1996, pp. 215–227.

[Mylōnas] Μυλωνάς, Κ., *Ιστορία του Ελληνικού Τραγουδιού* [History of Greek Song], Athens, Κέδρος [Kedros], 1985.

[Notaras] Νοταράς, Γ., "Απόλυτη Ρήξη" [Total Rupture] in *7 Ημέρες: Η Ελλάδα τον Εικοστό Αιώνα: 1950-1970* [7 Days: Greece during the 20th Century: 1950–1970], Athens, Καθημερινή [Kathēmerinē], 2001, pp. 131–134.

Papaioannou, J. G., *Jani Christou and the Metaphysics of Music*, London, Chester, 1970.

[Rōmanou], Ρωμανού, Κ., "Η Βρώσις του Εμβάμματος (The Messing of the Dressing). Η Νέα Μουσικολογία" [The Messing of the Dressing. New Musicology], *Μουσικολογία* [Mousikologia], 10–1, 1998, pp. 158–168.

——, *Ιστορία της Έντεχνης Νεοελληνικής Μουσικής* [History of Greek Art Music], Athens, Κουλτούρα [Koultoura], 2000.

——, "Η Μουσική 1949-1974: Η Ελληνική Πρωτοπορία" [Music in the Years 1949–1974: Greek Avant-Garde] in Β. Παναγιωτόπουλος [V. Panagiōtopoulos] (ed.), *Ιστορία του Νέου Ελληνισμού: 1770-2000, 9* [History of New Hellenism: 1770-2000, 9], Athens, Ελληνικά Γράμματα [Ellēnika Grammata], 2003, pp. 259–268.

[Sliōmes] Σλιώμης, Θ., "Γιάννης Χρήστου: Η *Μουσική του Φοίνικα*, η Μουσική της Πρώτης Συμφωνίας" [Jannēs Chrēstou: *Phoenix Music*, Music of the First Symphony], *Μουσικά* [Mousika], 5, 2000, pp. 55–58.

Slonimsky, N., "New Music in Greece", *Musical Quarterly*, 51, 1965, pp. 225–235.

Subotnik, R. R., *Developing Variations: Style and Ideology in Western Music*, Minneapolis, University of Minnesota Press, 1991.

[Symeōnidou] Συμεωνίδου, Α., *Λεξικό Ελλήνων Συνθετών* [Dictionary of Greek Composers], Athens, Φίλιππος Νάκας [Philippos Nakas], 1995.

Turner, B. S. (ed.), *Theories of Modernity and Postmodernity*, London, Sage, 1990.

[Vrondos] Βρόντος, Χ. Σ., *Diabolus in Musica: Δοκίμια για την Ελληνική Μουσική* [Diabolus in Musica: Essays on Greek Music], Athens, Gutenberg, 1983.

[Zapheiropoulou] Ζαφειροπούλου, Β., *Γιάννης Χρήστου: Αναπαράσταση ΙΙΙ ή Ο Πιανίστας* [Jannēs Chrēstou: Anaparastasis III or The Pianist], unpublished seminar paper, Athens, Department of Music Studies, University of Athens, 2004.

[Zervos] Ζερβός, Γ., "Μοντερνισμός και Μεταμοντερνισμός: Περιγραφή και Προοπτικές των Κινημάτων που Επικράτησαν στη Μουσική του Αιώνα μας" [Modernism and Postmodernism: Description and Perspectives of Movements that Dominated the Music of Our Century], *To Τέταρτο* [To Tetarto], 1, 1987, pp. 41–45.

——, "Προβλήματα Μορφής και Περιεχομένου στη Σύγχρονη Έντεχνη Ελληνική Μουσική Δημιουργία" [Problems of Form and Content in Modern Greek Art Music Creation], in *Προβλήματα και Προοπτικές της Ελληνικής Μουσικής* [Problems and Perspectives of Greek Music], Athens, Παπαγρηγορίου-Νάκας [Papagrēgoriou-Nakas], 1999, pp. 133–158.

Index of Persons

Abendroth, Hermann 50
Adam, Adamantinē (miledi) 116
Adam, Frederic 115
Adamēs, Michalēs (or Adamis, Michalis) 189,
194–197, 199, 201
Adamis, Michalis (*see* Adamēs, Michalēs)
Adler, Guido 169, 181
Adorno, Theodor W. 168
Aeschylus 194, 200
Albéniz, Isaak 51
Albini, Srećko 20, 49
Albright, Daniel 201
Alsmeier, Judith 180
Amar, Licco 41, 50
Andrōnēs, Dēmētrios 120
Angelomatē-Tsougarakē, Helenē 102
Anōgeianakēs, Phoebos 138
Ansorge, Conrad 51
Antōniou, Theodōros 201
Apostolidēs, Tatsēs 178
Aragon, Louis 51
Aramis (pseudonym of Periclēs Aravandinos)
132
Aravandinos, Periclēs (*see* Aramis)
Aretino, Guido 105
Aristeidēs, Iōannēs 100, 102, 103, 105, 122
Arrau, Claudio 46, 51
Arsenović, Teodora 36
Askētopoulou (Evelpidou), Nellē 166, 169, 171,
183
Asteriadou, Maria 179
Augerēs, Marcos 158
Auner, Joseph 201

Bach, Johann Sebastian 50–51, 74
Bach, Richard D. 201
Bachauer, Gina 190
Bajić, Isidor 20, 22, 30, 65
Bakić-Hayden, Milica 29
Bandur, Jovan 30, 39, 42, 49–50
Baranović, Krešimir 30, 31, 40–41, 49–50, 52
Barbakē, Maria 120
Bartók, Béla 74, 77, 175, 176, 182, 183
Bastašić, Andrija 31
Baton, Rhené 40, 50
Battagel, Marco 109, 115
Becht 145
Becker, Günter 177
Beer-Walbrunn, Anton 145
Beethoven, Ludwig van 37–38, 44, 46, 50–51,
112, 118, 122, 156, 175
Bellini, Vincenzo 18, 119
Belonis, Yannis (or Belōnēs, Ioannēs) 127, 129,
182
Benakēs, Manōlēs 166, 167, 168, 169, 171, 179,
181
Berg, Alban 190
Bergamo, Marija 63, 70, 72
Bergamo, Petar 89
Berlioz, Louis Hector 50, 114
Bešević, Alisa 45
Bichsel, Michel 181
Binički, Stanislav 20, 22, 29, 30, 37–40, 45
Blodek, William 30
Bogdanović, Ognjen 93, 94
Bogojević, Nataša 93, 94
Bonaparte, Joseph 121
Bonaparte, Napoleon 113, 120